"This is not a profession that you choose.

It chooses you."

-Norman Van Aken, *Becoming a Chef*

The Best of Art Culinaire

Issues 1-14

Project Coordinator and Executive Editor: Kimberly C. Ahto

Editor: Christine L. Failla, Recipe Testing: Stephanie Smith

Culinaire Inc.

PO Box 9268

Morristown, New Jersey 07963

Distributed by Culinaire Inc.

973-993-5500

Library of Congress Cataloging-in-Publication Data

The Best of Art Culinaire, Issues 1-14 Culinaire Inc.

p.   cm

Includes index.

ISBN 0-9623729-3-5

1. Cookery (The Best of Art Culinaire)

1. Title

TX 1174.T74 1999

Printed in Korea

First Edition

1 2 3 4 5 6 7 8 9 10

The Best of

Art Culinaire

Issues 1 - 14

Foreword by
Anne Byrn

Recipes by
Kimberly C. Ahto
Christine L. Failla
Anne Byrn
Ellen N. Brown

Illustrations by
Charles Perkalis
Bo Jia

Photography by
Zack Feuer
Andreas Elsner
Ciara O'Shea
Franz Mitterer
Joseph Saget

Culinaire Inc.
Morristown, New Jersey

大蒜 GARLIC 茱 H

CONTENTS

INTRODUCTION

From Seattle to Savannah, Edinburgh to Andalusia, Naples to Lanai, chefs nourish, educate and continue to enlighten us. The food they create is as beautiful as poetry, music and art. It is food conceived of the heart and enjoyed with good friends. It is food you don't learn by flipping through books. Or do you? With proper training, great chefs can pick up new ideas from looking at books and magazines.

Thirteen years ago, as Ritz-Carlton's corporate executive chef, I decided the culinary profession needed the ultimate food magazine. We needed an inspirational tool of the highest quality. Here artful plates might be showcased so that up-and-coming chefs without the economic resources to dine their way through three-star restaurants might simply pick up the magazine, soak in ideas, and create. Thus, *Art Culinaire* was born.

Our mission has been the same, then and now—to be a source of inspiration and information for our readers. *Art Culinaire* has achieved this through a glossy hardcover format and an emphasis on innovative photography and intriguing layouts that raises each issue and its featured cuisine to a unique level of artistry. Because so many readers have asked for copies of those early magazines, we are publishing this compilation of our first fourteen issues titled *The Best of Art Culinaire, Issues 1-14.*

Over a decade has passed since our first issue spotlighting the great chefs of New York appeared. Many of those chefs have moved on to other establishments, and their passionately cultivated legacies, along with many new faces, have come into their own. Our industry is exploding with potential, and we represent the front lines in the revolution.

Around the globe, larger cities and smaller markets are experiencing their own booms. As worldwide travel and international communication become commonplace, food and culture naturally evolve. India, the Far East, London, Miami, Seattle, Northern Africa, Mexico and Washington, D.C. are hot-spots. Chefs learn and change with global knowledge, ultimately affecting the way we eat. Yet some ideas remain constant. In this book, we have highlighted the best of these ideas from our first fourteen issues. Here too, you will find basic soups, stocks, breads, and vinaigrettes to get you started. Also included are details of new ingredients and chefs.

Reader loyalty inspired this special issue. Reader loyalty, too, enables *Art Culinaire* to maintain professionalism while keeping abreast of current culinary movements, something essential in an industry-oriented culinary publication. All too often, food related publications extend their focus to dining table accoutrements. *Art Culinare's* style is simply the food, free from food stylist's attention. We showcase food able to be presented in real restaurants, to real patrons. Dishes are and always have been photographed immediately after the chef places them in front of the camera. Each page of the magazine reveals food as it would appear before your guests. And the recipes that go with those photos are written with the same clarity.

To all the chefs who have contributed talents to *Art Culinaire,* a warm thank you. Thank you for hospitality in your restaurants, for sharing your recipes, and your culinary knowledge. Professional culinarians, craftsmen, and artisans, these chefs were our inspiration for *Art Culinaire* and they continue to influence the magazine's direction. May our relationship continue so we may reflect, and perhaps inspire, the ever-evolving movements that shape the culinary arts.

Franz Mitterer, Publisher

Although there are many references to the reverence for which both the ancient Greeks and Romans held fine food while all other art forms were being renewed during the Renaissance, the culinary arts and its artists were all but overlooked until the 19th century. Today, however, the creativity of chefs has been compared to that of composers and painters. While it is impossible to define culinary genius as it is to set criteria for those who strive for excellence in their appeal to our other senses, we can explore what makes a chef great. The modern restaurant is the arena in which the chef's genius is demonstrated. However, it is in cookbooks - the scripts for their plays, the scores for their symphonies - that the ephemeral experience of eating the chef's great food is recorded. Here the dishes contribute to the permanent opus of the world's culinary history.

The first cookbook, written in Latin and compiled by Platina, the Vatican librarian, was *De Honesta Voluptate.* It was published in Italy in 1475, and the translation that appeared in 1505 sparked interest amongst the French. This Italian influence on French cookery was later reinforced by the intermarriage in 1533 between the royal families of the two nations. After Catherine de Medici married the Duc d'Orleans, later Henri II, Montaigne's writings contained glowing reports of Florentine chefs in the French court. Catherine de Medici brought her kitchen staff to France as part of her dowery. Most food historians consider, however, François Pierre de La Varenne to be the first great chef of modern times. His *Le Cuisinier François*, published in 1651, introduced such delicacies as butter in pastry dough. But at the same time, he advised restraint in sauces. They could be as simple as deglazing a pan with wine or lemon juice.

It is La Varenne's style of cooking that remains the underpinning of classic French cuisine. This knowledge is essential for any chef. And while writers today may argue if Lyon or Los Angeles is the food capital of the world, there is no question that it was in France that the standards for gastronomy began after the French Revolution. In 1789, for example, there are records of merely 100 restaurants in Paris, and that number grew to more than 500 by 1804. The bourgeoisie wanted the meals formerly reserved for the nobility, and with the downfall of the aristocracy there were chefs on the market to meet this demand.

Perhaps the greatest of the world's gourmet writers, Jean Anthelme Brillat-Savarin (who was professionally a lawyer, but was a constant observer of all things gastronomic through his friendship with his cousin, the famed Madame Recamier) wrote in *Physiologie du Goût,* published a year before his death in 1826, that "few among those who go to restaurants realize that the man who first opened one must have been a man of genius and a profound observer."

It was Brillat-Savarin's writings that elevated eating from a fueling of our bodies for energy to an appreciation of the sensual potential of each bite of food we consume. Chefs, in fact, appeal more to our senses than artists in any other field. Their creations first must appeal to our eyes, documented in the 20th century through scientific studies about the rate of salivation at the sight of food. The secondary reaction is through the aroma of a dish. Only after our noses have given the signal that the eating experience will be enjoyable, do our taste buds enter into this psychological chain reaction. An appreciation of these responses, built into every dish that leaves the kitchen, is part of what makes a great chef. The blessing of talent may have been nurtured since childhood, since many chefs acknowledge their desire to become a chef started at an early age. For others, it was signaled by an eating experience nearing perfection. But appreciation of the finished dish is only part of what makes a great chef. American food writer and cookbook author Robert Farrar Capon captured another quality when he wrote "no artist can work simply for

results; he must also like the work of getting them. Not that there isn't a lot of drudgery in any art - and more in cooking than in most - but that if a man has never been pleasantly surprised at the way a custard sets or flour thickens, there is not much hope of making a cook of him." Indeed, not only is there drudgery involved in cooking, there are also long hours and working conditions that strain the body. Wolfgang Puck begins his day at dawn with a trip to the fish markets of Los Angeles to personally eyeball the eyes of the fish to be filleted for diners at Spago that evening. During the course of an evening the heat generated by salamanders and saute stations can become brutal, yet each plate at the end of the evening must be presented to diners with the same perfection as those created without fatigue before the pace quickened.

A great chef, to bring this task to fruition, must also be a leader of his staff and a communicator of his ideas. Part of this communications skill develops with a chef's own training. As parents use their childhood as reference points for teaching their own children, so the arduous years of learning the menial tasks of a kitchen become the foundation for how a chef communicates with the staff. Through this process, everyone learns how the completed dish should look and taste. Great chefs, too, communicate standards for excellence in terms of the quality of the product used in the kitchen and how that product is handled during each step of the cooking process. This includes selection and storage, how food is handled and at what temperature it is cooked. The chef cannot be the multitude of hands in the kitchen preparing the ingredients for each dish; the staff must know from training and watching exactly how to handle each stage of food preparation. Chefs today control the genesis of their ingredients. In the United States, one trailblazer has been Larry Forgione at An American Place in New York. Forgione founded American Spoon Foods, a Michigan-based company that provides a range of products from wild mushrooms to fruit preserves to domestic buffalo.

The ingredient needs of each chef and style of cooking is based on a philosophy, and it is the complexity of this philosophy that separates the truly great chefs from the competent cooks. For many chefs the standard by which they judge themselves is the figure who epitomized the intellectual side of the chef's profession and the respect a chef could accrue with patrons - Georges Auguste Escoffier (1846-1935). His *Le Guide Culinaire* included more than 5,000 recipes and forms the foundation for classic French cooking and its techniques.

During the decades between Escoffier's death and the evolution of modern French cooking in the kitchens of such masters such as Louis Outhier, Paul Bocuse and Roger Vergé, many of his tenets became distorted. Sauces were made heavier and restaurants substituted complexity for competence. However, Escoffier's philosophy remains true: "The greatest dishes are the simple dishes."

Simplicity certainly does not imply austerity. As 19th century French writer Jean-François Revel wrote: "To as great a degree as sexuality, food is inseparable from imagination." And actualizing the concepts from a vivid imagination is where chefs derive a great percentage of their pleasure. The reflection on this pleasure is part of their personalities. They are generally robust and happy people; a happy chef is a good chef. They do not brood over their creations as do artists working in other creative forms. Food is giving, food is caring, food is sharing. As Brillat-Savarin wrote: "The discovery of a new dish does more for the happiness of mankind than the discovery of a star." And it is in the kitchens of great chefs that the culinary galaxies are nurtured.

Soup

Nearly a century ago, Madame Seignobes advised, "The quality of the soup should foretell that of the whole meal." Ironic that this dish - made from a limited number of basic ingredients, easy to prepare and adaptable to each chef's unique culinary style - is upheld as such a respected harbinger of courses to follow. Yet, the reasoning behind this belief lies in soup's sheer simplicity. Soups may be elemental to each chef's repertoire, but they are not necessarily all that successful. They demand tried-and-true cooking methods - just like roasted chicken, flaky pie crust, chicken stock and mashed potatoes. Take a close look at soup, and you'll see the chef's background and expertise.

If we had to choose a single quality that endears soup to our palates and busy life, it would be versatility. Soup can be prepared ahead and frozen until needed. It can be clear and delicate, like a consommé, or rich and creamy, like a bisque. There are even numerous ways to thicken soup. Starches, egg yolks, legumes, natural gelatins, puréed vegetables and simple reduction methods can be used to achieve the desired consistency. And served hot, lukewarm or cold, soup is comfort food. It is a latenight snack. It is a refreshing dessert. Or it is an elegant starter, as is the case with chef Jean-Georges Vongerichten's Duck Consommé with Foie Gras Ravioli. The soup combines the intense flavor of a carefully constructed duck stock with the crystal beauty of a flawlessly clarified consommé. Delicate fois gras ravioli and a brunoise of vegetables provide visual and textural interest.

Soup, too, connects us with culinary traditions of the past. It is a medium through which today's chefs express their individual interests and experiment with innovative ingredient combinations. Take Gerard Maras' Guinea Hen and Oyster Gumbo. Using out-of-the-ordinary guinea hen with oysters, Maras successfully transcends traditional Creole gumbo.

Originally called a "potage" or simply "broth," soup was prepared from a combination of liquids, meats and vegetables. When the meats and vegetables were cooked, they were removed from the broth and taken to the table. Here they were served alongside the broth, which was poured into bowls over pieces of bread.

The word "soup" is derived from the earliest meaning of the word "sop." And its etymology is also rooted in the verb "to soak." Later, soup came to refer to a "piece of bread soaked in liquid" as well as "broth poured on to bread." It is this second definition that manifested itself in 17th century England, and thus became most familiar to us, according to *The Diner's Dictionary: Food and Drink from A to Z.*

Soup has endured the years because no matter the ingredients used, or the chef who prepares it, or the time of year, it is easy to assemble and quite beautiful. Plus, on its own, with a sandwich, as a first course or as a unique ending to a meal, soup is both nutritious and enjoyable. Over the years, *Art Culinaire* has featured many delicious interpretations of soup, from a delicate Cold Tomato Soup with Caviar and Crayfish to a hearty Monkfish Bouillabaisse. In this issue, we feature those soups that are distinctively innovative and that collectively bring together a balance of cooking styles and techniques. We hope that these soup recipes inspire you to explore your own unique combination of ingredients.

Chicken Stock

Yield 1 gallon

8 pounds chicken bones, carcasses preferred
Water to cover bones
1 pound mirepoix
6 quarts cold water
1 aromatic sachet

For the stock, blanch bones by covering completely with water and bring to a quick boil. Shut off heat and drain bones, removing surface scum. Add mirepoix to bones, and cover with 6 quarts cold water. Add sachet and bring to a lazy boil, simmering for 4-5 hours. Skim stock as needed. Do not stir. Strain the stock, cool, and store appropriately. Discard bones or make a remouillage.

Brown Chicken Stock

Yield 1 Gallon

8 pounds chicken bones, carcasses preferred
6 quarts cold water
fi cup vegetable oil
1 pound mirepoix
4 ounces tomato paste
1 aromatic sachet

For the stock, rinse the bones in cold water and dry completely. Brown the bones in a roasting pan until dark. Remove bones from roasting pan, and reserve pan. Place bones in stock pot, covering with cold water. Bring stock to a lazy boil. Combine the mirepoix and the vegetable oil in the reserved roasting pan and caramelize the mirepoix on the stovetop. Stir in tomato paste, and cook until mixture achieves a deep mahogany color, about 30 minutes. Add mirepoix and sachet to stock. Deglaze roasting pan and add to stock. Simmer stock 4-5 hours, skimming as needed. Do not stir. Strain the stock, cool, and store appropriately. Discard bones or make a remouillage.

Brown Veal Stock

Yield 1 Gallon

8 pounds veal joint bones
6 quarts cold water
fi cup vegetable oil
1 pound mirepoix
4 ounces tomato paste
1 aromatic sachet

For the stock, rinse the bones in cold water and dry completely. Brown the bones in a roasting pan until dark. Remove bones from roasting pan, and reserve pan. Place bones in stock pot, covering with cold water. Bring stock to a lazy boil. Combine the mirepoix and the vegetable oil in the reserved roasting pan and caramelize the mirepoix on the stovetop. Stir in tomato paste, and cook until mixture achieves a deep mahogany color, about 30 minutes. Add mirepoix and sachet to stock. Deglaze roasting pan and add to stock. Simmer stock 4-5 hours, skimming as needed. Do not stir. Strain the stock, cool, and store appropriately. Discard bones or make a remouilliage.

White Beef Stock

Yield 1 gallon

8 pounds beef bones cut into 3-inch lengths
Water to cover bones
1 pound mirepoix
6 quarts cold water
1 aromatic sachet

For the stock, blanch bones by covering completely with water and bring to a quick boil. Shut off heat and drain bones, removing surface scum. Add mirepoix to bones, and cover with 6 quarts cold water. Add sachet and bring to a lazy boil, simmering for 4-5 hours. Skim stock as needed; do not stir. Strain the stock, cool, and store appropriately. Discard bones or make a remouilliage.

Fish Stock

Yield 1 gallon

4 ounces butter or olive oil
11 pounds whitefish bones
1 pound white mirepoix
10 ounces mushroom trimmings
4 quarts cold water
1 quart white wine
1 bouquet garni

For the stock, heat the oil. Add the bones and mirepoix. Cover and sweat for 10 minutes. Add the mushroom trimmings. Cover and sweat for 5 minutes. Stir in the water and wine, add the bouquet garni, and bring to a gentle simmer. Simmer for 40 minutes, skimming as necessary; do not stir stock. Strain the stock, cool, and store appropriately. Discard bones.

Vegetable Stock

Yield 1 gallon

2 ounces vegetable oil
8 ounces onions, chopped
8 ounces leeks, chopped
4 ounces celery, chopped
3 ounces green cabbage, chopped
3 ounces carrots, peeled and chopped
3 ounces turnip, peeled and chopped
3 ounces tomato, chopped
5 garlic cloves, crushed
5 quarts cold water
1 aromatic sachet
1 teaspoon fennel seeds, crushed
2 whole cloves

For the stock, heat the oil. Add the vegetables, cover and sweat for 10 minutes. Stir in the cold water, sachet, fennel seeds and cloves. Bring to a lazy boil, and simmer for 40 minutes. Strain the stock, cool, and store appropriately. Discard vegetables.

Lexicon

Mirepoix: A basic flavoring ingredient in stocks and sauces. Standard ratio of two parts onions to one part carrots and celery, rough chopped to appropriate size.

White Mirepoix: Equal parts onions, leeks, celery, and parsnips. Alternatively, two parts onions to one part celery and one part leeks. White mirepoix adds more delicate flavors than straight mirepoix, and is often used in sauce preparation.

Aromatic Sachet: A wrapped and tied packet of cheesecloth containing cracked peppercorns, bay leaves, crushed garlic cloves, thyme and parsley stems.

Bouquet Garni: A stalk of celery stuffed and tied with bay leaves, parsley and thyme stems.

Clarification: A mixture containing mirepoix, ground meat or fish, an acid such as tomato or lemon, and herbs and spices bound together by frothy egg whites. The clarification is stirred into warm or cold stock which is brought to a simmer and allowed to reduce. The clarification mixture draws the impurities from the stock and traps them into the delicate web-like structure formed from the coagulating proteins. The result is a crystal-clear, fat-free broth.

Remouillage: Rewetting. The second preparation of a stock from bones which have already been used. A fresh mirepoix and a new aromatic sachet should be used. Remouillage is not as strong as stock prepared from fresh bones, but can be used, among other things, to start a new stock. It can also be reduced and used to fortify another stock, soup or sauce.

The following chefs contributed to the contents of this volume:

Paul Albrecht

Jean Banchet

Andrea Bell

Dennis Berkowitz

Antoine Bouterin

Henk Bruggeman

Jeffrey Buben

Peter Bührer

Jean-Marc Burillier

Yannick Cam

Kathy Casey

Richard Chamberlin

Roland Czekelius

Roberto Donna

Bradley Ogden

Charlie Palmer

Richard Chamberlin

Jean-Louis Palladin

Peter Bührer

Gerard Maras

Richard Ehrenreiter
Dean Fearing
Larry Forgione
Ralph Gerhard
Hervé Guillaume
Hartmut Handke
Ingo Holland
Jean Joho
Kenneth Juran
Franz Klampfer
Horst Klein
Emeril Lagasse
Christer Larsson
Gilbert Le Coze
Gerard Maras
Valentino Marcattilii
Gualtiero Marchesi
Georges Masraff
Douglas McNeill
Ferdinand Metz

Jeff Moogk
Patrick O'Connell
Bradley Ogden
Louis Outhier
Jean-Louis Palladin
Charlie Palmer
Gerard Pangaud
Cindy Pawlcyn
Georges Perrier
Alfred Portale
Pierre Prevost
Paul Prudhomme
Wolfgang Puck
Philippe Reininger
Seppi Renggli
Michel Rostang
Alain Sailhac
Ezio Santin
Maurizio Santin
Charles Saunders
Guenter Seeger
Susan Spicer
Eisuke Sugai
Emile Tabourdiau
Tadayuki Takahashi
Takashi Tamara
Heiji Tamura
Teruaki Tamura
Simon Teng
Matthew Tivy
Paolo Vai
Wolfgang von Wieser
Jean-Georges Vongerichten
Barry Wine

Seafood Minestrone 222

Crayfish Consommé
with Saffron Ravioli

223

13

Guinea Hen and Oyster Gumbo

Callaloo Soup

226

Consommé of Wild Mushroom with Shrimp and Shallot Flan

Salad

Do madmen toss great salads? If they are today's chefs they not only stir up one terrific salad, but they elevate salad from something for diners to graze on while the "real food" is being prepared to a dazzling, healthy course that stands on its own. The original salads were greens tossed simply with salt. In Rome they were known as "sal," the Latin word for salt. In Middle English the word became "salade." And from there a salad was known as "sallet" in England, whereas today a salad is called "salata" in Greece and Turkey, "salat" in Norway and Denmark and "salada" in Portugal.

Largely, the ingredients depend on the locale. It makes sense that English salads might be of watercress and salad burnet, that the mesclun greens of the countryside might form the basis of French salads, and that American salads might become this hodgepodge of various styles much depending on what region of the country you're exploring. For example, an apple and celery salad became all the rage at the Waldorf-Astoria hotel in New York City. The Caesar salad was born on the West Coast. In the heartland of the country, potato salads satisfied people who worked the farmlands. And in the Southeast you find a plethora of chicken or crab salads, a throwback to the post Civil War days when a salad was composed of meat or seafood and surrounded by a few herbs or greens from the garden. And although the esteemed late food writer M.F.K. Fisher once wrote that salads "should follow the main course of a meal," consist of "fresp crish garden lettuces tossed at the last with a plain vinaigrette," it was the French who originated this notion. To them a salad must contain some bitter greens, serve as a broom for the stomach, a cleanser for the palate before dessert.

These green salads are traditionally dressed with a light vinaigrette of oil and vinegar. And here all sorts of room for variation exists. What will the oil be? Walnut, olive, grapeseed or pumpkin seed? And the vinegar? Will it be a light Asian rice vinegar, a robust red wine, a sweet yet substantial balsamic from Italy? And the seasoning? Along with salt, there is pepper, chopped fresh herbs, garlic, mustard, you name it. Thanks to the burgeoning cottage gardening industries worldwide, possibilities abound with the salad ingredients themselves. Especially in climates such as California of warm days and cool nights, lettuce is as comfortable growing year 'round as are the myriad other food crops that flourish in this western state. Here small farmers have been supplying restaurants with greens and other vegetables and fruits for quite some time. The obvious pioneer in this local gardening movement was Berkeley's Alice Waters, cookbook author and founder of the legendary Chez Panisse restaurant. Waters realized many years ago that restaurants needed to work alongside gardeners at delivering the freshest, healthiest and most flavorful product to customers. "With the notable exception of Chinese and Japanese markets that even in the early seventies emphasized flavor and quality," says Waters in *The Farm-Restaurant Connection/Our Sustainable Table,* we really had nowhere to turn but to sympathetic gardeners who either already grew what we needed or would undertake to grow it for us."

And while today's chefs have changed the way we go about gathering the ingredients for salad, they, too, are changing the way we construct it. With the addition of succulent pieces of lobster or seared slices of lamb, today's salad is turning into a light summer entrée. With the emphasis on healthier fare, more and more restaurant patrons are looking to the salad section of the menu for their main course. Are they selecting salads because salads are actually healthier for them (and thus influencing chefs to offer more salads), or is it because restaurants are offering so many more delectable salad choices? This could be a topic of discussion, something on the scale of the chicken and egg. What's unarguable is that salads are fun to eat and create and an indication of the chef's imagination.

Flavored Vinegar

Yield 4 cups

4 cups neutral-flavored vinegar, such as white wine vinegar
1 cup flavoring agent, such as herbs, fruit or vegetables

For the vinegar, heat the vinegar to 100°F in a medium sauce pan. Stir in the flavoring agent, and steep for 30 minutes to 1 hour, depending on flavor intensity. Strain, cool as store at room temperature. Discard remaining residue.

Fruit Oil

Yield 2 cups

2 cups fruit juice
2 cups neutral flavored oil
2 tablespoons acidic fruit juice

For the oil, strain the juice and place in a non-reactive pan. Reduce over medium heat until desired consistency. Remove from heat, and stir in oil and acidic fruit juice. Cool and store at room temperature. Note: This oil is not uniform; it appears "broken". The oil can be emulsified by using a whisk or hand blender.

Herb Oil

Yield 4 cups

For the herb paste:
6 cups mild herb stems and leaves
fi cup neutral flavored oil
For the herb oil:
1 cup herb paste
4 cups neutral flavored oil

For the herb paste, blanch the herbs in boiling water for 30 seconds. Drain the herbs and shock them in ice water until completely cool. Drain the herbs, and dry well. In the bowl of a food processor fitted with the metal blade attachment, combine the herbs and oil, pureeing until smooth. Reserve.

For the herb oil, combine the herb paste and oil, and blend until smooth. Cover tightly and allow oil to settle a room temperature for 24 hours. Strain oil through a filter or cheesecloth. Store refrigerated for up to 7 days. Discard herb paste.

Root Oil

Yield 4 cups

1 cup minced garlic, ginger, horseradish, shallot, leek, scallion
  or onion
4 cups neutral flavored oil

For the oil, in a non-reactive saucepan, heat the oil to 100°F. Stir in the minced root. Allow to steep up to 2 hours, depending or desired intensity. Strain the oil, cool, and store at room temperature for up to 3 days. Discard root residue. Note: For food safety reasons, garlic oil should be kept refrigerated and made fresh daily.

Spice Oil

Yield 4 cups

5 cups neutral flavored oil
fi cup ground spice
Water as needed

For the spice oil, in a non-reactive saucepan, heat the oil to 100°F. Combine the ground spice and water as needed to make a thick paste. Stir paste into warm oil. Transfer oil to a container, cover and allow to steep for 3 days at room temperature. Use a ladle to remove the oil, paying careful attention not to disturb the spice residue. Strain the oil through cheesecloth or a coffee filter. Store covered up to 7 days. Discard spice residue.

Vegetable Juice Oil

Yield 3 cups

1 cup vegetable juice
2 cups neutral-flavored oil

For the vegetable juice oil, in a non-reactive saucepan, heat the oil to 100°F. Stir in the vegetable juice, and mix well. Note: This oil is not uniform; it appears "broken". The oil can be emulsified by using a whisk or hand blender.

Vinaigrette

Yield 4 cups

1 cup white wine vinegar
3 cups vegetable oil
Salt and pepper to taste

For the vinaigrette, whisk the vinegar and seasonings in a medium bowl. Slowly drizzle in the oil, whisking until mixture is uniform. Season to taste.

Emulsified Vinaigrette

Yield 5 cups

1 ounce pasteurized egg yolks or 1 egg yolk
1 tablespoon prepared mustard
1 quart vegetable oil
1fi cups white wine vinegar
Salt and pepper to taste

For the vinaigrette, using either the whisk or hand blender, combine the egg yolk and mustard in a large bowl and whisk until frothy. Drizzle in half the oil and whisk to combine. Drizzle in the vinegar; whisk vigorously. Drizzle in the remaining oil and whisk to form an emulsion. Add the salt and pepper to taste.

Lexicon

Vinegar: An acid derived from the oxidization of any product which first ferments into alcohol. The term "vinegar" comes from the French terminology *vin aigre* meaning "sour wine." Vinegar is typically made from wine, but can also be made from fruit, honey, rice, grains, and malt.

Oil: Any of innumerable liquids derived from plant and animal substances which are greasy, slick, and sticky.

Vinaigrette: A temporary emulsion sauce made from 3 parts oil or liquid fat to 1 part acid.

Emulsion: A uniform mixture of fat and another liquid formed through either heat or agitation. An emulsion is formed mechanically; it does not naturally occur. Lecithin, typically found in egg yolks or mustard, acts as the binding agent, stabilizing the two liquids.

Temporary emulsion: An emulsion as previously described without the emulsifier. A temporary emulsion will eventually separate into two distinct liquids.

Oils to use:	Vinegars to use:
Corn	Wine
Vegetable	Vinegar
Peanut	Herb-infused Vinegar
Sesame	Malt Vinegar
Safflower	Cider Vinegar
Grapeseed	Champagne Vinegar
Hazelnut	Balsamic Vinegar
Pumpkin Seed	Lemon Juice
Walnut	Lime Juice
Avocado	Pineapple Juice
Almond	Pineapple Vinegar
Bacon Fat	Grapefruit Juice
Soybean	Rice Vinegar
Palm	Sherry Vinegar
Coconut	Sweet Wine Vinegar

Cindy Pawlcyn

Seppi Renggli

Hervé Guillaume

Kathy Casey

Guenter Seeger

Dennis Berkowitz

Paul Albrecht

Scallop and Truffle Salad　　229

Scallop Salad 229

Pheasant Salad
with Cranberries   230

Lobster, Zucchini
and Bean Salad   230

30

Baked Pepper
and Artichoke Salad

Warm Lamb Salad with White Beans 232

Bean Salad
with Charred Lamb   233

Seasonal Greens with Quail Eggs   234

Vegetable Sorbet Salad 235

Appetizer

The aim is "to whet the appetite with-out complete-ly satisfying it." Curnonsky](a.k.a. Maurice Edmond Sailland) in Larousse Traditional French Cooking.

If soups are an indication of the talent of a chef, then appetizers are the gauge of a chef's wit and whimsy. Here colors, textures and flavors are mixed and mingled in seemingly effortless style. Nothing is taken too seriously, and yet well-executed appetizers become serious food, indeed. For in just one bite, the diner is taken on a culinary adventure, our senses are teased *en route*, and in the end our palate is pleased and we await, with grand expectation, the main course.

Often the appetizers are so alluring, we banish all thoughts of a main course. Take traditional Spanish tapas, the little dishes of skewered seafood, room temperature potato omelette and marinated mushrooms, made popular in Spanish bars and taverns. Coming from the Spanish *tapar*, meaning "to cover," it is said these appetizers were designed by some clever chef who placed one piece of food on top of a glass of sherry for the patron to sample. The tapas were satisfying to the hungry patron and to the tavern owner since their saltiness encouraged more drink. It's not uncommon to make an entire meal from just tapas. But the appetizers we share with you are grander than simple tapas. Take Herb Pasta with Crawfish, one of the appetizer recipes we have chosen to reprint, featured in our sixth magazine. The crimson crawfish resemble red poppy petals and form a delicate flower, which is brillantly complemented by fresh green herbs placed strategically around the plate. The herb theme is repeated in the pasta, where leaves shine through gossamer-thin pasta dough. Cut into individual circles, the pasta frames the crawfish. But at the same time, each round is a complete composition, reminiscent of a meticulously crafted botanical print.

The word by which most people know appetizers is the French *hors d'oeuvre,* which literally translates into "outside of work." Although the tiny bite of splendid food might seem outside the realm of traditional cooking, it plays an important part in the evolution of the modern meal. But appetizers also use up bits of shrimp, pasta, asparagus or sweet potatoes, "leftovers which could not properly be served at the table." Many a young chef has been told to take this mystery box of leftovers from the cooler and create something spectacular. Something so extraordinary that it will first please the eyes. Presentation in *hors d'oeuvres,* Curnonsky writes, is critical. Just look at recipes such as Foie Gras and Sweetbreads in Aspic from our premier issue, and Feuillete of Oysters from our eleventh magazine. Delicious yes, but also dazzling at which to look.

As chefs focus on the aesthetic appeal of their food, they are finding it possible to compose attractive plates not by fussing with the food, but merely by showcasing the inherent beauty and flavor of the ingredients. In the case of the above-mentioned recipes, that would be spotlighting the exquisite foie gras and sweetbreads or the pristine, fresh oysters, still scented of the sea. While complicated dishes may have been attention-getters in the past, today's chefs and their patrons are increasingly focused on simplicity. Yet chefs today continue to experiment with architectural presentations much like young children play day-in-and-day-out with building blocks. The food seems larger and taller than life, and it's tricky just getting it from the kitchen to table. But, all is well as long as the food tastes good. Taste, ultimately, is the bottom line. Nearly obsolete is the concept of puréeing glistening scallops into an opaque colorless mousse and then molding this mousse into some shape that only halfway resembles the mollusk.

Roberto Donna

Andrea Bell

Franz Klampfer

Horst Klein

Valentino Marcattilii

Millefeuille of Artichoke and Duck Liver 236

Terrine of Chanterelles and
Baby Leeks

236

Terrine of Duck with Lentils 237

Terrine of Smoked Eel ⬤237

Terrine of Seafood with Saffron Sauce 238

Terrine of Herring and Cabbage 239

48

Terrine of Goose and Truffle 〔240〕

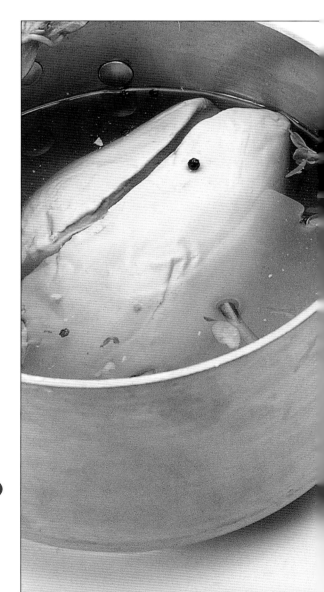

Foie Gras Poached in Gewürztraminer 〔241〕

"Baeckeofe" of Snails and Sauerkraut 243

Carpaccio with Truffles 239

52

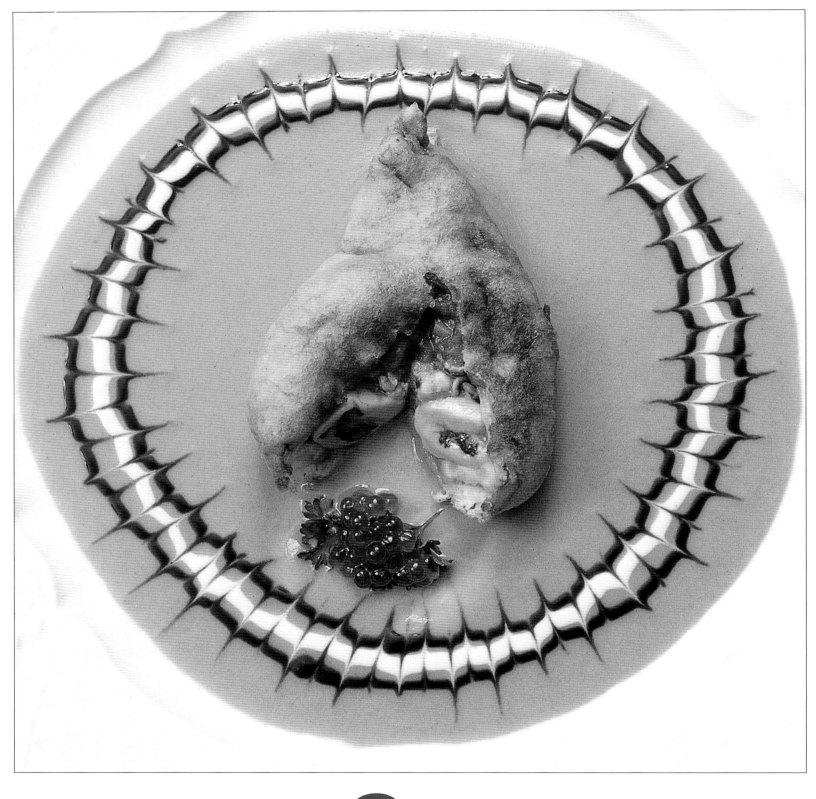

Oysters with Zucchini Flowers 242

Feuilleté of Oysters 244

Ravioli of Foie
Gras with Asparagus 244

Black Bean Pancake with Crabmeat 245

Goose Liver Braised in Sauerkraut 247

Pasta Pouches
with Fresh Seafood 247

59

Salmon Medallion in Shiitake Shell 250

Medley of Mushrooms 250

Gratin of Asparagus 251

64

Frogs Legs'
with Grapefruit 252

Wild Mushroom Gratin 252

Curried Oysters with Cucumber Sauce 253

Marinated Tuna with
Maui Onions and Avocados 253

American Foie Gras with Country Ham 254

Ricotta Cheese and Wasabi Pizza

Belgian Endive with Marinated Salmon 255

Garlic Custard
with Mushrooms **256**

Pasilla Chiles
with Avocado Salsa **256**

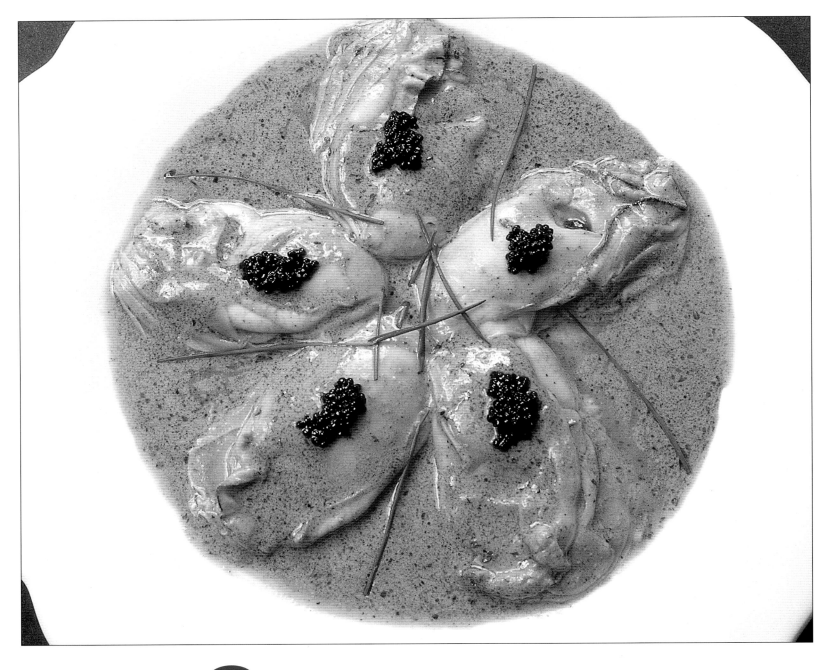

Oysters Trufant

Marinated Halibut

Oysters Maras 257

Tuna Carpaccio with Pesto 258

Gravlax with Mustard Sauce 259

76

Main Course

Today the terms "entrée" and "main course" are interchangeable. But step back into 17th century France, and you will find the words had other meanings. According to Escoffier, dinners à *la Française* included "relèves" and "entrées." Relèves were what we know as the main course, and entrées were what we now call appetizers.

"The first service of a dinner for twenty people, for instance, was comprised of eight or twelve entrées and four soups, all of which were set on the dinner table before the admission of the diners. As soon as the soups were served, the relèves, to the number of four, two of which consisted of fish, took the place of the soups on the table; they relieved the soups, hence their name, which is now, of course, quite meaningless." To further backtrack, food historian Raymond Sokolov writes in his book, *Why We Eat What We Eat,* that traditional French service evolved out of the "smorgasbordish anarchy of Medieval dining." It was "a table oriented self-service meal with a bewildering number of dishes."

French service turned into an exceedingly complicated performance of courses. Each course had its own French name. And in order to fully showcase the course, there were architectural table decorations including elaborate centerpieces. But enough was enough. Russian service came along to simplify matters. The greatest change with Russian was that in each course only one dish was served. For this style of service, serving platters were brought out from the kitchen, proudly displayed to the table of diners and then the waitstaff served up individual portions from a buffet table rolled in front of the dining table. Yet even this style of service had its absurdities. Such as even if a diner was eating alone and had ordered something that could have easily been plated in the kitchen, the procedure remained. Often waiters performed crucial finishing stages of actual cooking at tableside. It took decades for Russian service to totally replace French service. And the movement led to what has has ultimately been beneficial to today's cuisine - allowing chefs to perfect each individual dish instead of concentrating on a vast array of dishes.

Over the years, the serving of food has been greatly modified. We have for the most part lost the serving platters and deft waiters and now cuisine is focused on the individual plate. With today's focus on simplification, the menu usually centers on a main dish, preceeded by an appetizer or followed by a salad, cheese or dessert.

It's sometime difficult to make the distinction between appetizer and main course. As cuisine becomes less formal, the lines separating courses tend to fade and we become more relaxed as how we view the make-up of the meal. Nevertheless, main courses still anchor a meal. They influence side dishes. They influence our choice of appetizer. They affect our choice of wine. And considering the main courses we are offering here in this volume, they are indications of the creative talents of today's chefs and the beauty of their respective cuisines.

The main course is exactly what it is billed: the star of the show, the pinnacle of the dining experience. No matter the size of the dish, the main course presents several important components, one of which is the sauce. Some time ago, sauce was an afterthought. Today it is a fundamental detail in the construction of a plate, for the aroma and glisten of the sauce beholds an invitation to the character of the dish. Every element serves a specific purpose, but it is the sauce which enhances the delicate flavors of a dish, imparting a light or rich luminosity to the sum of its parts. Sauce making is a well-developed skill—one could say it is an art. Understanding basic technique enables us to later customize flavors with the addition of garnish.

According to Escoffier, the father of modern cuisine, sauce is an integral component to the dish. If basic technique is adopted, many variations are possible. Garnishes are added to change the flavors of dishes, and different aromatics can be used, resulting in a completely new sauce. Techniques like reduction of a well-flavored stock produce a rich glaze, to be used sparingly in order to add a powerful punch of flavor. A consistent base preparation is the only requirement—from there, the sky's the limit. The following recipes illustrate Escoffier's simple technique, and of course, the derivations are endless.

Brown Sauce

Yield 1 Gallon

For the brown roux:
3 ounces clarified butter
8 ounces flour
Salt and pepper to taste
For the brown sauce:
3 ounces vegetable oil
1 pound mirepoix
3 ounces tomato paste
1fi gallons brown veal stock
1 aromatic sachet
Salt and pepper to taste

For the brown roux, in a medium sauté pan, heat the clarified butter. Stir in the flour to make a paste, season to taste, and cook until roux is medium brown, about 15 minutes; reserve.

For the brown sauce, in a medium stock pot, heat the vegetable oil to smoking and caramelize the mirepoix, about 10 minutes. Stir in the tomato paste, and cook until the mixture is a deep mahogany color, about 15 minutes. Stir in the reserved roux. Whisk in the brown veal stock. Add the aromatic sachet, and bring to a simmer. Cook over medium-low heat for at least one hour, skimming the surface as necessary, until sauce reduces enough to coat the back of a spoon. Remove the aromatic sachet, and strain the sauce. Season to taste.

White Sauce (Béchamel)

Yield 1 Gallon

For the white roux:
8 ounces clarified butter
1fi cups finely chopped onions
10 ounces flour
Salt and pepper to taste
For the white sauce:
5 quarts cold milk
1 bay leaf
1 onion studded with 10 cloves
Salt and pepper to taste

For the white roux, in a large saucepan, heat the clarified butter. Add the onions; cover and sweat until translucent, about 15 minutes. Stir in the flour to make a paste, season to taste, and cook 3 minutes. Maintain the heat.

For the white sauce, whisk the cold milk into the onion roux. Bring to a simmer, adding the bay leaf and studded onion. Simmer over low heat for 45 minutes to cook out the roux. Strain the sauce, discarding the onion and bay leaf. Season to taste.

Velouté Sauce

Yield 1 Gallon

For the pale roux:
8 ounces clarified butter
10 ounces flour
Salt and pepper to taste
For the velouté:
5 quarts cold chicken, fish or white beef stock
1 bay leaf
1 aromatic sachet
Salt and pepper to taste

For the pale roux, in a large saucepan, heat the clarified butter. Stir in the flour to make a paste, season to taste, and cook 1 minute. Maintain the heat.

For the velouté sauce, whisk the cold stock into the roux. Bring to a simmer, adding the bay leaf and aromatic sachet. Simmer over low heat for 1 hour to cook out the roux. When the sauce coats the back of a spoon, strain the sauce and discard the bay leaf and sachet. Season to taste.

Fresh Tomato Sauce

Yield 1 Gallon

1 cup olive oil
1 pound mirepoix, finely chopped
fi cup garlic, finely chopped
5 pounds tomatoes, peeled, seeded and chopped
1 cup basil leaves, finely sliced
1 cup parsley, chopped
Salt and pepper to taste

For the tomato sauce, in a large sauce pan, heat the olive oil to smoking and add the mirepoix. Cook 3 minutes, and stir in the garlic. Cover and sweat vegetables until translucent, about 20 minutes. Stir in the tomatoes, and cook 30 minutes, or until sauce is fragrant. Just before service, stir in the basil and parsley. Season to taste.

Hollandaise Sauce

Yield 1 Quart

For the reduction:
4 ounces cider vinegar
1 teaspoon black peppercorns, crushed
³/₄ cup water

For the sauce:
12 egg yolks
3 cups clarified butter
Water as needed
3 teaspoons lemon juice
Salt and pepper to taste

For the reduction, in a small sauté pan over high heat, reduce the cider vinegar and peppercorns until dry. Add the water and reduce by half. Strain, and reserve.

For the sauce, in a medium stainless steel bowl set over a simmering water bath, whisk the egg yolks and reduction until frothy. Gradually whisk in the clarified butter a few drops at a time until a thick and homogeneous emulsion forms. At this point, the butter can be added in larger quantities. If mixture becomes too thick, thin it down with a little bit of water. Stir in the lemon juice, and season with salt and pepper. Serve immediately.

Dean Fearing

Jean Joho

Larry Forgione

Emeril Lagasse

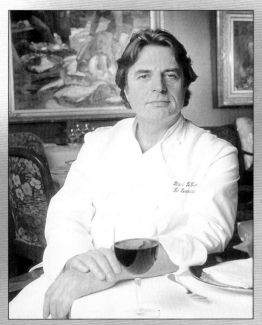

Gilbert Le Coze

Wolfgang Puck

Michel Rostang

83

Seafood

If you want to get some idea of how seafood has evolved into one of the most precious ingredients at a chef's fingertips, take a look at the recipes we share with you from our first 14 issues. In those early issues chefs were poaching, steaming and sautéing. In later years the popularity of grilling and roasting would catch on. And we witnessed the growing use of underutilized, also known as "trash" fish, like skate and sea robin.

Used successfully in the most classic French preparation, such as Poached Turbot with Buerre Noisette, seafood also lends itself to contemporary Asian influences such as Pan Fried Lobster with Curry Sauce or Grilled Butterfish Yuan Style. And as diners and chefs become more health conscious, seafood becomes more present on the menu, especially since much seafood has been found to contain the beneficial Omega-3 fatty acids, believed to lower cholesterol. Yet, still there is much we don't know about just how seafood gets from the water to our table. Environmentalists have raised red flags about the methods used by fisherman to keep up with the growing consumer demand for fish. The most poignant issue involves the shrimping industry and the endangered sea turtles, which become trapped in nets unless boats are equipped with Turtle Excluder Devices (TEDs).

Fish farming, too, has had its share of criticism. What seems to be the logical answer to our growing demand and dwindling wild supply of seafood has grown so rapidly that few standards are in place to enforce it. Aquaculture may be the answer over time, but environmentalists argue that too many people get involved in fish farming for the short term, and in the process destroys mangroves - the ecosystems of trees and shrubs found along a salt-water coastline. In addition, consumer activists continue to remind us that seafood, unlike beef or poultry, doesn't go through the government inspection process before we purchase it. Much of that, however, is changing. Kathy Snider, spokesperson for the National Fisheries Institute, says the Food and Drug Administration has implemented a new inspection program for seafood which became effective at the end of 1997. The program is based on what is known as HACCP or Hazard Analysis Critical Control Point. This identifies critical control points that occur in the processing and handling of food and requires that processors of fish and fishery products take preventative measures be taken to avoid food safety hazards before they happen. This might include taking temperatures of cooked and uncooked seafood, improving employee sanitation practices and evaluating the storage conditions of frozen food. A HACCP plan will cover each location where fish and fishery products are processed.

The seafood industry also has been given the option of having their product graded by the National Marine Fisheries Service (NMFS). But this voluntary program must be paid for by the fishery or manufacturer. Of course, if the manufacturer complies, the grading can be used as a marketing tool. And for the 600 seafood varieties, the NMFS has some 23 grading standards. As of yet, there are no standards for crab, oysters and sea urchin. Which is even more reason to be careful to eat and cook only very fresh fish. Uncooked seafood should always be stored in ice, in the lowest part of the refrigerator. It shouldn't be allowed to soak in water. And it is safest to purchase whole fish, with bones and gills intact, so you can see what you are getting. Leftover trim can be used to make stock and fish mousse.

The freshest fish will be plump with bright scales. It will have clear bulging eyes. It will have pinkish gills and a sweet aroma. Shellfish, too, should smell sweet and briny. Mollusks bought in the shell should always be alive with closed shells, or they should close quickly in response to gentle pressure. Crab, lobster and crayfish, unless purchased cooked, should be alive. And if you assure that your fish is fresh, make sure you don't overcook it. In Wolfgang Puck's classic Tempura Sashimi, tuna is lightly battered and deep-fried to only cook the outside so that the inside remains raw. In other dishes, like Grilled Swordfish and Sea Robin with Chanterelles, the fish might not be served raw, but you can bet the chefs didn't let it overcook one minute, or else the subtle textures and flavors of the seafood creations would be lost.

Grilled John Dory with Basil Vinaigrette 263

Lobster with Ginger Sauce 263

King Crab Pasta
with Italian Parsley 264

White Alaskan Salmon with Spicy Pecan Butter   264

91

Roasted Monkfish with Vegetables — 265

Steamed Salmon with Black Bean Sauce — 266

Fricassee of Cod 266

Seared Codfish 267

Sea Robin Tails   268

Monkfish with
Fennel and Star Anise 269

Sautéed Sea Robin with Chanterelles 270

Black Bass with Port
Wine Sauce   270

Striped Bass with Thyme Flowers 270

Seared Bluefish with
Melon Relish 271

Pike with Sauvignon Blanc Sauce 272

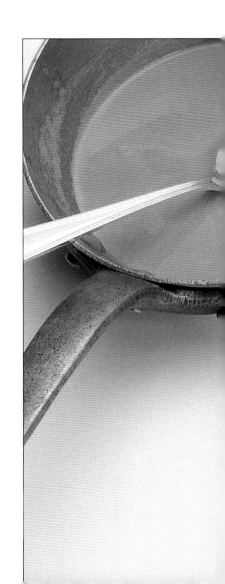

272

Shrimp with Carrot-Sauvignon Blanc Sauce 273

Shrimp Balls with Matsutake Mushrooms 274

Grilled Abalone　284

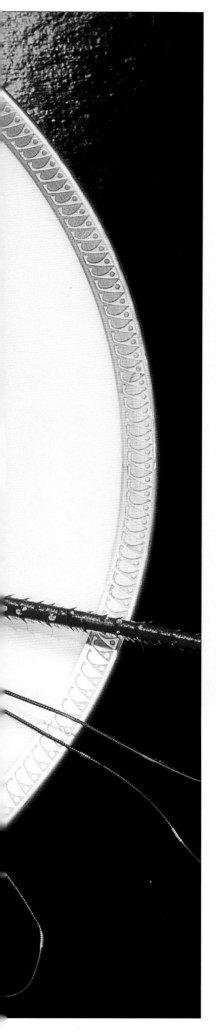

Barbecued Shrimp 277

Steamed Bok Choy with Seafood   278

113

Red Mullet with Fava Beans and Basil   281

Poached Turbot
with Brown Butter   282

Grilled Butterfish with Tempura 282

Open Ravioli 285

Crispy Salmon
with Herb Sauce   286

Sea Bass with
Red Beet Sauce   287

123

Poultry-Game-Fowl

The chickens our grandparents roasted, fried or simmered on Sunday bear little resemblance to the computerized, hormone-induced, mass-produced chickens most consumers purchase today. Not only have production methods switched to high gear to crank out the plumpest, roundest birds imaginable, but these modern chicks have little taste. But then, a chicken is not a chicken is not a chicken.

For today so many kinds of chicken exist. They come with differing price tags. But simply, chicken can be classified in four groups. The first is the commercial chicken geared to the supermarket industry as described above. The second is "natural," meaning only that no traces of antibiotics or hormones can be found in the chicken. The third is "free range," defined by the U.S. Department of Agriculture as a chicken that has free access to the outdoors with a minimum of 10 feet per bird to roam and feed.

And the last is "organic," a term the USDA has yet to define, but meaning that these chickens have been raised on organic land with access to plenty of real sunlight. They have been fed on organic grains and water and have been allowed to grow at their own rate, which takes twice as long as the commercial chicken. Organic chicken is produced without hormones, growth stimulants, force feeding or antibiotics. And with just simple mathematics you can deduce that the cost of allowing a bird to grow slowly, naturally and humanely these days is expensive. In fact, the only certified organic chicken breeder in the United States is D'Artagnan. Ariane Daguin of D'Artagnan patiently waits for the USDA to recognize the organic poultry production and to set it apart from those chickens deemed "natural" or "organic." D'Artagnan chicken has been certified by the North East Organic Farmers Association of New York for the past three years. The USDA claims that organic will become a recognized term in the next few years. But in the meantime, confusion abounds. Presently, commercial chicken can be described as "natural" on the label. Organic chicken can be described as "natural" on the label. But the two have completely different textures, flavors, methods of production and pricetags.

Not as mainstream as chicken, but an important part of the restaurant's menu are other fowl - squab, quail and grouse. Along with sharing Chicken with Eggplant Ravioli and Foie Gras, we share Squab with Risotto, Roast Quail with Bean Ragout and Crepinette of Grouse. Their popularity increases as creative chefs devise intriguing ways to prepare them. And the same goes for venison. While it is technically red meat, it is an altogether different ingredient. New Zealand is the largest producer and exporter of farm-raised venison in the world. Some 85 percent of the venison imported in the United States comes from New Zealand. the forefront is Cervena, a venison company that lauds itself as feeding the venison only grass and slaughtering under three years of age to assure consistent size, texture and mild flavor. But domestic farm-raised venison is, too, a growth industry. In the decade the United States has gone from producing virtually no venison, some 150,000 pounds are produced here each year. One source is Millbrook Venison, a New York company that raises organically-fed and hormone-free venison.

The appeal for venison is understandable. It has all the protein of beef and lamb but is lower in fat and cholesterol. But because of this leanness and absence of internal marbling, venison doesn't baste itself while it cooks. Steaks and chops must be lightly cooked or they will lose their natural juices.

If you've ever been tempted to scoop up that road kill and serve it for dinner, think again. This is not what wild game is all about. Wild game is actually an old tradition. And as one of our most cherished resources, it is currently experiencing a fashionable recurrence. Long before our ancestors harvested wild grasses, they scoured the land, foraging for food and killing animals in order to survive. Wild game was a dietary staple for generations of people. A good kill was beneficial because it guaranteed food for the entire group. Now, we are fortunate enough to have food brought right to our doorstep, and the need to hunt for and gather our food has been nearly eliminated.

In less modern times, wild game was as seasonal as produce. The "season" depended on the birth of young animals and the laws within each community. During the past few decades, for example, venison was thought to be available only during autumn, when the deer hunting season opened. Today, however, wild game as we know it most likely refers to specific species of game which are raised on farms or ranches. The product is still wild because of the manner in which it is raised, but the flavors are distinctly different. The "gamey" flavors often associated with wild game are less pronounced in the farm-raised variety, and the quality of the meat is more tender and better in flavor. For example, a deer living in the wild is likely to eat a random diet consisting of "leaves, flowers, buds, acorns, and berries, but if food is scarce, the deer may resort to mucky swamp water, tree bark, rotted vegetation, and even animal excrement" (Ray 8). A deer raised in a controlled environment eats a strict diet of corn, grain, and greens, which has a positive effect on the flavor of the meat. The result is a near neutral product which adapts easily to menus, and which customers will be likely to enjoy because of its less pronounced flavor.

The best way to familiarize yourself and your customers with wild game is to experiment. Seek out knowledgeable resources, like purveyors who specialize in wild game, then purchase product and test different cooking methods. Educate yourself and ask questions. It is important to find out every aspect of the animal's life before harvest, such as the diet and environment of the animal, and the time between harvest and processing of the animal. An animal that was hunted to death would have had a flow of adrenaline through its body, making its meat taste very tough and unpleasant. An animal that rests in rigor before being dressed may deteriorate more quickly. Obviously, meat that has been harvested and processed consecutively will be of highest quality, while meat that experienced a delay between phases will be of lower and maybe even poor quality. Add wild game dishes to your menu sparingly—get feedback and look for the results as plates return to the kitchen. An excellent way to introduce wild game to your customers is to offer a special game and wine tasting. Or use game as an amuse-bouche. Guests love a small portion of wild game consommé as a way to taste some-thing of which they might not typically order a full portion. Use familiar products on these plates. Try adapting game to standard dishes—venison for beef, or quail for chicken or Cornish hen. It might take a while, but gradually your customers will adjust.

The Wild Side: A Brief Guide to Game

Unless using a moist-heat method of cooking, wild game is best served medium-rare to maximize texture and flavor. Take each cut of meat into consideration as you cook and be wary of lean to muscle ratio. Wild game is appreciated better if prepared slightly undercooked.
Source: Ray, Christopher. *The Wild Menu.* Wisconsin: Willow Creek Press, 1995.

Alligator: Light in color, firm in texture with strong flavor. Marinate and grill or grind into sausage. Works well with Cajun spices.

Antelope: Similar in shape to deer, but physically related to goats. Finely grained meat, mild tasting. Herbal, tastes "sweet" like veal. Broil, braise, grill, roast, or sauté.

Bear: Carnivorous animal. Coarse, dark red meat has fat content similar to pork. Braise and roast. Strong flavor—not for wild game beginners.

Boar: Less fatty than pork. Young boar is tender, with dark red meat. Sweet, nutty, and intense flavor. Braise, broil, grill, or roast.

Buffalo: Also called bison and believed to have descended from wild cattle. Substitute for beef. Less fat marbling than beef; lean in texture and flavor. Sauté or grill over high heat.

Caribou: Small animal, close in size to the deer. Finely grained, herbal flavor resembling veal. Broil, braise, grill, roast, or sauté.

Deer: Herbal flavor, velvety-textured meat. Similar to beef. Broil, braise, grill, roast, or sauté.

Elk: Second largest member of the deer family. Dark and coarsely grained. "Sweet," distinctive flavor. Broil, braise, grill, roast, or sauté.

Moose: Largest member of the deer family. Harvested mature, after four years of age. Dark, intense, mature meat. Rich marbling and flavor. Braise or roast.

Duck: Meaty, rich flavor. Fatty, chewy meat. Breasts are best suited to grill or broil; serve medium-rare as meat toughens if overcooked. Braise or preserve legs. Roast whole duck.

Goose: Lean bird with dark, sweet meat. Slight game taste with buttery flavor. Braise or roast.

Hare: Larger than rabbit with coarser texture and richer, "gamier" flavor. Low in fat. Braise.

Musk Ox: Related to the buffalo. Limited availability. Less regulated harvesting methods result in a rich tasting, gamey meat. Sauté or grill over high heat.

Ostrich: Lean red meat comparable to an excellent quality beef. Low in fat. Grill or sauté.

Partridge and Grouse: Light flavor reminiscent of the forest. Most favored of the wild game birds because of its true wild game qualities. Roast or grill.

Pheasant: Delicate flavor and texture. Fruity and herbal qualities. Braise or roast over low heat.

Quail: Small, light, delicate bird. Juicy, light-textured, and mildly flavorful. De-bone and stuff; roast over high heat.

Rabbit: Similar to chicken, easily digestible. Low in fat. Braise, broil, grill, roast, or sauté.

Rattlesnake: Light and chewy meat, herbal flavor resembling chicken. Braise or sauté.

Squab (Pigeon): Commercial birds are featherless. Rich, dark, moist meat. Intense game flavor. Stuff and roast at high heat.

Wild Turkey: Lean in fat and taste similar to commercial turkeys; versatile. Braise, broil, roast, or sauté.

Alfred Portale

Paul Prudhomme

Alain Sailhac

Georges Perrier

Ezio Santin

Grilled Marinated Quail · 290

132

Chicken with Eggplant Ravioli and Foie Gras

Roast Quail with Bean Ragoût   291

Crépinette of Grouse   292

137

Ragoût of Rabbit with Artichoke 294

Chicken Breast with Cèpes and
Flageolet Beans

295

143

Squab with Risotto 295

Venison Loin with Peppercorn Crust 296

Chicken Breast with Pinto Beans   296

Veal

Veal needs little explanation. It is the most delicate, elegant and versatile of meats. It has the ability to marry with limitless flavors, from red cabbage and Riesling to country ham and rosemary to fresh basil and mozzarella. It is the stuff of which classics are made, from Austrian Wiener Schnitzel, breaded veal scallops cooked in the style of Vienna, to Veal Marsala, perfumed of the rich, smoky Italian wine. Veal, too, is complemented by most any spice on the shelf, and there is no fresh herb that doesn't adapt well to veal. Especially sage in the Roman classic Saltimbocca, meaning "jump in the mouth," in which finely sliced veal is sprinkled with sage and topped with thinly sliced prosciutto before sautéeing in butter and braising in white wine. But should you want to hold back on the butter and prosciutto, veal adapts well to low-calorie cuisine. Chef Georges Masraff successfully creates a "diet" veal dish with a mere 180 calories. It captures the piquant flavor of citrus, the succulence of veal and the crispness of fresh zucchini.

If any group of people claim to love veal more than others it would have to be the Italians. They love veal because it is harmonious, blending with the various sauces and textures on the Italian plate. According to the 19th century gourmand Grimond de la Reynière, veal is "the chameleon of the kitchen." It's neutral, allowing for tomatoes, garlic, zucchini, sage, prosciutto, whatever, to shine through. In fact, at one time, historians theorized that the names "veal" and "Italy" were somehow related, that Italy was named for the "calf land" or "grazing land." And to further confuse everyone, there was talk that the Austrian Wiener Schnitzel was actually an Italian dish that originated at a church dinner in Milan in 1134. Regardless of its roots, or the people who claim to have prepared the first veal, the veal we eat today has grand variation, from poor to superior. This depends on how and what the calf is fed, and how young it is when slaughtered.

Veal sold in the United States is technically any calf that is slaughtered up to four months of age and is either farm-raised or formula-fed. Formula-fed veal of the European tradition, on the other hand, is fed dry milk solids blended with fat and water. Movement is restricted to arrive at complete tenderness. While these calves get up to 350 pounds, their flesh is white, tender and delicate. And yet the movement towards more humanely raised animals has led to the current farm-raised calves such as those at Summerfield Farm in Virginia. Calves are allowed to suckle, in addition to walking and foraging. Their flesh is pink, with a stronger flavor and coarser texture. It is a veal that many people have grown to prefer.

Distinguishing veal from other types of young beef can be confusing. Bob veal is slaughtered at less than 21 days of age, with these young calves weighing 150 pounds or less. These calves have never been allowed to eat grass or grain. But when calves are slaughtered at between four and nine months they are termed "baby beef." The flesh is pinkish red and coarse. The USDA grades veal based on how much fat is between the ribs and the flank, how thick and full the carcass is, and how the lean muscle tissue is colored and textured. Obviously, the United States and France have different methods of rearing calves. According to Larousse Gastronomique, the highest quality veal should be that raised on mother's milk alone. It should smell of milk and have satiny white fat. At the time that Larousse was first published, the St. Etienne calves were prized. They received a combination of mother's milk and protein supplements. The Lyon calves were weaned and fattened indoors, whereas the most prized calves, those from Limosin, were raised exclusively at the udder. No doubt that when the Beef Industry Council coined the slogan, "Veal, It's Worth Going Out For," it had surveyed chefs. Veal has always had a place of honor at European tables, and if you look at the veal recipes we share in this issue - from shanks to chops to medallions - you will see that veal is not only elegant, it is versatile.

Medallions of Veal with Sweetbread Terrine 298

Medallions of Veal with Country Ham and Rosemary Cream 298

Grilled Veal Loin with Beans 299

Roasted Veal Shank with Riesling ⟨300⟩

154

Roasted Veal Tenderloin with
Arugula and Grilled Wild Mushrooms

301

Lamb-Pork

The roasting of a whole lamb or whole pig is cause for celebration in many parts of the world. There is something grand about a garlic-and- rosemary-studded whole lamb sizzling on a spit, dripping fat into the fire, or of a suckling pig searing over hickory. The aroma wafts thick in the air. These are memorable, heady food experiences. In the Mediterranean that lamb might be sliced and served up with a glass of red wine. In the Deep South, that pork would be pulled from the bone, tossed with a peppery vinegar sauce and washed down with a cold glass of iced tea. Obviously, no matter the locale, people have connected to roasting lamb and pork for generations.

According to Alexandre Dumas in *Dumas on Food,* the Greeks thought so highly of lamb, that "few feasts were given without roast lamb being the most important dish." Lamb was savored, sacrificed, and it was bartered. In the Bible's book of Genesis, Abraham gave Abimelech seven lambs as a token of their covenant. Even today, the focus of the Greek Easter table is a roasted lamb. And the most popular Greek street food of all - the gyro - is based on lamb. An oversized "tourney" of lamb roasts slowly over an open flame. Slices are shaved off to order, and the meat is layered with creamy yogurt and fresh garlic on soft pita bread. In *Italian Food,* by Elizabeth David, the author describes how Sardinian shepherds excelled in spit-roasting meat. They roasted it underground in a pit lined with "branches and leaves... they then cover it with a light layer of soil, upon which they burn a big fire for several hours." Who knows how often the owner of a stolen sheep sat around the fire under which his sheep was cooking, never dreaming the people who invited him were precisely the ones who robbed him! But don't think the rest of the world doesn't adore lamb. Waverly Root writes in his food history/dictionary called *Food,* that the Middle East has long been home to lamb. The oldest find of domesticated sheep bones was from 9000 B.C. and was found in Iraq. These sheep were killed before they were a year of age. Root notes that as much as we like to believe that prehistoric man was a gross creature, he obviously discerned the flavor difference in lamb and mutton.

The passion for lamb, however, seems to wane when you head west. Root says Americans are "sulky towards lamb." The British eat five times as much lamb as Americans. Although the American west produces some excellent lamb, Americans don't like lamb because they don't get the chance to taste it often, says Root. What most Americans call lamb is what Europeans would call "mutton." By definition, lamb is sheep that is not more than a year old. But what Root points out is that once a lamb produces its first two teeth by its first birthday, a "natural taste-changing development occurs at this age in sheep." The French and Italians eat the youngest lamb. A lamb that has never tasted grass in Italy is called *abbacchio,* a true suckling lamb. But in France it's a bit more complicated. French lambs are not slaughtered until they weigh 15½ pounds. From here until 22 pounds, the lamb is called *agneau de lait,* and the lamb is from five to seven weeks old. If the lamb has not been weaned, but it's possible that it might have eaten some grass, it would be called *agneau blanc.* And if it is certain this lamb has eaten some grass, it would be a *broutard,* and the lamb would have reached about three months of age.

Pork, on the other hand, is a welcome ingredient at most any age. Although the younger, suckling pigs, are prized for spit-roasting. Grimod de la Reynière called the pig an "encyopedic animal, veritable walking repast. One throws no part of it away, even to the feet, one eats it all." Without a doubt, pork has been the most important meat in the world. Without it, there would be few cuisines. The leading pork-eating nation is China, although many of you might have guessed the United States, what with the impact pork has had on the evolution of the American diet.

Pork has remained a cook's friend because it is economical. There is no waste. Not only for its meat is it prized, but its skin can be turned into leather, its glands into pharmaceuticals, its hair into upholstery and insulation. Pork can be cooked fresh, smoked, lightly salted or air-dried, as those fine prosciuttos of Italy, that take eating pork to another dimension.

Jean-Georges Vongerichten

Hartmut Handke

Christer Larsson

Patrick O'Connell

Ferdinand Metz

Lamb Loin with
Black Trumpet Mushrooms 306

Glazed Pork Shanks 305

Loin of Lamb with Lentils   308

Grilled Loin of Lamb   308

Lamb Shank with Persillade 309

Beef

It's no surprise that once the American public grew more concerned about fat and cholesterol, farmers tried to raise leaner cattle. Today's beef is 27 percent leaner than beef produced a decade ago. That is made possible by new feeding methods and the role of genetics, developing cattle with more lean muscle and less fat. Whereas cattle farmers used to make money on the sheer weight of livestock, bigger is no longer better. Federally established yield grading looks at how cutable the cattle is.

According to chef Anthony Ligouri, meat fabrication instructor at the Culinary Institute of America in Hyde Park, N.Y., beef is yield graded to determine how much saleable meat is obtained from boneless and semi-boneless trimmed retail cuts of the round, loin rib and chuck. It is based on the amount of internal fat (marbling) and external fat in relation to total carcass weight. Then, beef is broken down into eight quality grades to describe how palatable it will be. Since this is a voluntary practice paid for by the packer, not all beef sold will be quality graded. The eight grades are prime, choice, select, standard, commercial, utility, cutter and canner. The quality is based on the age of the animal, the amount of marbling in lean muscle and the bone ossification and color.

Just to prove how precious prime beef is, only five percent of the cattle graded will be deemed prime. Prime beef comes from cattle that is less than three years old, and it has the most marbling. Thus, it is the most tender beef and the most flavorful. But it is usually only available in fine restaurants and from specialty butchers.

Choice and select, on the other hand, are more readily available at wholesale and retail outlets. Most of the beef sold in supermarkets has been graded choice up until the last few years when the beef industry has responded to the public's quest for lower fat and cholesterol foods by marketing select beef. It is leaner than prime or choice, but without the internal fat, it is also a lot less juicy and flavorful. The remaining grades of beef from standard on down to canner go into myriad processed products.

Certified Angus Beef is a little different than regular choice beef. Not only must the beef come from Angus cattle, but it must have modest, evenly distributed marbling, have a yield grade of three or leaner, and have come from young cattle, from nine to 30 months in age. According to Bill Wylie, director of the foodservice division for Certified Angus Beef, of the U.S. beef that is judged to be choice, some 70 percent of it falls into the lowest acceptable marbling range allowed by the USDA. Certified Angus Beef has more marbling than regular choice beef, plus the program is monitored by the American Angus Association. Long before Angus Beef was certified, our prehistoric ancestors were hunting wild ox for food. The domestic cattle as we know them are descendants of these ox. Cattle have been domesticated for more than 40 centuries, according to the Larousse Gastronomique.

In the Middle Ages, dishes for nobility were prepared using the best cuts of beef. Tournedos, chateaubriand, filet en croute and the beef rib roast are classics. In 1756 the Duke of Richelieu chose the menu for a famous meal that was given for his illustrious prisoners during the Hanoverian War. The 12 dishes of the first course and the 10 dishes of the second course all contained beef. Possibly the Duke's intent was to kill them off with clogged arteries? That would have shortened their prison sentence!

The most fatty and the most prized beef in the world comes from the Kobe cattle farms in Japan. Here cattle enjoy a luxurious regimen of rich grains, hearty beers and end their day with a relaxing massage. The workers are encouraged to speak to the cattle in stress-free, calm dialogue. Violent language or actions are not tolerated. In the end, the happy cow is a mighty tasty cow. And the Japanese people serve up this razor-thin sliced Kobe beef as a rare treat, indeed.

Maurizio Santin

Susan Spicer

Eisuke Sugai

Barry Wine

Wolfgang von Wieser

175

Sirloin with Sauce Bordelaise

 310

178

Roast Tenderloin of Beef Venison Style   311

Tournedo of Beef with Roquefort 311

Fillet of Beef with Country Ham and Oyster Sauce 312

Grilled Sirloin Steak 312

Medallions of Beef with Ancho Chili Sauce 313

Pasta-Bread

The staff of life, the foundation on which diets have been built - bread. Isn't the breadwinner the head of the family? And aren't we in the Christian Lord's Prayer asked to be given our daily bread before we are asked to be delivered from evil? To take bread out of one's mouth is to tear someone away from something he is about to enjoy. To have your bread buttered on both sides is to prosper. The metaphors could go on. For bread is the foodstuff that has sustained populations. And the flour that is mixed, moistened and leavened into bread is also the basis for pasta, another important anchor of the diet, and a food more increasingly eaten now that dietitians are urging us to adhere to a Mediterrean diet and consume more complex carbohydrates.

The first record of pasta was in ancient Rome where a type of pasta called *laganum* was made. It was a cake made from strips of dough, similar to lasagna, and it was adopted from the Greeks. The pasta as we know it entered Italian cooking in 800 A.D. when the Arabs invaded Sicily. The first recorded mention of pasta was in 15 A.D. in Italy when a Sicilian geographer surveyed land and mentioned the word *itriya*, the Arabic name for pasta. He said the land would be suitable for growing wheat to turn into pasta. And pasta is still called *tria* in the Sicilian dialect. Elsewhere in Italy, it is just called pasta, a word used to describe all 300 of the shapes and lengths of this durum semolina product. That rigid semolina grain is what makes pasta so deliciously chewy. Most American pastas are not produced with durum semolina; thus, they are often gummy and flavorless when cooked. Imported Italian pasta, on the other hand, is quite durable and has excellent flavor and texture. Look for those made in the old pasta factories where machines with brass dies as opposed to newer non-stick dies extrude the various shapes. Martelli from Tuscany and Rustichella from Abruzzo are two such producers. Because these pastas are extruded through brass, they have a coarser texture. And this rough exterior not only gives the pasta a more chewy texture, but it allows it to hold onto the sauce. Times are a changing, unfortunately. Much of the Italian pasta is manufactured in big, modern plants with machinery that automatically extrudes, cuts, dies and packs the product.

Fresh pasta, on the other hand, gives a chef more freedom to create a product with a special flavor, color, shape or filling. It does have a limited shelf life and can only be refrigerated for up to two days. If you choose to go this route, you will need to carefully select the flours you begin with. Look for semolina flour, but let your imagination roam. Try pasta with whole wheat flour, cornmeal, rye flour, ground chickpeas and other specialty grains.

But don't think Italians are the only ones who forged their cuisine on a flour-based product. The Germans have spaetzle. The Poles have pierogi, and the Asian countries have all sorts of noodles made from wheat, rice and soy flours. Yet with all this variety, sometimes the simplest preparation of pasta is the best. Such as noodles tossed with fruity olive oil and a shaving of good Pecorino Romano cheese.

In terms of feeding people worldwide, another important grain is rice. In fact, rice feeds more people than pasta. The sheer varieties of rice available today is amazing. In the long grains, you can sample aromatics grown in the United States, such as basmati and jasmine, or imported Indian basmati and Thai jasmine. Short-grain Asian sticky rices are perfect for eating with chopsticks. And the medium-grain rices fold beautifully into paella. Perhaps one of the most beloved rices is the Italian arborio, a round short-grain rice, traditionally grown in the Po valley.

Here the famous risotto was born. Risotto, known as "porridge of the gods," in northern Italy, is made by slowly cooking arborio rice on top of the stove, constantly adding simmering broth or other liquids. The rice is said to be done when it is creamy overall, yet each grain still a little *al dente*, or firm to the bite. Or, if you shake a pan of risotto, it should undulate like a wave, called *al onda*. Making risottos in restaurants isn't easy, because the traditional recipes calls for someone to stand there at the stove constantly stirring it until done. But some chefs have discovered how to cook risotto in the oven. This frees up the chef. But regardless of the method, risottos have got to be served up at once or they lose their creaminess. The classic Risotto alla Milanese has an intriguing history. The legend dates to 1574, when an artisan named Zafferano was working on the stained glass in Milan's Duomo. Because he added saffron to his paints, his co-workers teased him and said one day he would go so far as to add saffron to his risotto. For his daughter's wedding feast, he did add saffron to the risotto. The bright yellow risotto looked like gold coins.

The word cereal—what does it mean? We think of it as a breakfast food, prepackaged and precooked, a product that in no way represents the cereals of ancient peoples. Our cereal is sweet and turns milk pink or brown. Their cereals began as tall grasses that covered the land, swaying gently in the wind. Cereal, known to civilization as early as 8000 B.C., is named for Ceres, the Roman goddess of agriculture, and includes any plant from the grass family which yields an edible seed or grain. Grains are an historical presence. Barley is thought to pre-date wheat, having been a mainstay in the diet of ancient Greeks and Romans..

The tall grasses were cut, and the kernels separated from the stalks. The kernels were roasted, and stone tools were used to smash apart the kernels. The sperm was separated from the germ and the husk. The parts were either ground into flour, roasted and dried, soaked or crushed. Different crushing techniques were employed for different parts of the grain, resulting in a multitude of products requiring a variety of cooking methods.

It is known that early peoples foraged for food and, in their travels, noticed that the wild grasses they cut down were not reproducing; instead, bare spots remained. But, by chance, some of the seeds transported by the wind had begun to reproduce, and soon the grasses grew tall once again. Eventually, these peoples began to sow grass seeds, remaining in the area for the season to reap the results of their efforts: "It is no exaggeration to say that the beginning of agriculture marked the beginning of civilization, for once freed from constant foraging, our ancestors could devote their strength to building cities and the systems necessary for their survival," says Marlene Bumgarner in her *Book of Whole Grains*.

Grain is essential to our diet, representing nearly 80% of what we consume daily. Wheat is our most familiar cereal grain, providing us with the bulk of our intake. It appears in everything from the obvious, like pasta and bread, to less suspicious items like soup and beer. It is versatile and has many uses. Cereal grains in general pair well with greens and meats, creating balanced yet diverse plating combinations. But wheat is only one type of grain. There are dozens more, and they, too, have many uses. It's time for us to shed the milk from our cereal and take a more serious look into our oldest food source.

Whole grains are often used in the preparation of bread. A "soaker" is prepared by combining whole grains with liquid which rests for 8 - 12 hours. The grains absorb the liquid, making it easier for them to be incorporated into the bread dough. Alternatively, a quick "soaker" can be prepared by using the following methods, keeping in mind to undercook the grains.

Grains can be cooked using a variety of methods, but boiling or steaming is the preferred method. Water or stock can be used for cooking. The general rule for cooking grains is to season the cooking liquid, *not* the finished product. There are certain exceptions, however. Amaranth, whole grain rye, wheat berries, and brown rice should *not* be cooked in salted liquid—the salt toughens the outer husks of these grains, preventing liquid absorption and making the finished product unpalatable.

Lexicon

Cereal Grains: Any plant from the grass family which yields a seed which can then be ground into flour.

Bran: The partly ground husk of wheat or other grain, separated from flour by sifting through a fine sieve. Varieties include oat bran, rice bran, or wheat bran.

Endosperm: Nutritive outside material of cereal grain.

Flour: Finely ground meal of a grain.

Germ: Embryo of a plant in its early stages, contained within the cereal grain.

Groats: Hulled, whole kernels of grain, usually oats, buckwheat, rye, or barley.

Hominy: Whole, hulled corn from which the bran and germ have been removed by processing the whole kernel in a lye bath.

Husk: The dry outside covering of a seed, or as in corn, a group of seeds.

Kasha: Mush made from whole or coarse cracked grain, especially buckwheat.

Kernel: A whole seed grain.

Meal: The edible part of any grain ground coarse, unsifted.

Wheat Flour: Ground meal from the wheat kernel. Wheat flour comes in many formulas. Hard flours, or flours with a high protein content, are most suitable for bread baking. Soft flours have a high starch content and a low protein content and are best used for cakes and quick breads.

Yeast: Yeast is a living micro-organism which feeds on sugar to form carbon dioxide and alcohol. It is essential to certain types of bread product. Yeast is available both fresh and dried. Yeast also occurs naturally in the air in some locations, in particular, vineyards and on grapes.

Sugar: Sugar is essential to the breadmaking process, as it accelerates development of the dough by providing food to the yeast. Too much sugar, however, can kill the yeast.

Salt: Salt provides flavor and strengthens the gluten net which develops when the protein in flour is combined with liquid.

Additional Source: London, Mel and Sheryl. *The Versatile Grain and Elegant Bean*. New York: Simon and Schuster, 1992.

Lexicon

Cereal Grains: Any plant from the grass family which yields a seed which can then be ground into flour.

Bran: The partly ground husk of wheat or other grain, separated from flour by sifting through a fine sieve. Varieties include oat bran, rice bran, or wheat bran.

Endosperm: Nutritive outside material of cereal grain.

Flour: Finely ground meal of a grain.

Germ: Embryo of a plant in its early stages, contained within the cereal grain.

Groats: Hulled, whole kernels of grain, usually oats, buckwheat, rye, or barley.

Hominy: Whole, hulled corn from which the bran and germ have been removed by processing the whole

Grain	How to Buy:	Volume of Liquid per 1 cup:	Approximate Cooking Time:	Approximate Yield:
	Whole Grain	3 Cups	25 Minutes	2½ Cups
	Pearled	3½ Cups	35 Minutes	3¼ Cups
	Grits	4 Cups	20 Minutes	3⅔ Cups
	Rolled Flakes	3 Cups	22 Minutes	2⅔ Cups
	Unroasted Whole	2 Cups	12 Minutes	4 Cups
	Groats	3 Cups	12 Minutes	2⅓ Cups
	Creamy Kernel Grits	4 Cups	10 to 20 Minutes	3¾ Cups
	Kasha	6 Cups	30 Minutes	8 Cups
	Cornmeal	5 Cups	2½ to 3 hours	3 Cups
	Whole Hominy	2½ Cups	25 to 30 Minutes	4 Cups
	Grits	2 Cups	25 to 30 minutes	4 Cups
	Whole Grain	2¾ Cups	25 Minutes	3 Cups
	Whole Groats	3½ Cups	15 Minutes	3 Cups
	Steel Cut	2¾ Cups	10 Minutes	2½ Cups
	Rolled Flakes	2 Cups	12 to 15 Minutes	3 Cups
	Whole Grain	3 Cups	20 to 30 Minutes	3 Cups
	Arborio	1½ Cups	25 Minutes	3 Cups
	Basmati	1¾ Cups	25-30 Minutes	4 Cups
	Converted	3 Cups	40 Minutes	4 Cups
	Long-Grain Brown	1½ Cups	18 Minutes	3 Cups
	Long-Grain White	2½ Cups	35 to 40 Minutes	4 Cups
	Short-Grain Brown	1½ Cups	30 Minutes	3 Cups
	Short-Grain White	3 Cups	30 to 45 Minutes	4 Cups
	Wild	3¼ Cups	60 Minutes	2 Cups
	Whole Grain	3½ Cups	35 to 40 Minutes	2⅔ Cups
	Grits	3 Cups	25 to 30 Minutes	2⅔ Cups
	Rolled Flakes	3 Cups	15 Minutes	3 Cups
	Whole Grain	3 Cups	70 Minutes	2½ Cups
	Whole Berries	3½ Cups	50 to 60 Minutes	3 Cups
	Cracked Wheat	2⅓ Cups	15 Minutes	2¾ Cups
	Couscous	1 Cup	10 Minutes	2 Cups
	Bulghur	2½ Cups	15 to 30 Minutes	3 Cups

Macaroni with
Caviar and Onions 314

Farfalle with
Mozzarella
and Pepper Vodka 315

190

Risotto with
Saffron and Gold Leaf   316

Angel Hair Pasta with Chanterelles   315

"Alper" Macaroni 315

Mushroom Wontons 316

193

Plain Brioche 317

194

Fruit Brioche 317

Vegetable Brioche 318

195

Dessert

If there be any poetry at all in meals, or the process of feeding, there is poetry in the dessert.

- Isabella Beeton

A talented woman, no doubt, but Mrs. Beeton lived in 19th century England when people just didn't wax eloquently about custards and cakes and soufflés and sherbets. However, Mrs. Beeton found art in their assembly. For to her, desserts not only tempted the palate, but they pleased the eye. By definition, the dessert is the course that appears last on the menu, after empty dishes from previous courses have been removed. Thus, the word dessert comes from the French verb *desservir*, to clear the table. It is the final course, the last act of the finely constructed play, the ending chapter of the book. It is the difficult time for a chef, a time when appetites are satisfied, when a course is needed to restore the palate and leave a lasting impression. Although many dessert courses in the world are composed of cheese and nuts, especially in England where port is sipped, most desserts are sweet. Even if their main ingredient is fresh fruit, this fruit is invariably sweetened with a syrup or a caramel sauce or a sweet custard.

Sugar, it seems, signals the meal's end. And this is more than sheer coincidence. For according to the Time-Life researchers who assembled the book, *Classic Desserts*, the development of modern desserts is inseparable from the increasing availability of sugar. Sugar was widely used in India in the 4th century B.C., and its use spread throughout the Muslim world. But elsewhere in the world, sugar was a rarity. Honey was the sweetener in most European recipes. The ancient Romans mixed honey with eggs to make the predecessor of the dessert omelet as we know it.

But with the Moorish conquest of the Iberian peninsula in the 9th century, Europeans were introduced to sugar. It was so precious that it was referred to as the "white gold." In the 11th century, the use of sugar expanded a little when the Crusaders returned from the Holy Land with sugar cane and refined sugar. Yet, it was expensive sprinkled on every dish.

Only in the 15th century had Italian cooks learned from the Arabs how to use sugar discriminately, saving it for special occasions. These sweets were eaten by those who could afford the high pricetag of sugar. And if a host wanted to really impress his guests he might serve sweet dishes any chance he could just so people might think he was financially successful. It wasn't until the Spaniards colonized the Caribbean and began growing sugar cane on a grand scale there did the European sugar supply increase enough to make it affordable to the masses.

And yet separating the dessert course from the rest of the meal took time. It wasn't until the middle of the 19th century that people accepted the notion of a menu, eating foods in a specific order. Not only was this menu ultimately beneficial to the diner - he or she knew what food was coming and ate foods at the proper temperature - but it helped chefs out too. They could carefully select courses that complemented each other.

And desserts caught on, not only because people developed an affinity for sweet things, but because even in the worst of times, a sweet conclusion to a meal was like a happy ending to a fairytale. The sugar of that day, however, wasn't like the granulated sugar of today. It was in the form of hard rock loaves, and the loaf had to be pounded with a mortar to make powder. This is a task that might seem tame today, considering how much care and skill goes into making à la carte desserts such as those we share in this chapter. Consider the skill involved in Ricotta Quenelles with Strawberry Coulis or Chocolate Symphony. And yet the trick remains to present a dessert that looks simple. A dessert in which the raw ingredients shine through. A dessert that reflects the meal, leaves your imagination wandering. A dessert that reads like poetry.

Desserts might also be comforting, remind us of yesteryear, but have a slightly new slant. Or they might have regional identity when fresh, local produce is in season, whether it be cranberries from New England, loganberries from the Pacific Northwest or limes from the Florida Keys. Then desserts truly become poetic postscripts to the meal.

Note: Since baking is a more precise science than cooking, ingredient quantities are listed as weights rather than cup measurements.

Pie Dough

Yield 20 ounces

13 ounces bread flour
½ tablespoon salt
11 ounces cold butter, sliced
⅓ cup ice water

For the dough, combine the flour and salt in a large bowl. Using your fingertips or a pastry blender, cut the butter into the flour, until the mixture resembles cornmeal. Be careful not to over-work the dough as the heat from your hands will soften the butter, preventing proper coating of the flour. Stir half of the ice water into the flour mixture and mix quickly to form a lumpy ball of dough. Add remaining ice water as needed.

To roll the dough, on a smooth lightly floured surface, turn dough out of bowl. Portion dough and roll immediately to desired size and thickness. Line pie or tart pans with dough, and allow to rest in refrigerator for 30 minutes before blind baking at 350°F or filling.

Short Dough

Yield 2 pounds

15 ounces butter at room temperature
6 ounces granulated sugar
1 egg
1 pound bread flour

For the dough, in the bowl of an electric mixer fitted with the dough hook, cream the butter and sugar until incorporated. Add the egg and mix on low speed until combined. Add the bread flour and mix until just uniform. Do not overmix this dough. Remove dough from bowl, flatten into a disc, cover and allow to rest in refrigerator until dough is firm enough to roll. Just-mixed dough can be piped into cookie shapes and refrigerated until ready to bake.

To roll out short dough, remove chilled dough from the refrigerator, and portion. Lightly flour a smooth flat surface with bread flour, and roll out dough to desired thickness. Use dough to line tart pans or cut into cookie shapes.

To finish the dough, preheat oven to 350°F, and bake tart shells or cookies until dough is fragrant and turns golden brown.

Choux Paste

Yield 2 pounds

2 cups water
2 cups milk
1 pound butter
1½ pounds bread flour
1 quart whole eggs

For the choux paste, in a large saucepan, over medium heat, combine the water, milk and butter and bring to a boil. Remove pan from the heat, and, using a wooden spoon, stir in the flour until mixture forms a paste and pulls away from sides of the pan. Allow mixture to cool slightly. Stir in the eggs one at a time until a stiff paste is formed. Alternatively, place paste in the stainless steel bowl of an electric mixer fitted with the paddle attachment. With the mixer on low speed, beat eggs in one at a time until absorbed.

To finish the choux paste, preheat the oven to 425°F. Line a sheet pan with parchment paper and, using a piping bag, immediately pipe paste into desired shapes. Bake 10 minutes or until fully puffed. Reduce heat to 350°F and bake until done, about 10 minutes more.

Pastry Cream

Yield 1½ quarts

1 quart milk
3 ounces butter
8 ounces sugar
3 eggs
2 egg yolks
3 ounces cornstarch

For the pastry cream, in a large saucepan, combine the milk, butter and half of the sugar bringing it to a boil over medium heat. In a medium stainless steel bowl, combine remaining sugar, eggs, egg yolks, and cornstarch. Stir until smooth with a wooden spoon. When milk mixture has boiled, reduce heat to low. Temper the egg mixture by adding one third of the hot milk mixture into the eggs. Stir the tempered eggs back into the hot milk mixture, and return saucepan to the heat. Bring mixture to a boil and cook for three minutes, stirring constantly. Remove from the heat, place mixture in an ice bath and chill to cool. Stir constantly and cover with plastic film to avoid forming a skin.

Lemon Curd

Yield 2 quarts

16 eggs
3 pounds sugar
1 cup grated lemon zest
3 cups lemon juice
1½ pounds butter cut into small pieces

For the lemon curd, in a large stainless steel saucepan, whisk together the eggs and sugar until smooth. Stir in the lemon zest, juice and butter. Place the saucepan over medium heat, and bring the mixture to a boil, stirring constantly with a wooden spoon. Cook mixture for three minutes, or until curd has thickened enough to coat the back of a spoon. Remove from the heat, and cool in an ice bath, stirring constantly or covering with plastic film to avoid forming a skin.

Ganache

Yield 3 cups

1 pound chocolate
2 cups heavy cream, hot

For the ganache, finely chop the chocolate and place in a stainless steel bowl. Pour the hot heavy cream over the chocolate, stirring to combine. Use warm ganache to glaze cakes or pastries. Or, refrigerate ganache until set and scoop and roll to form truffles.

Caramel Sauce

Yield 1 quart

1½ pounds granulated sugar
⅓ cup plus two tablespoons water
1 teaspoon lemon juice
3 tablespoons light corn syrup
2¼ cups heavy cream, hot
4 tablespoons butter

For the caramel sauce, in a large saucepan over high heat, combine the sugar, water, lemon juice, and corn syrup. Bring to a boil, brushing down the sides of the pan with a pastry brush dipped in cool water to remove any sugar crystals. Reduce heat to medium, and cook to desired caramel color. Remove pan from the heat, and carefully add the hot heavy cream to the caramel, stirring constantly. Return caramel sauce to low heat, and cook, stirring constantly, to remove any lumps. Remove pan from heat, and stir in butter until a smooth sauce is formed. Reserve warm until ready to use.

Swiss Meringue

Yield 2 quarts

1 pint egg whites at room temperature
2 pounds granulated sugar

For the meringue, in a large saucepan, prepare a simmering water bath. In the stainless steel bowl of an electric mixer, combine the egg whites and sugar, and place over the water bath. Whisk mixture by hand until sugar has dissolved completely, being careful not to heat mixture above 110ºF. Remove bowl from the water bath, and, using an electric mixer fitted with the whisk attachment, whip mixture to desired peak stiffness.

Italian Meringue

Yield 2 quarts

2 pounds granulated sugar
1 cup water
1 pint egg whites at room temperature

For the meringue, in a heavy stainless steel saucepan, combine the sugar and water and bring to a boil. Cook until the temperature reaches 240ºF on a candy thermometer. In the stainless steel bowl of an electric mixer fitted with the whisk attachment, whip the egg whites to soft peaks. Lower the speed of the mixer, and pour the syrup in a steady stream down the inside of the bowl into the whites, being careful to avoid the whip. Return the speed to high and whip 1 minute or until meringue is firm.

French Buttercream

Yield 4 pounds

1½ pounds granulated sugar
½ cup water
12 egg yolks
2¼ pounds sweet butter at room temperature
4 teaspoons vanilla extract or alternate flavoring

For the buttercream, in a medium saucepan, combine the sugar and water. Cook over medium heat until the temperature reaches 240ºF on a candy thermometer. While syrup is boiling, pour the egg yolks into the stainless steel bowl of an electric mixer fitted with the whip attachment. Whip yolks on high until light and lemon-colored, having at least doubled in volume. Lower the speed of the mixer, and pour the syrup in a steady stream down the inside of the bowl. Return speed to high, and whip until mixture has cooled slightly, about 2 minutes. Add the softened butter to the yolks in ¼ cup increments, or as fast as the butter can be incorporated into a uniform mixture. Stir in the vanilla.

Cheese Strudel with Sauce Anglaise   319

Grape Strudel
with Riesling Sauce   320

202

Apple Strudel 321

Chocolate Strudel
with Eggnog 321

Apple Cranberry Cobbler 322

Salzburger Soufflé 322

Prune and
Apricot Fritters
with Red Wine Sauce 323

Ginger Custard with Warm Berries 325

Chocolate Tart 325

Poached Pear in Phyllo 326

Orange Scented Raspberry Gratin ⬬326⬭

Timbale of Chocolate with Berries and Mint Cream

Apricot Ravioli with Peach Sauce 328

Tiramisu 329

Rock of Hazelnut 329

Chocolate Symphony 330

213

Trio of Chocolate Mousses

331

Ricotta Quenelles with
Strawberry Coulis

331

Apricot Ravioli with Sabayon

332

Frozen Apricot Soufflé Le Cirque 333

Bartlet-Pear Granité

333

Passion Fruit Mousse with Orange Brioche 334

Pear Strudel

335

Gratin of Cream Cheese and Mangoes 334

Chocolate Walnut Tea Cake 336

220

Fog City Brownie with Chocolate Sauce   336

Lemon-Poppy Seed Pound Cake   337

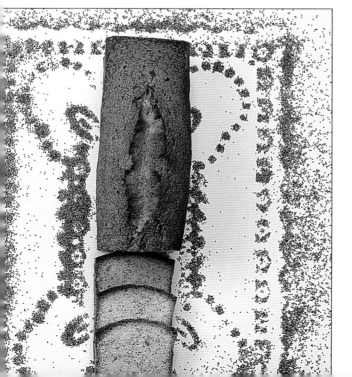

Chocolate Bag with White   337
Chocolate Mousse

221

Seafood
Minestrone

(Serves 4)

For the vegetables:

1 zucchini, sliced half-moon on the bias
1 summer squash, sliced
1 red bell pepper, diced
1 yellow bell pepper, diced
1 green bell pepper, diced
½ small eggplant, diced
1 rib celery, sliced into strips
½ cup haricot verts, sliced on bias
½ cup fennel, cut into diamonds
¼ cup carrots, cut with parisienne scoop
¼ cup turnips, cut into ripple slices

For the soup:

2 cloves garlic, crushed
1 small onion, sliced into rings
1 leek, white part only diced
Olive oil
¾ pound squid, cleaned and slit lengthwise and scored
¾ pound octopus, cooked and sliced on the bias
2 cups fish stock
2 cups chicken stock
Bouquet garni of fennel, carrot, thyme sprig and bay leaf
1 cup cooked pasta, shaped into curls and pre-cooked
½ cup pesto sauce

For the vegetables, blanch all and shock in ice water. Set aside.

For the soup, sweat garlic, onion and leek in olive oil in a saucepan. Add vegetables, squid, and octopus and stir. Add stocks, bouquet garni and pasta. Bring to a boil. Remove from heat and infuse with pesto sauce. Adjust seasoning to taste.

Cold Tomato Soup with Crayfish
and Caviar

(Serves 4)

For the crayfish:

1 pound carrots, peeled and chopped
1 pound onions, peeled and chopped
2 tablespoons butter
2 cups dry white wine
2 cloves garlic, peeled and chopped
1 bay leaf
10 juniper berries
3 sprigs fresh cilantro, stemmed and chopped
3 quarts water
30 crayfish

For the soup:

2 pounds ripe tomatoes, peeled, seeded, and diced
2 tablespoons tomato paste
2 tablespoons sherry vinegar
2 teaspoons sugar
Celery salt and black pepper to taste

For the garnish:

Chopped tomatoes
Caviar
Chives

For the crayfish, in a large saucepan, heat the butter, add the carrots and onions, and sauté until softened. Add the white wine, bring to a boil, and reduce by ¾. Add the garlic, bay leaf, cilantro, and water, bring to a boil, and cook for 40 minutes. Add the crayfish, cook for two minutes, and remove from the pan with a slotted spoon. Remove the meat from the tails and set aside, reserving the court bouillon for another use.

For the soup, in the bowl of a food processor fitted with the metal blade attachment, add the tomatoes, tomato paste, vinegar, and sugar, and purée until smooth. Transfer to a large bowl, season, and set aside in the refrigerator to chill.

To serve, ladle some of the soup in a bowl and spoon some of the diced tomatoes in the center. Alternate spoonfuls of caviar and crayfish tails around the tomatoes and garnish with chives.

Crayfish Consommé with Saffron Ravioli

(Serves 6)

For the filling:

½ stick unsalted butter

1 large red onion, peeled and thinly sliced

1 pound savoy cabbage, shredded

½ pound celery, chopped

1 tablespoon fresh thyme

5 pounds crayfish, boiled and tails de-veined and reserved
   (save bodies for making consommé)

2 tablespoons sherry

2 tablespoons cognac

1 sprig parsley, stemmed and chopped

For the saffron pasta:

2 pinches saffron threads

¼ cup dry white wine

2 eggs

1½ cups durum flour

½ cup semolina flour

¼ teaspoon salt

For the squid pasta:

¾ cup durum flour

¼ cup semolina flour

½ teaspoon salt

1 packet squid ink*

1 egg

1 tablespoon water

For the consommé:

5 pounds crayfish shells

1 onion, peeled and diced

1 small leek, cleaned, and chopped

4 carrots, peeled and chopped

4 stalk celery, chopped

1 6-ounce can tomato paste

2 cups fresh tomato juice

6 cups chilled fish stock

½ cup dry sherry

3 bay leaves

3 sprigs thyme

6 sprigs parsley

1½ cups egg whites

½ pound lean ground veal

For the garnish:

Minced chives

Diced tomato

*Available in gourmet markets

For the filling, in a large sauté pan, heat the butter, add the onion, cabbage and celery, and sauté until softened. .Add the thyme, crayfish tails, sherry, cognac, and parsley, and sauté until the crawfish are cooked through. Remove from the heat, season, and set aside to cool.

For the saffron pasta, in a small saucepan, add the saffron and white wine and bring to a boil. Reduce the heat to low and simmer until almost all of the liquid has evaporated. Remove from the heat and set aside to cool. Add the eggs and whisk to combine. Combine the dry ingredients on a work surface and place the egg mixture in the center. Knead for ten minutes, cover with plastic wrap, and set aside for 30 minutes. Roll through a pasta machine until it is set at the thinnest setting, and set aside.

For the squid pasta, combine the dry ingredients and then incorporate the squid, egg, and water, using a fork. Follow the instructions for the saffron pasta, cut into linguini-sized strips, and reserve.

To finish the ravioli, lay the saffron pasta on a work surface, and place the squid linguini on top in a crisscross pattern. Roll the finished sheets one at a time through the thinnest setting of the pasta machine. Place one tablespoon of the filling 3-inches apart on a sheet of pasta. Top with a second sheet, cut into squares, and seal the edges.

For the consommé, in a medium saucepan, add all of the ingredients and mix thoroughly. Bring to a boil, reduce the heat, and gently simmer for one hour. Carefully ladle the consommé through a cheesecloth-lined sieve and keep warm.

To serve, cook the ravioli in salted boiling water for two minutes. Drain, and divide into heated soup bowls. Ladle the consommé over the ravioli, and garnish with chives and tomato.

Three Bean Gazpacho with Cucumber-Crab Salad

(Serves 4 to 6)

For the red gazpacho:
3 red tomatoes, seeded
2 red bell peppers, stemmed, seeded, membranes removed, and chopped
1 clove garlic, peeled and minced
1 sprig basil, stemmed and chopped
2 shallots, peeled and chopped
Juice of 1 lemon
2 cucumbers, peeled and chopped
3 tablespoons cooked lentils
3 tablespoons cooked black beans
3 tablespoons cooked split peas
Salt and pepper to taste

For the yellow gazpacho:
3 yellow tomatoes, seeded
2 yellow bell peppers, stemmed, seeded, membranes removed, and chopped
1 clove garlic, peeled and minced
1 sprig basil, stemmed and chopped
2 shallots, peeled and minced
Juice of 1 lemon
2 cucumbers, peeled and chopped
3 tablespoons cooked lentils
3 tablespoons cooked black beans
3 tablespoons cooked dried split peas
Salt and pepper to taste

For the crab salad:
4 ounces lump crabmeat
1 cucumber, peeled and julienned
1 red bell pepper, stemmed, seeded, membranes removed, and julienned
½ bunch chives, chopped
1 red tomato, seeded and julienned
1 yellow tomato, seeded and julienned
2 tablespoons peanut oil
1 tablespoon champagne vinegar
Salt and pepper to taste

For the garnish:
Lump crabmeat
Thyme sprigs
Black beans

For the red gazpacho, in the bowl of a food processor fitted with the metal blade attachment, add the tomatoes, pepper, garlic, basil, shallots, lemon juice, and cucumbers, and purée until smooth. Incorporate the beans and pulse, season, and set aside in the refrigerator to chill.

For the yellow gazpacho, repeat procedure as for the red gazpacho and set aside in the refrigerator to chill.

For the crab salad, in a medium bowl, toss together all of the ingredients, season, and set aside in the refrigerator to chill.

To serve, ladle each variety of soup side by side in a bowl. Spoon some of the salad in the center of the bowl and garnish the soup with crab, thyme, and black beans.

Bündner Barley Soup with Lamb

(Serves 4)

For the soup:
1 small onion, chopped
1 stick celery, chopped
1 carrot, chopped
½ leek, chopped

For the soup garnish:
1 carrot, finely diced
¼ leek stalk, finely diced
1 stick celery, finely diced
2 tablespoons butter
½ cup heavy cream
1 ounce barley, precooked in salt water
2 ounces Bündnerfleisch, diced
Marjoram
1 lamb loin, cleaned and trimmed
1 tablespoon butter
Salt and pepper to taste

1 tablespoon butter
2 ounces bacon
2 ounces barley
½ cup dry white wine
2 quarts beef broth

For the soup, sauté the vegetables in butter and bacon until golden brown. Pour off excess fat, add the barley and deglaze with the white wine. Add the broth and simmer over low heat for 1½ hours. Purée in a blender and strain. Set aside.

For the soup garnish, sauté the finely diced vegetables in two tablespoons of butter. Add the cream, bring to a boil and add the strained soup. Add the barley, Bünderfleisch and season to taste with salt and pepper and marjoram. Keep soup warm.

Sauté the lamb loin in butter on each side for three minutes, until pink. Remove and keep warm.

To serve, ladle soup into bowls and top with thinly sliced lamb loin. Garnish with marjoram.

Corn and Oyster Soup with Dill

(Serves 6)

For the soup:

6 tablespoons unsalted butter

4 cups corn kernels

2 teaspoons kosher salt

1 teaspoon freshly ground white pepper

¼ teaspoon Tabasco sauce

4 cups fish stock or clam juice

2 cups heavy cream

18 Blue Point oysters, shucked and liquor strained and reserved

For the garnish:

Corn kernels

Dill sprigs

For the soup, in a large saucepan, heat the butter, add the corn, salt, pepper and Tabasco, and sauté for ten minutes. Incorporate the stock and cream and bring to a boil. Reduce the heat and simmer for 30 minutes. Remove from the heat and cool slightly. Transfer to the bowl of a food processor fitted with the metal blade attachment and purée until smooth. Strain into a saucepan, return to the heat, and bring to a simmer. Incorporate the oysters and liquor and simmer until the edges of the oysters begin to curl. Remove from the heat, season, and keep warm.

To serve, place three oysters in a soup bowl and fill the bowl with some of the soup. Sprinkle the oysters with corn and garnish with dill sprigs.

Duck Consommé with Foie Gras Ravioli

(Serves 4)

For the consommé:

6 cups duck stock

4 ounces ground duck meat

1 stalk celery, diced

1 carrot, peeled and diced

½ medium onion, peeled and minced

2 tomatoes, chopped

5 egg whites, lightly beaten

Salt and pepper to taste

For the ravioli:

1 pound semolina flour

6 eggs

1 tablespoon olive oil

½ teaspoon salt

6 ounce slice foie gras

1 egg yolk beaten with 1 tablespoon water

For the dish:

1 tablespoon unsalted butter

1 small carrot, peeled, diced small, and blanched

1 small white turnip, peeled, diced small, and blanched

1 small zucchini, diced small and blanched

1 ounce black truffle, diced small

Salt to taste

For the garnish:

Tarragon leaves

For the duck consommé, in a large saucepan, over medium heat, bring the stock to a simmer and maintain the heat. In a large bowl, combine the duck meat, celery, carrot, onion, tomatoes, and egg whites and stir well to combine. Gently pour the meat-mix into the hot stock and stir gently once. Maintain a gentle simmer and gently stir once or twice to make sure the meat-mix is not sticking to the bottom of the saucepan. Once a "raft" forms on the surface of the stock, make a small whole to one side to prevent boil-ing. Maintain a simmer for 15 more minutes. Remove from the heat and set aside to cool for ten minutes. Using a ladle, gently spoon the consommé through the hole in the "raft" and strain through a coffee filter-lined mesh sieve. Make sure not to disturb the "raft" during the straining process as this may cause clouding in the final consommé. Return the consommé to medium heat, season, and reserve, keeping warm.

For the ravioli, in the bowl of an electric mixer fitted with the metal blade attachment, combine the flour, eggs, oil and salt and mix on low speed until a rough dough pulls free from the sides of the bowl. Turn the dough onto a lightly floured work surface and knead until smooth. Cover with plastic wrap and set aside in the refrigerator for 30 minutes. Transfer the dough to a lightly floured work surface and divide into four pieces. Roll each piece ¼-inch thick and roll through a pasta machine according to manufacturer's instructions to form four long sheets. Using a decorative cookie cutter, cut 24 circular pieces, set aside on a lightly floured work surface, and cover with plastic wrap. Heat a large sauté pan over medium high heat, season the foie gras, and sear on both sides until golden brown. Remove from the heat and using a slotted spatula, transfer the foie gras to a cutting board. Cut the foie gras into 12 equal pieces and set aside, keeping warm.

To assemble the ravioli, place a piece of foie gras onto the center of 12 pasta circles. Brush the edges of each with egg wash, place one of the remaining pasta circles on top, press gently to enclose the foie gras, and reserve.

For the dish, in a medium sauté pan, melt the butter over medium heat, add the carrots, celery, and turnips and sauté until tender. Remove from the heat, add the truffle, and toss to combine. Season and reserve, keeping warm.

To finish the ravioli, bring a large saucepan of water to a boil, add the ravioli, and simmer until cooked, about three to five minutes. Remove from the heat, drain, and set aside.

To serve, arrange three ravioli in the bottom of a soup bowl and ladle some hot consommé on top. Place a spoon of sautéed vegetables in the center and garnish with tarragon.

Guinea Hen and
Oyster Gumbo

(Serves 12)

For the guinea hens:
2 2½-pound guinea hens
Salt and pepper to taste
2 gallons rich, dark chicken stock

For the gumbo:
¼ cup melted butter
5 onions, peeled and chopped
6 green bell peppers, stemmed, seeded, and chopped
4 red bell peppers, stemmed, seeded, and chopped
28 ounces canned plum tomatoes
6 cloves garlic, peeled and minced
1 bunch celery stalks, chopped
4 bay leaves
4 sprigs thyme, stemmed and chopped
1 teaspoon red pepper flakes
1 tablespoon Creole seasoning
Reserved guinea hen stock

For the roux:
2 cups vegetable oil
3 cups flour
4 cups reserved hen stock

For the dish:
4 leeks or 12 wild leeks, cleaned and sliced
1 tablespoon hot pepper sauce
3 pints shucked oysters, drained
2 tablespoons filé powder
Cooked rice

For the guinea hen, preheat the oven to 400 degrees. Season the hens with salt and pepper and place in a roasting pan. Set the pan in the oven and roast for 35 minutes or until the skin is well browned and crisp. Remove from the oven, transfer the hens and drippings to a large saucepan, and cover with the chicken stock. Bring to a boil over high heat, lower the heat and simmer for one hour, skimming any residue that rises to the surface. Remove the hens from the saucepan and set aside on a cutting board to cool slightly. Strain the stock and reserve. Remove the meat from the guinea hens and reserve.

For the gumbo, in a large sauté pan, heat the butter over medium high heat, add the onions, peppers, tomatoes, garlic, celery, bay leaves, thyme, red pepper, and Creole seasoning and sauté for ten minutes, or until the vegetables have softened. Add the hen stock, (remove 4 cups for the roux), to the pan and bring to a boil. Reduce the heat and simmer for 30 minutes.

For the roux, in a medium saucepan, heat the oil over high heat, add the flour and bring to a boil. Reduce the heat and simmer, stirring constantly, until the mixture is the color of deep mahogany. Whisk in the stock and pour the mixture into the gumbo mixture. Bring to a boil over high heat, lower the heat and simmer for 30 minutes, skimming off any grease that rises to the surface. Add the leeks and continue to simmer for ten minutes. Add the hot pepper sauce, oysters, reserved guinea hen meat, and file powder, and simmer until the oysters are cooked to desired doneness. Remove from the heat and serve with rice.

Callaloo
Soup

(Serves 6)

For the soup:
12 ounces salt pork, diced
2 quarts water
4 tablespoons clarified butter
1 medium onion, peeled and diced
2 cloves garlic, peeled and minced
15 pods okra, stemmed and sliced into ¼-inch rounds
30 fresh callaloo or spinach leaves
1 bouquet garni
3 land or stone crabs, cooked and shelled
½ cup butter

For the garnish:
Fresh callaloo leaves
Crab claws

For the soup, in a large saucepan, add the salt pork, cover with water and bring to a boil. Reduce the heat and simmer for one hour. In a medium sauté pan, heat the butter, add the onions and garlic and sauté until softened. Remove from the heat, add to the salt pork, and bring the mixture to a boil. Incorporate the okra, callaloo leaves, and bouquet garni and return to a boil. Reduce the heat and simmer for 30 minutes. Add the crab, incorporate the butter, and remove from the heat.

To serve, ladle some of the soup into a bowl and garnish with fresh callaloo leaves and crab claws.

Monkfish
Bouillabaisse

(Serves 4)

For the bouillabaisse:
1½ quarts water
2 pounds monkfish bones and skin
1 medium fennel bulb, trimmed and cut in half
1 medium onion, coarsely chopped
1 cup dry white wine
White pepper to taste
50 strands saffron

For vegetables:
4 small new potatoes, cleaned
1 large carrot, peeled and sliced
2 small zucchini, sliced
2 small turnips, sliced

For the fish:
1½ pounds monkfish, cut into medallions

For the garnish:
½ red bell pepper, seeded, blanched and minced
Italian parsley sprigs

For the bouillabaisse, combine water, fish bones, fennel, onion and wine. Season to taste with white pepper. Bring to a boil. Simmer uncovered for 20 minutes. Strain and reserve liquid. Stir in saffron so that broth turns a pale golden color. When ready to serve, bring broth to a simmer. Steam vegetables in it for ten minutes. Steam fish medallions five minutes remove from the heat and set aside. To serve, ladle broth into large bowls. Divide vegetables among the bowls. Add fish medallions. Scatter red pepper pieces and Italian parsley on top of the soup.

Consommé of Wild Mushroom with
Shrimp and Shallot Flan

20

(Serves 4)

For the consomme of wild mushrooms:
5 cups lobster consomme
2 quarts water, for blanching mushrooms
2 cups small fresh honey mushrooms (don't eat raw honey mushrooms)

For the shallot flan:
Unsalted butter, for flan molds
¼ cup heavy cream
¼ cup milk
Salt water (1 tablespoon coarse sea salt mixed with 3 cups water), for cooking shallots
6 medium-size shallots, peeled
2 large eggs
Fine sea salt and freshly ground black pepper

For the lobster quenelle mixture:
1 (1 to 1½ pounds) active live Maine lobster
3 ounces sea scallops, rinsed and small tough muscle on the side of each removed
½ teaspoon fine sea salt
Freshly ground black pepper
½ cup heavy cream
½ teaspoon finely sliced chives, optional
2 cups consommé or water, for poaching the quenelles

For the Santa Barbara shrimp:
12 large, unpeeled Santa Barbara shrimp tails (about 10 ounces), peeled and de-veined

For the mushroom consommé, place the consommé in a medium-size pot and bring to a simmer. Meanwhile, bring two quarts water to a boil in a separate pot and blanch the mushrooms for 15 seconds to clean them, stirring constantly. Immediately transfer mushrooms with a slotted spoon to the simmering consommé (discard blanching water) and very slowly simmer for 30 minutes. Line the chinois with a double thickness of damp cheesecloth and strain the mushroom consommé through it into a bowl; reserve drained mushrooms for garnishing the soup bowls. Refrigerate consommé and mushrooms separately. (This may be done several hours ahead.)

For the shallot flan, heat oven to 300 degrees F. Generously butter four flan molds. Combine the cream and milk in a small pot. Add the shallots and boil until tender, about ten minutes; drain. Purée in a food processor with the eggs, the scalded cream-milk mixture, and a generous amount of salt and pepper until smooth. Strain purée through the chinois, using the bottom of a sturdy ladle to force as much through as possible. Pour purée into the prepared molds and place molds in a small baking pan; add enough boiling hot water to come up the sides of the molds 1¼ inches. Bake uncovered in the preheated oven until done, about 50 minutes. To test doneness, after 45 minutes of cooking, remove a mold from the oven, loosen sides of flan with a thin flexible-bladed knife in one clean movement and invert onto a plate; if done, the flan will hold its shape and when cut in half, the center will be solid, not runny. Remove cooked flans from the oven and let them sit in the hot water for at least ten minutes or up to about 30 minutes, then unmold and serve promptly. Makes four flans, plus one flan for testing doneness.

For the lobster quenelles, ease the lobster, head first, into a large pot of boiling water. Promptly cover pot and cook for precisely one minute. Immediately drain on paper towels and let cool briefly. Protecting your hands with thick dish towels, twist off the head and claws, then remove the tail and claw meat

recipe continued on next page

from the shells. Process the lobster meat in a food processor with the scallops, half teaspoon of the salt, and a generous amount of pepper until smooth. Add half cup of the cream and continue processing until well blended; do not overmix. Strain mousseline through the strainer, using a rubber spatula to force as much through as possible; the strained mousseline should yield about one cup. Stir in the chives if using. Refrigerate if not using immediately. (Mousseline can be prepared several hours in advance.)

To form and cook quenelles, to form the quenelles, mold one scant teaspoon of the mousseline into a quenelle shape using two hot teaspoons and cook in an uncovered pan of hot (not simmering) water for five minutes. Before continuing, check the quenelle for seasoning and texture. If under-seasoned, add more salt and pepper to the remaining mousseline. If rubbery in texture, add one more tablespoon of cream to the mousseline, whisking until barely blended. Do not add too much cream as the quenelles will lose their shapes.

For the Santa Barbara shrimp, steam and peel the shrimp, in a covered steamer over rapidly boiling water. Steam the shrimp until the shells turn pink, about five minutes; do not over-cook. Immediately transfer to a large bowl. When cool enough to handle, separate each head section from the tail by gently twisting the head section off. Then peel away the remaining shell from the tail meat. Cover and refrigerate tails until time to reheat. (The shrimp may be steamed several hours in advance and kept refrigerated.)

To assemble the dish and serve, begin to reheat the mushroom consommé over medium heat. Unmold a flan into the center of each of four wide ovenproof soup bowls; arrange a portion of the reserved mushrooms from infusing the consommé around each flan. Next, arrange three shrimp tails and three drained quenelles around each flan. Cover each bowl with aluminum foil and heat in a 400 degree oven for four minutes, or until the food is heated through. Remove bowls from oven, uncover and serve promptly, ladling about ¾ cup soup into each bowl at the table.

Scallop and Truffle Salad

28

(Serves 4)

For the salad:

¾ pound large sea scallops

½ ounces canned black truffles, trimmed and sliced into thin rounds

2 tablespoons sherry wine vinegar

⅓ cup olive oil

Reserved truffle juice

Salt and pepper to taste

½ pound mixed salad greens

For the garnish:

Scallop roe

Chervil sprigs

Frisée

For the salad, poach the scallops in one and a half cups of lightly salted water for 2 minutes, or until they are firm but only three fourths cooked through. Remove from pan with a slotted spoon, reduce the liquid to four tablespoons, and set aside to cool. Thinly slice the scallops and set aside. In a small bowl, add the vinegar, oil, juice from the truffles, and poaching liquid and whisk to combine. Season and set aside.

To serve, toss the salad greens with the vinaigrette. Place some of the greens in a tight mound on a plate arrange the scallop slices over the greens in a circles. Arrange another circle of truffles on top of the scallops and brush the scallops and truffles with some of the vinaigrette. Place some scallop roe on top of the truffles and garnish with a sprig of chervil and frisée.

Scallop Salad with Mustard

(Serves 4)

For the salad:

1 teaspoon Dijon mustard

1 teaspoon champagne vinegar

1 teaspoon lemon juice

5 tablespoons olive oil

Salt and pepper to taste

¼ pound assorted salad greens

12 leaves Belgian endive, julienned and blanched

¼ pound carrots, peeled, julienned, and blanched

¼ pound turnips, peeled, julienned, and blanched

For the dish:

12 sea scallops, each sliced transversely into three pieces:

2 tablespoons unsalted butter

1 tablespoon mustard

1 sprig tarragon, stemmed and minced

2 tablespoons fish stock

Salt and cayenne pepper to taste

For the salad, in a small bowl, add the mustard, champagne, lemon juice, salt, and olive oil, and whisk to combine. Season and set aside. In a medium bowl, toss the greens with the vinaigrette and set aside. Divide the greens between four salad plates, arrange the blanched vegetables on top, and set aside.

For the dish, prepare a steamer, heavily butter four small ramekins and line with the scallop slices. In a small bowl, whisk together the butter, mustard, tarragon, and fish stock, pour over the ramekins, and season. Place the ramekins in the steamer and cook for three minutes. Remove from the steamer and set aside.

To serve, unmold a ramekin onto the center of the salad.

Roasted Pheasant Salad with Cranberries

(Serves 2)

For the pheasant:
1 pheasant, cleaned
Salt and pepper to taste

For the marinade:
1/2 cup chicken stock
1/2 medium onion
2 teaspoons thyme
2 bay leaves

For the sauce:
1 tablespoon olive oil
2 shallots, chopped
2 tablespoons Madeira wine
2 cups veal stock

For the sauerkraut:
4 tablespoons sauerkraut
2 tablespoons shredded cabbage
2 tablespoons shredded carrot

For the horseradish:
Oil for frying
2-inch piece of fresh horseradish, cut into ribbons

For the dressing:
1 teaspoon raspberry vinegar
1 tablespoon walnut oil
1/2 sprig tarragon, minced
White pepper to taste

For the cranberries:
4 tablespoons Madeira wine
1/2 cup cranberries

For the salad greens:
2 cups mixed fresh salad greens

For the pheasant, cut up bird, separating the breast portions. Separate and joint the legs and break up the carcass. In a large bowl, place chicken stock, onion, thyme and bay leaves. Add breasts and cover well with marinade. Place in refrigerator overnight.

For the sauce, heat oil in a large frying and when hot add pheasant legs, skin-side down and brown well. Add carcass pieces and cook until dark brown. Add shallots and continue cooking until they are golden but not burnt. Remove bones and meat. Deglaze pan with Madeira, scraping up pieces on pan bottom. Add veal stock and simmer 30 minutes. Strain sauce and return it to a clean pan. Reduce until sauce lightly coats the back of a spoon.

For the sauerkraut, drain well and toss with shredded carrots and cabbage.

For the horseradish, heat oil for frying. Drop ribbons of horseradish into oil and then drain. Set aside.

For the dressing, whisk raspberry vinegar into walnut oil. Mix in tarragon and white pepper to taste. Set aside.

For the cranberries, heat Madeira in small saucepan and add cranberries. Cook until tender.

To finish, the pheasant heat oven to 425 degrees. Warm Madeira sauce over low heat. Drain pheasant breast from marinade and dry well. Place skin-side down in a roasting pan and roast 15 minutes. Mount sauerkraut in middle of each serving plate. Toss greens with walnut oil dressing until coated. Remove pheasant from oven and separate from the skin. Slice breasts thinly on the bias and overlap on the sauerkraut. Split dressed among plates. Garnish plate by drizzling sauce over pheasant and scatter cranberries over sauce.

Lobster, Zucchini and Bean Salad with Ginger Vinaigrette

(Serves 1)

For the lobster:
1 rib celery, chopped
1 carrot, peeled and chopped
1 onion, peeled and chopped
1 clove garlic, peeled and chopped
1 bunch thyme
1 bay leaf
1 cup white wine
1 quart water
Salt and pepper to taste
1½-pound lobster

For the ginger vinaigrette:
2-inch piece ginger, peeled and minced
Juice of ½ lemon
2 tablespoons corn oil
Salt and pepper to taste

For the salad:
Reserved sliced lobster tail
1 zucchini, scored, thinly sliced and blanched
½ mango, peeled, pitted, and thinly sliced into rounds
Reserved ginger vinaigrette

recipe continued on next page

Lobster, Zucchini and Bean Salad

with Ginger Vinaigrette

continued from previous page

For the dish:
¼ cup string beans, blanched
¼ cup enoki mushrooms
Reserved ginger vinaigrette

For the garnish:
Chive oil
Lobster coral

For the lobster, in a large saucepan, combine all of the ingredients and bring to a boil. Reduce the heat and simmer for ten minutes. Increase the heat and return to a boil, add the lobster and cook for eight minutes or to desired doneness. Remove, from the pan and set aside to cool. Remove the tail meat from the shell, thinly slice into rounds, and set aside.

For vinaigrette, combine all of the ingredients and whisk until well incorporated. Season and set aside.

For the salad, in a medium bowl, combine the lobster, zucchini and mango, toss with ¾ of the vinaigrette, and set aside.

For the dish, in a small bowl, combine the mushrooms and green beans, toss with the remaining vinaigrette, and set aside.

To serve, alternate slices of lobster, mango, and zucchini in a circular pattern on a plate and mound some of the beans and zucchini in the center of the circle. Drizzle the plate with chive oil and garnish with lobster coral.

Baked Pepper and Artichoke Salad

(Serves 4)

For the salad
1 lemon, halved and juiced
4 5-ounce artichokes, stemmed, trimmed, chokes and inner leaves removed
2 red bell peppers, stemmed, quartered, and grilled
2 yellow bell peppers, stemmed, quartered, and grilled
2 green peppers, stemmed, quartered, and grilled
1 cup fresh shelled peas
Dressing, if desired

For the salad, in a large saucepan of boiling salted water, add the lemon juice to the water and bring to a boil. Add the artichokes, bring to a simmer, and cook until tender, about eight to ten minutes. Remove with a slotted spoon and shock in an ice bath. Add the peas to the saucepan and cook for about three minutes. Drain and shock in an ice bath.

To serve, place an artichoke in the center of a plate and arrange alternating strips of red, yellow, and green pepper around it. Fill the artichoke with the peas allowing some to spill onto the plate. Dress the salad with vinaigrette if desired.

Lamb, Endive and Arugula Salad

(Serves 4)

For the curry vinaigrette:
Juice of 1 lemon
2 teaspoons curry powder
½ cup olive oil
Salt and pepper to taste

For the lamb:
1 pound young lamb shoulder, trimmed and tied
2 tablespoons olive oil
Salt and freshly ground black pepper to taste
1 shallot, peeled and minced

For the salad:
4 medium beets, cooked and thinly sliced into rounds
4 Belgian endive, cored and leaves separated
2 bunches arugula, stemmed

For the vinaigrette, in a small bowl, combine the lemon juice and curry powder. Gradually add the oil, whisking to incorporate, season, and set aside.

For the lamb, prepare a hot grill. Brush the lamb with oil and season. Grill to desired doneness, remove from the heat, and set aside to rest for ten minutes before carving. Thinly slice the lamb and toss with the shallot and a little of the reserved vinaigrette. Season and set aside.

To serve, arrange the beet slices in a circular pattern on a plate. Alternate layers of endive leaves , lamb slices, and arugula, and drizzle with the vinaigrette.

Warm Lobster Salad with Black Truffle Vinaigrette

(Serves 4)

2 black truffle, fresh or canned,
½ cup walnut oil
4 lobsters (1-1¼ pounds each)
4 cups salad greenns, washed and dried (a mix of colors and textures such
 as radicchio, red leaf, mach, etc.)
2 tablespoons butter
4 tablespoons balsamic vinegar
Salt and freshly ground pepper to taste

Marinate the truffles overnight in the walnut oil. The next day, cook the lobsters in boiling salted water or court bouillon by plunging them in head first. When the liquid returns to a boil, reduce the heat to medium and cook, covered, for seven to ten minutes, depending on the weight of the lobster.

Remove the lobster from liquid and allow to drain until cool enough to handle. Remove meat from tail and remove vein running up the back of the tail. Cut tail meat into six slices. Crack and remove meat form claws and large leg joints. Reserve bodies for stock or discard. Cover meat and keep warm.

Remove truffles from oil and peel them with a sharp paring knife. Reserve the peels for later use. Slice the peeled truffles thinly. Melt butter in small skillet over low heat, and add truffle slices to warm lobster. Remove pan from heat and set aside.

Combine walnut oil, truffle peelings, vinegar and salt and pepper in a blender for 30 seconds. Drizzle four tablespoons of the vinaigrette over the lobster.

To serve, arrange salad greens on 4 plates with the lobster and truffle slices. Pass the remaining dressing separately.

Warm Lamb Salad with White Beans

33

(Serves 4)

For the beans:
¼ pound dry white beans, soaked overnight and drained
1 large black truffle, sliced
1 bunch chives, minced
2 teaspoons olive oil
Salt and freshly ground black pepper

For the spinach:
3 teaspoons olive oil
1 clove garlic, peeled and minced
1 bunch spinach, stemmed and washed
Salt and freshly ground black pepper

For the truffle vinaigrette:
4 tablespoons extra virgin olive oil
4 tablespoons aged sherry vinegar
4 tablespoons truffle juice
1 large black truffle, chopped
2 tablespoons rich lamb stock
Salt and freshly ground white pepper
1 teaspoon chopped chervil
1 teaspoon chopped chives

For the shallot custard:
6 eggs
1¾ cups heavy cream
1¼ cups purée of roasted shallots
Salt and freshly ground white pepper

For the lamb:
2 teaspoons olive oil
2 lamb filets, boned and trimmed
Salt and freshly ground black pepper to taste

For the dish:
2 cups assorted salad greens

For the garnish:
Diced tomato
Sliced Truffle
Mint sprigs
Chive sprigs

For the beans, cook the beans in boiling salted water until tender. Drain and place in a medium bowl. While the beans are still warm, toss with the truffle, chives, and olive oil. Season and set aside, keeping warm. For the spinach, in a large sauté pan over high heat, heat the oil, add the garlic and spinach, and sauté until wilted. Remove from the heat, season, and set aside, keeping warm.

For the shallot custard, lightly butter four 4-ounce ramekins and set aside. Preheat the oven to 350 degrees. In a medium bowl, add the eggs and cream and whisk until combined. Incorporate the shallot purée, season, and fill the prepared ramekins three fourths full. Set in a water bath , place in the oven, and bake for 12 to 15 minutes or until the custards are set. Remove from the oven and set aside, keeping warm.

For the vinaigrette, in a small bowl, whisk together the oil, vinegar, truffle juice, chopped truffle, and lamb stock. Add the herbs, season, and set aside.

For the lamb, season filets with salt and pepper and set aside. In a large sauté pan over high heat, heat the oil, add the lamb, and sear to desired doneness. Remove from the heat and set aside keeping warm.

To serve, place a stainless steel ring mold on a plate. Spoon some of the white beans in the bottom of the mold and arrange some of the spinach on top. Thinly slice the lamb and arrange on top of the spinach, overlapping slightly in a circular pattern. Unmold a shallot custard and set beside the lamb. Mound some of the salad greens next to the lamb and drizzle some of the vinaigrette on top. Garnish lamb with diced tomato, truffle slices, and mint and chive sprigs.

Tuscan Pasta Salad

(Serves 6)

For the filling:
8 ounces ricotta cheese
4 ounces mascarpone cheese
8 ounces gorgonzola cheese
4 ounces freshly grated Parmesan cheese
1 small sprig parsley, stemmed and chopped
1 small clove garlic, peeled and minced
Salt and pepper to taste

For the pasta:
1 recipe Egg Pasta
½ recipe reserved filling

For the zucchini flowers:
½ recipe reserved filling
30 small zucchini flowers
Flour for dusting
3 tablespoons olive oil

For the salad:
¼ pound haricots verts, blanched
6 ounces smoked veal, thinly sliced
6 ounces garbanzo beans
¾ cup pesto

For the filling, in the bowl of an electric mixer fitted with the paddle attachment, add all of the ingredients, and beat until smooth. Remove from the mixer and set aside.

For the pasta, divide the dough in half, shape half into radiatore using an electric pasta machine, and roll the other half into two sheets through the thinnest setting of a pasta machine. Place a sheet of pasta on a work surface and spoon half of the reserved filling 2-inches apart on the sheet. Cover with a second sheet, press to seal and cut into ravioli. Bring a large pot of salted water to a boil, add the ravioli and cook for two minutes. Remove with a slotted spoon, and transfer to a bowl of ice water. Add the radiatore to the pan and boil for 90 seconds. Drain, and cool in the ice water. In a large bowl, toss the pasta with the haricots verts, veal, garbanzo beans, and pesto and set aside.

For the zucchini flowers, place the remaining filling in a pastry bag, and pipe into the zucchini flowers. Dust with flour and set aside. In a large sauté pan, heat the oil, add the flowers, and sauté until golden brown and crisp. Remove from the pan and keep warm

To serve, spoon some of the pasta in a shallow bowl and garnish with zucchini flowers.

Bean Salad with Charred Lamb

(Serves 6)

For the lamb:
¼ cup salad oil
2 lamb loins, cut from the eye of the rack
Salt and pepper to taste

For the vinaigrette:
3 cloves garlic, peeled and minced
2 shallots, peeled and minced
2 tablespoons coarse mustard
Juice of 1 small lemon
½ cup sherry wine vinegar
1¼ cup walnut oil
Salt and freshly ground pepper to taste

For the salad:
¾ pound haricot verts, stemmed and blanched
4 artichoke hearts, steamed in lemon water and sliced
4 ounces mushrooms, cleaned, stems removed, and sliced
2 Belgian endive, leaves separated and thinly sliced
2 tomatoes, peeled, seeded, and sliced
1 cup Nicoise olives, pitted and chopped
1 small bunch fresh basil, stemmed and minced

For the garnish
Parmesan shavings
12 nasturtium flowers

For the lamb, heat the oil, add the lamb, and sear on all sides, turning frequently so the exterior is completely charred and the interior is still rare. Transfer to a cutting board and set aside

For the vinaigrette, in a small bowl, add the garlic, shallots, mustard, lemon juice and vinegar. Slowly whisk in oil, and season to taste with salt and pepper. Allow to sit at room temperature, covered.

For the salad, in a small bowl, combine all of the ingredients and toss with the vinaigrette. Season and set aside.

To serve, mound some of the green bean salad on a plate and arrange lamb slices in a circle on top. Sprinkle with Parmesan cheese and garnish with nasturtiums.

Seasonal Greens with Quail Eggs

(Serves 4)

For the basil-walnut vinaigrette:
1 small bunch basil, stemmed and chopped
2 tablespoons Dijon mustard
1 egg yolk
Juice of ½ small lemon
1 clove garlic, peeled and minced
1 shallot, peeled and minced
¾ cup walnut oil
¾ cup vegetable oil
¼ cup champagne vinegar
Salt and pepper to taste

For the salad:
4 cups salad greens
1 tomato, cored, seeded, and sliced
8 yellow pear tomatoes, halved
⅓ cup crumbled Oregon blue cheese
⅓ cup toasted walnuts
12 leaves Belgian endive
1 small red onion, peeled and thinly sliced
12 fresh quail eggs, lightly poached

For the garnish
4 sprigs fresh basil
Pea tendrils

For the basil-walnut vinaigrette, in a small bowl, add the egg yolk and mustard and whisk to combine. Slowly add oil and vinegar in a steady stream, whisking constantly until emulsified. Incorporate the lemon, garlic, shallots, and basil, season, and set aside.

For the salad, in a large bowl, toss the salad greens, tomatoes, cheese, and walnuts with the vinaigrette and set aside.

To serve, arrange three endive leaves on a plate and place a mound of salad in the center. Place some of the onions and three quails eggs on top, and garnish with basil sprigs and pea tendrils.

Smoked Tuna with Grilled Shiitake Salad

Serves 4

For the dish:
3 ounces peanut oil
1 teaspoon dark sesame oil
2 tablespoons soy sauce
3 tablespoons balsamic vinegar
1 small clove garlic, peeled and minced
6 ounces shiitake mushrooms
6 ounces enoki mushrooms
1 carrot, peeled and julienned
1 small red onion, roasted and thinly sliced
2 scallions, thinly sliced
Juice of ½ lemon
8 ounces smoked tuna, thinly sliced

For the garnish:
Chervil sprigs

For the dish, in a medium sauté pan, add the oils, soy sauce, vinegar, and garlic, and bring to a boil. Add the shiitake mushrooms and sauté for three minutes, or until the mushrooms are tender. Remove from the heat and set aside to cool. Transfer to a large bowl, add the enoki mushrooms, carrot, red onion, scallion, and lemon juice and toss to combine.

To serve, arrange two ounces of sliced tuna on a plate like petals of a flower. Mound some of the salad in the center of the plate and garnish with chervil sprigs.

Vegetable
Sorbet Salad

(Serves 6)

For the sorbets:
1 bunch carrots, peeled and diced
2 bunches red beets, cooked, peeled and diced
1 bunch celery, trimmed and diced

For the salad:
1 tablespoon finely chopped truffle
2 tablespoons truffle juice
1 tablespoon sherry vinegar
¼ cup grapeseed oil
2 tablespoons hazelnut oil
⅛ teaspoon of Dijon mustard
Salt and white pepper to taste
6 cups mixed young lettuce (radicchio, mâche, bibb, and arugula)

For the garnish:
Carrot juice
Beet juice
Chervil sprigs

For each of the three sorbets, purée each vegetable in a food processor fitted with a metal blade attachment until as liquefied as possible. Strain the liquid, season, and set aside. Reserve some of the carrot and beet juice for the garnish. Freeze each juice in an ice cream machine according to the manufacturer's directions and form each sorbet into six quenelles. Place on a parchment-lined sheet pan and keep in the freezer until ready to serve.

For the salad, in a small bowl, whisk together all of the ingredients, season, and set aside.

To serve, toss the lettuce with the dressing and arrange in the center of a chilled plate. Place a quenelle of each of the sorbets on the greens, drizzle the plate with the reserved carrot and beet juice, and garnish with chervil sprigs.

Poppyseed Lasagna Salad
with Crayfish

(Serves 6)

For the lasagna:
2 pinches saffron threads
¼ cup hot water
2½ cups semolina flour
2 eggs
2 teaspoons olive oil
Pinch of salt
⅛ cup toasted poppy seeds
Flour for kneading
2 tablespoons olive oil
60 live crayfish

For the vinaigrette:
½ cup fish stock
¼ cup champagne vinegar
1½ cups grapeseed oil
1 teaspoon Dijon mustard
Salt and pepper to taste

For the garnish:
Italian parsley
Dill sprigs
Basil sprigs
Whole chives
Cilantro sprigs

To make the lasagna, soak the saffron in hot water for 20 minutes. Strain the juice and reserve. In the bowl of a food processor fitted with the metal blade attachment, add the flour, eggs, olive oil, and reserved saffron broth, and process until the dough forms a ball. Transfer to a lightly floured work surface and knead by hand to incorporate the poppy seeds. Continue to knead for five minutes, lightly dust with flour, and set aside to rest for one hour. Bring a large saucepan of salted water, court bouillon, or fish stock to a boil, add the crayfish, and cook for one minute. Remove from the pan and set aside to cool slightly. Break the tails from the bodies, remove the tail meat from the shells, and reserve. Reserve the bodies and tail shells for later use.

For the vinaigrette, in the bowl of a food processor fitted with the metal blade attachment, add the fish stock, vinegar, oil, mustard, and purée for ten seconds. Transfer to a small bowl, season and set aside.

To finish the pasta, using a pasta machine, roll the dough into long strips, ending with the thinnest possible setting. Cut the sheets of pasta into 12 equal triangles, place on a parchment-lined sheet pan, and set aside to dry for 15 minutes. Bring a large saucepan of salted water to a boil, add the pasta, and cook for 15 seconds. Drain, toss the triangles gently with oil, and reserve.

To serve, place a triangle in the center of the plate and top it with ten crayfish. Lightly brush the vinaigrette over the tails and place another triangle on top, folding back one corner to reveal the crayfish. Brush the pasta with additional vinaigrette and garnish with fresh herbs tossed in the remaining vinaigrette.

Mille-Feuille of Artichoke and Duck Liver

(Serves 6)

For the duck liver:
1 pound duck liver
Salt and pepper to taste

For the aspic:
1½ tablespoons unflavored gelatin
½ cup cold water
½ cup warm Sauternes wine

For the mille-feuille:
6 cooked artichoke hearts, sliced
Salt and pepper to taste

For the garnish:
Herb mayonnaise
Madeira and truffle sauce
Seasonal greens
Parsley

For the duck liver, season trimmed duck liver with salt and pepper. Bake in a terrine at 350 degrees F for about 30 minutes or until just pink. Remove and set aside.

For the aspic, soften gelatin in cold water. Add warm Sauternes and stir until dissolved.

For the mille-feuille, season sliced artichoke hearts with salt and pepper. Slice liver the same size as your terrine. Pour some aspic in bottom of terrine and arrange artichoke slices on top. Alternate liver and artichokes, pouring aspic between each layer until terrine is full. Pour aspic over all to keep freshness in. Chill until firm.

To serve, pour herb mayonnaise and truffle sauce onto serving plate. Top with a slice of mille-feuille and garnish with greens and parsley.

Terrine of Chanterelles and Baby Leeks

(Serves 15)

For the chicken aspic:
1 quart chicken stock, clarified and seasoned
½ ounce unflavored gelatin, softened

For the terrine:
1 tablespoon walnut oil
4 pounds chanterelles, washed, trimmed and halved
2 shallots, peeled and finely diced
1 bunch Italian parsley, stemmed and minced
3 bunches baby leeks, blanched

For the garnish:
Walnut oil
Sherry vinegar
Minced chervil

For the chicken aspic, in a medium saucepan, add the chicken stock and bring to a boil. Remove from the heat, add the gelatin, and stir until dissolved. Set aside to cool to room temperature.

For the terrine, line a triangular terrine mold with plastic wrap and set aside. In a medium saute pan, heat the oil, add the chanterelles, and saute until softened. Deglaze the pan with two cups of the chicken aspic and bring to a boil. Reduce the heat and simmer until the liquid is reduced by half. Incorporate the shallots and parsley, remove from the heat, and set aside to cool. Dip the leeks in the remaining aspic and line the bottom and sides of the mold, pressing the leeks as closely together as possible. Fill the terrine with the cooled mushroom mixture and cover with more of the leeks dipped in aspic. Wrap the terrine in plastic wrap and refrigerate for at least six hours or until completely set.

To serve, unmold the terrine and slice into ½-inch pieces. Place a slice of terrine on a plate, drizzle with oil and vinegar, and sprinkle the plate with minced chervil.

Terrine of Duck Breast with Lentils

45

(Serves 4)

For truffle vinaigrette:
1 teaspoon chopped truffles
1 tablespoon truffle juice
Juice of ½ lemon
1 tablespoon olive oil
½ tablespoon hazelnut oil
Salt and pepper to taste

For the aspic:
2¼ cups duck stock
5 gelatin leaves, bloomed in cold water

For the lentils:
7 ounces lentils
1 carrot, peeled and chopped
1 onion, peeled and chopped
1 clove
1 sprig thyme, stemmed and minced
1 bay leaf
1 cup corn kernels, blanched
4 ounces foie gras, cleaned and chopped
Reserved aspic
Salt and pepper to taste

For the terrine:
1 large carrots, peeled, thinly sliced, and blanched
3 boneless, skinless cooked duck breasts

For the garnish:
Mâche leaves

For the truffle vinaigrette, in a small bowl, combine all of the ingredients, whisk until well incorporated, and set aside. For the aspic, in a small saucepan, add the duck stock and bring to a boil. Reduce the heat and simmer until the mixture is reduced by two thirds. Add the softened gelatin leaves and stir to dissolve. Remove from the heat and set aside.

For the lentils, in a medium saucepan, combine the lentils, carrots, onion, clove, thyme and bay leaf cover with water and bring to a boil. Reduce the heat and simmer until the lentils are tender. Remove from the heat, strain, discarding the herbs, and set aside. Place in a medium bowl, add the corn, foie gras and reserve aspic and mix to combine. Season and set aside.

For the terrine, coat a triangular-shaped terrine with plastic wrap and line each side with carrot slices. Fill the terrine with layers of the lentil mixture and duck breasts, cover with some more of the carrot slices, place the lid on the terrine, and set aside in the refrigerator overnight. Remove from the refrigerator, unmold, and cut into ½-inch thick slices.

To serve, arrange a few mâche leaves on a plate and place a slice of the terrine on top. Drizzle the plate with some of the truffle vinaigrette.

Terrine of Smoked Eel

46

(Serves 16)

For the eels and curing mixture:
4 small eels, boned and skinned
3 cups chopped parsley
2 cloves garlic, minced
12 shallots, minced

For the smoking:
Dried Greek mountain tea
1 bay leaf, chopped
½ bunch thyme, chopped
1 bunch parsley, chopped
1 clove garlic, minced
5 shallots, minced
Cracked black pepper and salt to taste
3 cups white wine

4 bay leaves, chopped
½ bunch thyme, chopped
3 tablespoons sugar
½ cup salt
15 crushed green peppercorns

For the aspic:
Eel bones
Bouquet garni
1 leek, diced
1 onion, diced
1 rib celery, diced
1 cup white wine
Water to cover
Black peppercorns
2 tablespoons unflavored gelatin

recipe continued on next page

For the garnishes:

1 6-ounce jar ginko nuts

3 packages enoki mushrooms, cut into thirds

2 red bell peppers, cleaned and cut into 2-inch julienne strips

For the eels and curing mixture, save bones and head for stock. Combine parsley, garlic, shallots, bay leaf, thyme, sugar, salt and peppercorns. Cover a sheet pan with plastic wrap and spread half of the curing mixture on it. Place eels on top of cure. Spread remaining cure over eels and wrap in plastic. Refrigerate 24 hours.

For smoking eels and marinating them, scrape eels of the cure and remove all particles. Grease smoker racks well. Place eels on racks and don't allow to touch one another. Smoke over the tea until flesh is firm to the touch.

To prepare marinade, combine bay leaf, thyme, parsley, garlic and shallots. Place half of this in a pan, eels on top and season with salt and cracked pepper. Add remaining marinade, cover with white wine and set aside for two hours.

For the aspic, clean eel bones of any blood and rinse with cold water. Combine bones with more fish bones, bouquet garni, leek, onion, celery, wine, water to cover and peppercorns. Bring to a boil and reduce heat to a simmer. Simmer 40 minutes. Remove from heat, strain and allow to cool. Place one and a half cups stock in a bowl. Sprinkle gelatin over stock. Heat over a double boiler until gelatin is dissolved. Add gelatin to four cups warm stock and stir. Set aside.

For the garnishes, pat dry ginko nuts and season with salt and pepper. Blanch and shock peppers. Season with salt and pepper. To assemble terrine, dot terrine mold with butter and line with parchment paper. Place eels crosswise into the mold, allowing them to hang over the sides. Continue entire length of the mold. Alternate layers of garnish in the mold packing the pieces closely together. Add enough aspic to coat everything. Continue until terrine is filled to the top. Fold pieces of eel hanging from the sides of the terrine over the top. Wrap in plastic. Weigh down the terrine and chill overnight. To serve, slice and garnish with fresh herbs and greens.

Terrine of Seafood with Saffron Sauce

(Serves 10 to 12)

For the aspic:

2 tablespoons butter

3 pounds shrimp shells and/or lobster bodies

1 carrot, peeled and chopped

1 leek, trimmed and chopped

1 onion, peeled and chopped

2 cups each of chicken stock and veal stock

2 egg whites

3 tablespoons (3 envelopes) gelatin

For the terrine:

1 pound fresh salmon fillet, skin and bones removed

1 pound piece smoked salmon

Juice of 3 lemons

¼ cup olive oil

1 shallot, finely minced

¼ cup chopped fresh herbs, stemmed and minced

1 teaspoon olive oil

1 pound large spinach leaves, washed, stemmed, and blanched

3 bunches scallions, trimmed, and blanched

2 red bell peppers, roasted, stemmed, seeded, peeled and sliced

2 yellow bell peppers, roasted, stemmed, seeded, peeled and sliced

½ pound very thin asparagus tips, blanched

½ pound carrots, peeled, sliced, and blanched

½ pound snow peas, stemmed and blanched

For the sauce:

1 pound mussels, soaked, scrubbed and debearded

1 large pinch saffron threads, crushed

2 cups heavy cream

Salt and freshly ground pepper to taste

For the garnish:

Salad greens

Whipped cream

For the aspic, in a large sauté pan, heat the butter, add the shells, carrots, leeks and onions and sauté over low heat for ten minutes. Add the stocks and bring to a boil. Reduce the heat and simmer for 30 minutes, strain, and cool in an ice bath. Remove any fat that has risen to the top and set aside. In the bowl of an electric mixer fitted with the whip attachment, add the whites and one cup of the cooled stock and whip on high speed until frothy. In a medium saucepan, bring the remaining stock to a boil and slowly add to the egg white mixture in a steady stream, whisking constantly. Return the mixture to the saucepan and continue to whisk over medium-low heat. As soon as the eggs begin to turn white, stop whisking, reduce the heat to low, and allow to barely simmer for ten minutes. Sprinkle the gelatin over ¼ cup of cold water and set aside to soften for five minutes. Pour the stock through a cheesecloth-lined sieve, or through a paper coffee filter. Add the softened gelatin, stir until dissolved, and set aside.

For the terrine, cut the two types of salmon into ½-inch thick pieces. Place in a shallow pan and marinate with the lemon juice, olive oil, shallot, and herbs for at least two hours, or overnight. In a large sauté pan, heat the olive oil, and sear the fresh salmon pieces over high heat for 30 seconds on each side, keeping the center of the slices rare, and set aside. To assemble the terrine, line a 3x3x7-inch terrine mold with plastic wrap, allowing approximately 2½-inches to hang over the sides. Line the plastic wrap with the blanched spinach leaves, allowing the leaves to hang over the edges. Alternate layers of salmon and vegetables, brushing a thin layer of aspic between each layer. Enclose the terrine with the overhanging spinach leaves, wrap in plastic, and set aside in the refrigerator overnight.

recipe continued on next page

For the sauce, in a large saute pan, add the mussels and steam over high heat until they open. Remove the mussels with a slotted spoon and strain the liquid through a cheesecloth or paper coffee filter into a saucepan. Add the saffron and bring to a simmer. Reduce the broth by half and add the cream. Bring to a boil, remove from heat and season.

To serve, unmold the terrine onto a work surface and slice into ¹/₂-inch pieces. Spoon a pool of the sauce on a plate and set a slice of the terrine beside it. Garnish the terrine with salad greens and decorate the sauce with some of the whipped cream.

Terrine of Herring and Cabbage ⚫48

(Serves 12)

For the vinaigrette:
¹/₂ cup white vinegar
1 cup olive oil
2 shallots, peeled and minced
Salt and pepper to taste

For the cabbage:
1 small head white cabbage, leaves separated and blanched
12 ounces marinated herring
4 tablespoons grated horseradish
Salt and pepper to taste

For the terrine:
8 small leeks, trimmed and blanched
4 small carrots, trimmed and blanched

For the garnish:
Assorted salad greens and cherry tomatoes tossed with ¹/₃ of the vinaigrette
Cooked, peeled, and sliced potatoes sprinkled with ¹/₃ of the vinaigrette
  chopped chives, and scallions
Remaining reserved vinaigrette

For the vinaigrette, in a small bowl, combine all of the ingredients and whisk until well combined.

For the cabbage, set aside five large leaves for the terrine, finely julienned the remaining cabbage and place in a large bowl. Add the herring and horseradish, season, cover with plastic wrap, and set aside in the refrigerator to chill for 48 hours.

For the terrine, line a rectangular terrine mold with the reserved cabbage leaves, allowing the edges of the leaves to hang approximately 2¹/₂-inches over each side. Fill the terrine with alternating layers of the herring mixture, carrots, and leeks, enclose with the cabbage leaves, and place the lid of the terrine on top. Set in a water bath, place in the oven, and bake for one hour. Remove from the oven and set aside. Place a weight such as a light brick or a board over the terrine and set aside in the refrigerator to cool before slicing.

To serve, unmold the terrine and slice into 1 ¹/₂-inch pieces. Place a slice of the terrine onto a plate, spoon some of the vinaigrette beside it, and garnish with salad greens and potato.

Carpaccio with Truffles ⚫52

(Serves 6)

For the carpaccio:
1 bunch arugula, stemmed
¹/₂ head frisée, stemmed
¹/₂ small head red leaf lettuce, cored and leaves separated
4 celery hearts, sliced
2 tablespoons olive oil
1 tablespoon balsamic vinegar
Salt and pepper to taste
12 ounces beef tenderloin, frozen and very thinly sliced

For the garnish:
Sliced truffles
Diced celery heart

For the carpaccio, in a large bowl, toss together the arugula, frisée, and red leaf and set aside. In a small bowl, whisk together the oil and vinegar, season, and toss with the reserved greens.

To serve, mound some of the greens on a plate and arrange slices of the beef on top. Garnish the plate with truffle slices and celery.

Terrine of Goose and Truffle

(Serves 4)

For the goose:
1 breast and 1 deboned leg of goose
Riesling wine to cover
Salt and pepper to taste

For the dish:
4 medium potatoes
Salt and pepper to taste
1 whole truffle
½ onion, minced
1 tablespoon minced parsley
1 tablespoon minced carrot
8 ounces Riesling wine

For the garnish:
Assorted, dressed salad greens

For the goose, marinate meat overnight in Riesling wine to cover and season with salt and pepper.

For the terrine, slice potatoes ⅛-inch thick and season with salt and pepper. Slice goose and truffle the same thickness. Mix onion, parsley and carrot together.

In a ceramic mold, place a layer of potatoes, one of vegetables, a layer of goose and layer of truffle. Repeat three times. Add wine and a glass of water. Bake at 350 degrees for two and a half hours.

To serve, unmold the terrine, slice and serve with mixed greens.

Foie Gras and Sweetbreads in Aspic

(Serves 10 to 12)

1 pound veal sweetbreads, sliced
2 cups chicken stock
1¼ pounds foie gras (1 liver)
¾ teaspoon salt
¼ teaspoon white pepper
¼ teaspoon paprika
1 tablespoon green peppercorns, drained and rinsed
1½ tablespoons unflavored gelatin
1 cup brandy
2 fresh or canned truffles

Place chicken stock in a 2-quart saucepan and bring to a boil. Add the sweetbreads and lower the heat so they gently simmer for ten minutes.

Remove them with a slotted spoon and plunge them into a bowl of ice water to stop the cooking action. Rinse them well, place them in a colander over a bowl, and set a plate weighted with two or three cans over them. Chill weighted until cold. When cold, slice into arcs ½-inch thick and set aside.

Soak and clean the foie gras. Cut the foie gras into ½-inch thick slices. Mix together the salt, pepper and paprika and sprinkle both sides of the slices with the seasoning mixture.

For the foie gras, heat a 12 or 14-inch skillet or sauté pan over high heat and when hot add the foie gras slices, being sure not to crowd them in the pan. After 20 seconds turn the slices and then after an additional 20 seconds remove them from the pan with a slotted spatula or spoon. Set the slices on a wire rack over a dish and drain the fat from the skillet. Continue until all the foie gras slices are seared.

For the sweetbreads, leave a little of the foie gras fat in the pan and sauté the sweetbread slice over medium heat for 1½ minutes on each side, or until lightly browned. Pour the fat out of the pan and add the brandy. Reduce until only three tablespoons remain. Add the reserved chicken stock to the pan and stir in the gelatin and green peppercorns. Stir until all gelatin granules are dissolved. Place a thin layer of the aspic in the terrine and chill until set. Place a layer of the foie gras slices over the aspic, alternating with a layer of the sweetbread slices. Slice the truffles thinly and place them in a line down the center of the terrine when half the ingredients have been layered. Continue to layer the foie gras and sweetbreads and pour remaining aspic over the terrine, tapping it on the counter to insure the air pockets are filled, and place the terrine in the refrigerator, covered with aluminum foil.

Foie Gras Poached in Gewürztraminer

(Serves 4)

For the dish:

1 pound foie gras

2 sprigs purslane

1 teaspoon cracked black pepper

1 tablespoon julienne strips of ginger

Gewürztraminer to cover

2 tablespoons sugar

1 teaspoon cracked black pepper

½ lemon, juiced

Purslane for garnishing

For the foie gras, poach in a pan with purslane, pepper, ginger and Gewürztraminer to cover. Cook 30 minutes.

In saucepan, bring sugar and pepper to a caramel and deglaze pan with wine and drippings from foie gras pan. Reduce by half and finish sauce with lemon juice.

To serve, slice foie gras and layer with purslane on plate. Spoon sauce around.

Assortment of Italian Appetizers

(Serves 4)

For the spaghetti:

4 ounces spaghetti

1 teaspoon olive oil

4 chives, minced

3 tablespoons caviar

¼ small shallot, peeled and minced

For the scampi and cucumber salad:

11 ounces medium shrimp, shelled

¾ cup lemon juice

Salt and white pepper

1¼ cups olive oil

1 medium cucumber, scored and thinly sliced

For the sea bass and spinach roulade:

12 spinach leaves

2 teaspoons coarse-grain mustard

1 teaspoon water

¼ cup olive oil

4 ounces sea bass, thinly sliced

Olive oil

Salt and white pepper

For the marinated salmon:

1 2½ pounds-fillet salmon

6 tablespoons salt

1 cup granulated sugar

3 cups chopped fresh dill

4 cream cheese quenelles

For the sole with cauliflower:

8 ounces sole fillets, skinned and pin-boned and sliced into diamonds

2 cups cooked cauliflower florets

1½ tablespoons capers, soaked in water and drained

1 tablespoon black olives, pitted

1 tablespoon olive oil

Juice of ½ lemon

Salt and pepper to taste

Chervil sprigs

For the spaghetti, in a medium saucepan of boiling salted water add the pasta and cook until al dente. Drain and set aside to cool.

For the scampi and cucumber salad, prepare a steamer. Add the shrimp, cover, and steam to desired doneness. Remove from the steamer and set aside. In a medium bowl, whisk together the lemon juice, salt and white pepper and olive oil. Add the shrimp, toss in the vinaigrette, and set aside.

For spinach and sea bass roulade, in a medium bowl, whisk together the mustard, water, and olive oil, and set aside. Make 12 rolls of spinach, wrap a sea bass fillet around each roll, and brush with olive oil, Sprinkle with lemon, season, and set aside.

For the marinated salmon, in a small bowl, add the salt, sugar, black pepper, half of the chopped dill, and mix to combine. Coat the salmon with the mixture, wrap in plastic wrap, and set aside at room temperature for a few hours or until moisture excretes from the salmon. Place in the refrigerator to cure for 48 hours, turn, and add one more cup of the dill, and continue to refrigerate for an additional 24 hours. Remove from the refrigerator, slice thinly, and set aside.

For the sole with cauliflower, prepare a steamer, add the sole, and steam to desired doneness. Remove from the steamer, season, and set aside to cool. In medium bowl, whisk together the olive oil, lemon juice, and salt. Add the sole, cauliflower, capers, and olives, and set aside.

To serve, finish the spaghetti by tossing in the olive oil, and place a mound in the middle of a serving dish. Sprinkle with chives, spoon some of the caviar on top, and garnish with shallots. To finish the scampi, lay the cucumber slices in a circle on the serving dish and arrange a few shrimp on top. For the roulade, set three sea bass and spinach rolls on the plate and spoon some of the mustard vinaigrette on each roll. For the salmon, sprinkle the remaining dill on the salmon, arrange three slices on the plate and top with a quenelle of cream cheese. For the sole, arrange some of the sole, cauliflower, olives and capers on the plate, and garnish with chervil sprigs.

Oysters with Zucchini Flowers

(Serves 4)

For the ratatouille:

1 eggplant, peeled and diced

1 zucchini, peeled and diced

2 tablespoons salt

2 tablespoons olive oil

½ small onion, peeled and diced

1 small clove garlic, peeled and minced

1 tomato, peeled and diced

½ green bell pepper, stemmed, seeded, and diced

1 bouquet garni (celery, leek, thyme, and bay leaf)

For the tomato-butter sauce:

2 medium tomatoes, coarsely chopped

1 tablespoon tomato paste

1 cup fish stock

1 cup mussel juice or bottled clam juice

2 shallots, peeled and minced

1 mushroom, sliced

¼ cup white wine

2 tablespoons dry vermouth

1 cup heavy cream

8 ounces unsalted butter

Salt and pepper to taste

For the beignet batter:

1 cup plus 1 tablespoon all-purpose flour

1½ teaspoons vegetable oil

Pinch salt

⅓ cup beer

½ cup warm water

1½ teaspoons brandy

1 egg white

For the zucchini flowers:

Oil for frying

8 medium oysters, poached in their liquor and cooled

4 zucchini flowers

For the garnish:

Thinned mayonnaise with parsley purée added

Thinned mayonnaise

Parsley sprigs

Salmon roe

For the ratatouille, place the eggplant and zucchini in a medium bowl, sprinkle with salt, set aside covered with a weighted plate for one hour. In a large sauté pan over medium-high heat, heat the oil, add the onion and sauté until lightly caramelized. Reduce the heat to low and add the garlic, tomato, pepper, and bouquet garni. Squeeze the excess moisture from the eggplant and zucchini and add to the saucepan. Bring the mixture to a simmer, cover, and cook for one hour. Remove from the heat and set aside to cool.

For tomato-butter sauce, in a medium saucepan over medium-high heat, combine the tomatoes, tomato paste, fish stock, mussel juice, shallots, mushroom, wine, and vermouth and bring to a boil. Reduce the heat and simmer until the mixture is reduced by half. Remove from the heat, place in the bowl of a food processor fitted with the metal blade attachment, and purée until smooth. Place mixture in a saucepan over medium-high heat and incorporate the cream. Bring to a boil, reduce the heat, and simmer until the mixture is reduced by half. Remove from the heat, strain, and set aside, keeping warm.

For the beignet batter, in a medium bowl, combine the flour, oil, salt, beer, water and brandy. In the bowl of an electric mixer fitter with the whip attachment, add the whites and whip to stiff peaks. Remove from the mixer, fold into the flour mixture, and set aside.

To finish the zucchini flowers, fill a large sauté pan with 1-inch of oil, and heat to 375 degrees. Remove the pistol and stamen from the flowers, fill each flower with two oysters and a tablespoon of ratatouille, and wrap the petals around the filling to enclose. Dip the flowers in the beignet batter, place in the saute pan, and fry for two minutes, turning frequently until golden brown. Remove from the pan, set aside on a paper towel-lined sheet pan to drain, and keep warm.

To finish the sauce, bring the sauce to a boil, reduce the heat to low, and gradually add the butter, whisking to incorporate. Remove from the heat, season, and set aside, keeping warm.

To serve, spoon some of the sauce onto a plate and decoratively drizzle the green and white sauces around the perimeter. Slice a zucchini in ½ and place in the center of the plate. Garnish the dish with a sprig of parsley and spoon some salmon roe on top.

Oyster "Gâteau"

(Serves 4)

For the curry sauce:
1 cup fish stock
1 cup mussel juice or bottled clam juice
1 tablespoon curry powder
2 tablespoons white wine
2 tablespoons dry vermouth
10 oysters shucked and juices reserved
1 cup heavy cream
8 ounces unsalted butter, diced and room temperature
Salt and pepper to taste

For the puff pastry:
8 ounces puff pastry dough

For the zucchini:
2 medium zucchini, thinly sliced into rounds
Flour for dusting
Salt and pepper to taste

For the tomato concasse:
2 tablespoons olive oil
2 tomatoes, peeled, seeded, and diced
Salt and pepper to taste

For the oysters:
20 oysters, shucked and juices reserved

For the garnish:
Green sauce made by combining 1 tablespoons cooked parsley purée and
¼ cup mayonnaise thinned with water to purée consistency
Parsley sprigs

For the curry sauce, in a medium sauté pan over medium-high heat, combine the fish stock, mussel juice, curry powder, white wine, dry vermouth, oysters and juice and bring to a boil. Reduce the heat and simmer until the mixture is reduced by half. Incorporate the cream, bring to a simmer, and reduce by half. Remove from the heat, strain, and set aside, keeping warm.

For the puff pastry, preheat the oven to 400 degrees. On a lightly floured surface, roll the pastry to ⅛-inch thickness, and place on a parchment-lined sheet pan. Prick the pastry with a fork, cover with parchment and another sheet pan, and set aside in the refrigerator to chill for one hour. Place in the oven and bake for 12 minutes. Remove the top sheet pan and continue to bake for an additional five minutes, or until golden brown. Remove from the oven and set aside to cool. Cut the pastry into four circles 4-inches in diameter and set aside.

For the zucchini, lightly butter a parchment-lined sheet pan and set aside. Preheat the oven to 400 degrees. Lightly dust the zucchini rounds with flour and arrange the zucchini slices in an overlapping pattern to make a 4-inch round. Season and place in the oven to bake for six minutes. Remove from the oven and set aside to cool.

For the tomato concasse, in a small saucepan over medium-high heat, heat the oil, add the tomatoes, and sauté, stirring constantly, for five minutes. Remove from the heat, season, and set aside, keeping warm.

To assemble the gateau, preheat the oven to 300 degrees. Divide the tomato concasse between the puff pastry rounds and arrange a zucchini round on top. Place the sheet pan in the oven to keep warm. In a small saucepan over medium heat, poach the oysters in their liquor until edges curl. Remove from the heat and set aside. Remove the sheet pan from the oven, arrange a few of the oysters on top of the zucchini and set aside, keeping warm.

To finish the curry sauce, bring the saucepan to a boil over medium-high heat, reduce the heat to low, and gradually add the butter, whisking to combine. Season and set aside, keeping warm.

To serve, spoon some of the curry sauce onto a plate and decoratively drizzle some of the white and green sauces around the perimeter. Set a gateau in the center of the plate, spoon some more of the curry sauce on top, and garnish with a sprig of parsley.

"Baeckeofe" of Snails and Sauerkraut

(Serves 4)

For the Baeckeofe:
1 each potato and carrot, peeled
1 leek
4 tablespoons butter
1 cup Petit Gris snails
1 lamb tenderloin, sautéed rare and diced
1 braised calf's foot, precooked and diced
Salt and pepper to taste

7 ounces sauerkraut
2 tablespoons white wine
5 ounces pate brisée, rolled thin
Egg wash
Fresh herbs for garnishing

Cut potato and carrot into fine brunoise. Finely chop leak and sweat all in butter. Add snails, lamb and calf's foot. Season mixture with salt and pepper and combine with sauerkraut. Turn into a terra cotta terrine and add wine. Place pastry on top of the terrine and seal edges. Brush with egg wash. Bake at 350 degrees for 30 minutes. Garnish with herbs such as rosemary.

Note: "Baeckeofe" is an Alsatian word which, when translated, means baker's oven. All the ingredients of a dish were combined in a earthenware crock and then brought to the local baker for cooking in his oven.

Feuilleté of Oysters

(Serves 4)

For the puff pastry:
Flour for rolling
8 ounces puff pastry

For the seafood sauce:
1 cup fish stock
1 cup mussel juice
2 tablespoons white wine
2 tablespoons dry vermouth
2 shallots, peeled and chopped
1 mushroom, sliced
½ cup chopped sea scallops
1 cup heavy cream
8 ounces unsalted butter
Salt and pepper to taste

For the dish:
1 tablespoon olive oil
1 pound spinach leaves, blanched
Salt and pepper to taste
¼ pound baby white asparagus, trimmed and blanched
16 oysters, shucked and juices reserved

For the garnish:
Caviar
Diced tomato
Parsley sprigs

For the puff pastry, preheat the oven to 400 degrees. On a lightly floured surface, roll the pastry to ⅛-inch thickness, and place on a parchment-lined sheet pan. Prick the pastry with a fork, cover with parchment and another sheet pan, and set aside in the refrigerator to chill for one hour. Place in the oven and bake for 12 minutes. Remove the top sheet pan and continue to bake for an additional five minutes, or until golden brown. Remove from the oven and set aside to cool. Cut the pastry into four 2x4-inch rectangles and reserve.

For the seafood sauce, in a medium saucepan over medium high heat, add the fish stock, mussel juice, wine, vermouth, shallots, mushroom, and scallops and bring to a boil. Reduce the heat and simmer until the mixture is reduced by half. Add the cream and bring to a boil. Reduce the heat and simmer until the mixture is reduced by half or until the sauce coats the back of a spoon. Gradually add the butter and remove from the heat. Strain, season, and keep warm.

To assemble the feuilleté, arrange four of the pastry rectangles on a sheet pan. In a large sauté pan, heat the oil, add the spinach, and sauté until wilted. Remove from the heat, season and divide between the rectangles. Reheat the asparagus in boiling water, drain, and lay lengthwise on top of spinach. In a small saucepan over low heat, add the oysters and juice, poach until edges begin to curl, and arrange on top of the asparagus.

To serve, spoon some of the sauce on a plate, and place a feuilleté in the center. Spoon some more of the sauce over the oysters, and garnish with caviar, tomato, and a parsley sprig.

Ravioli of Foie Gras with Asparagus

(Serves 4)

For the ravioli:
2 cups unbleached flour
1 egg
1 egg yolk
2 tablespoons water
2 tablespoons olive oil
Pinch of salt
4 slices fresh foie gras (about 1/4 pound)
5 ounces fresh spinach, cleaned and stemmed
1 truffle, thinly sliced
1 egg, lightly beaten

For the dish:
1 bunch small white asparagus, cleaned and blanched
1 truffle, peeled, sliced, and sauteed in 3 tablespoons unsalted butter

For the ravioli, place the flour on a board and make a well in the center. Place the egg, egg yolk, water, olive oil, and salt in the well and mix with a fork. Incorporate all of the flour into the dough with a fork, and then knead the dough for ten minutes. Form into a ball, cover with plastic wrap, and set aside for 30 minutes. Roll through a pasta machine, ending with the thinnest possible setting, and set aside. In a small sauté pan, add the foie gras, and sear each side for 20 seconds. Remove with a slotted spatula and set aside. Add the spinach to the pan and sauté over medium heat until wilted. Remove from the heat and set aside. Place squares of foie gras, a little of the spinach, and a slice of truffle 3-inches apart on a sheet of dough. Brush the sheet with egg, cover with a second sheet, and press to seal. Cut out the ravioli with round cutters and set aside.

To serve, poach the ravioli in salted boiling water for three minutes and drain. Arrange some asparagus on a plate and place a few slices of truffle on top. Place a ravioli over the truffle slices and spoon some of the truffle butter on top.

Black Bean Pancake
with Crabmeat

(Serves 4)

For the pancakes:
½ cup liquid reserved from cooking black beans
¼ cup cornstarch
¼ cup all-purpose flour
2 eggs
½ cup milk
Salt to taste
1 teaspoon vegetable oil

For the salsa:
2 red bell peppers, seeded and membranes removed
1 yellow bell pepper, seeded and membranes removed
3 plum tomatoes
1 clove garlic
2 shallots, chopped
Juice of 1 lime
1 tablespoon fresh cilantro

For the crabmeat:
2 shallots, minced
1 red bell pepper, seeded, membranes removed and cut into julienne slices
1 tablespoon butter
½ cup heavy cream
1 tablespoon chopped cilantro
Juice of 1 lime
Salt and pepper to taste
12 ounces crabmeat

For the garnish:
Cooked black beans
Julienne slices of jicama
Julienne slices of assorted bell peppers

For the pancakes, mix all ingredients except oil in a stainless steel bowl. In a non-stick frying over medium heat add a teaspoon oil and pour one ounce batter into pan and roll around until it is spread thinly. Flip and cook until firm. Set aside four of these and save remaining batter for another use.

For the salsa, run all ingredients through a food grinder, season to taste and chill.

For the crabmeat, sauté shallots and pepper in butter in frying over medium-low heat. Add cream, cilantro and lime and cook until reduced slightly and thickened. Fold in crabmeat and season with salt and pepper.

To finish, spoon salsa onto four plates. Fold crabmeat mixture into pancakes and roll up. Place atop salsa and garnish with black beans, jicama and pepper strips.

Lamb Shank Ravioli

(Serves 6)

For the pasta dough:
5¼ cups all-purpose flour
Salt to taste
4 egg yolks
4 whole eggs
Water as needed

For the lamb shank filling:
2 lamb shanks
Salt and freshly ground black pepper
Olive oil for sautéing
Butter for sweating vegetables
1 medium carrot, peeled and chopped
1 rib celery, chopped
1 medium onion, chopped
4 cloves garlic, minced
1 large ripe tomato, chopped
1 bunch fresh thyme
Lamb stock
Dry white wine
¼ cup cooked and roughly chopped Swiss chard
2 tablespoons grated Parmesan cheese
3 or more tablespoons ricotta cheese
Salt and pepper if needed

recipe continued on next page

245

continued from previous page

For the ratatouille:
1 yellow squash, very finely chopped
1 zucchini, very finely chopped
1 red bell pepper, cored and minced
1 yellow bell pepper, cored and minced
1 small onion, minced
1 small eggplant, very finely chopped
Olive oil for sauteing
1 small ripe tomato, very finely chopped
2 cloves garlic, minced
2 sprigs fresh thyme
1 tablespoon chopped parsley
Salt and freshly ground black pepper

For the garlic butter sauce:
Reserved braising liquid
1 cup butter
2 cloves garlic, minced
½ teaspoon fresh savory
½ teaspoon fresh thyme
1 tablespoon chopped parsley
Salt and freshly ground black pepper

For the garnish:
Edible and herb flowers
Chervil leaves

For the pasta, place flour, salt and eggs in the bowl of a food processor. Mix lightly and add water. Pulse machine to bring dough together into a ball. Turn out onto a floured board and begin to knead for ten minutes. Wrap in plastic and allow to rest in refrigerator for one hour before rolling and cutting.

For the filling, season lamb shanks with salt and pepper and lightly brown in hot oil. Heat butter in a braising pot and add carrot, celery, onion and garlic. Sauté five minutes. Add browned lamb shanks, tomato, thyme and enough lamb stock and white wine to cover the meat by $\frac{2}{3}$. Bring liquid to a simmer, cover and cook at 350 degrees for an hour, until meat is tender. When cool enough to handle, remove meat from bones. Set aside. Strain and degrease braising liquid. Remove ½ cup and reduce to a glaze. Reserve rest of braising liquid for garlic butter sauce. Place shredded meat in a bowl with lamb glaze, swiss chard, parmesan and enough ricotta cheese to make a creamy, rich filling. Season if needed with salt and pepper.

To make the ravioli, roll out pasta on machine's lowest setting and cut into ravioli. Fill with lamb filling and set aside.

To make ratatouille, sauté all of the vegetables except tomato separately in olive oil. Transfer to baking dish and add tomato, chopped garlic and thyme. Season with salt and pepper. Bake uncovered at 325 degrees for 15 to 20 minutes. Before serving, correct seasoning, add a bit of olive oil to moisten and add parsley.

For the garlic butter sauce, combine butter, garlic, savory, thyme, parsley and salt and pepper in blender or food processor and purée. Mount warm reserved braising liquid with this butter.

To finish the ravioli, bring salted water to a boil and cook ravioli until tender. Drain and arrange in soup plates. Garnish with ratatouille and garlic butter sauce. Arrange herb flowers and leaves around edge of the sauce.

Ragoût of Morels with Pears and Foie Gras

(Serves 4)

For the ragoût:
7 ounces fresh morels
1 shallot, finely diced
1 tablespoon butter
½ cup dry white wine
¾ cup heavy cream
1 tablespoon sherry

For the pear:
1 pear, peeled, cored and sliced
1 tablespoon sugar
4 tablespoons water

For the foie gras:
4 slices raw foie gras, ¼ inch thick
2 tablespoons melted butter
Salt and pepper to taste

For the garnish:
1 tablespoon heavy cream, whipped
Italian parsley

recipe continued on next page

Ragoût of Morels with Pears
and Foie Gras

continued from previous page

For the ragoût, trim and wash the morels in order to remove all sand and impurities. Sauté the shallot in butter until translucent. Add the morels and deglaze with the white wine. Simmer over low heat until half the liquid has evaporated. Add the cream and continue simmering until the morels are tender. Season to taste with salt and pepper from the pepper mill. Finish with the sherry. Set aside and keep warm.

For the pear, put sugar and one tablespoon of water into skillet and while constantly stirring, caramelize the sugar until golden brown. Add the remaining three tablespoon of water and the pear slices, and simmer until the pears are tender. Set aside.

For the foie gras, season with salt and pepper, and brush with melted butter. Place on hot grill and mark. Do not over-cook.

To serve, place ragoût of morels on preheated plates and top with the grilled foie gras. Garnish with the pear slices and Italian parsley.

Goose Liver Braised
in Sauerkraut

(Serves 8)

For the sauerkraut:
1 cup goose fat
1 onion, peeled and thinly sliced
3 pounds sauerkraut, rinsed
1 cup white wine
5 ounces smoked and blanched bacon, diced
8 3-ounce pieces goose liver
Salt and pepper to taste

For the truffle sauce:
1 cup veal demi-glace
2 tablespoons Madeira infused with truffle peelings
2 tablespoons diced truffles
Salt and pepper to taste

For the garnish:
2 cups wild mushrooms sautéed in butter
Baby pearl onions, peeled and sautéed in butter
Young red-skinned potatoes, steamed, tossed in butter and chives

For the goose, preheat the oven to 350 degrees. In a large saucepan over medium-high heat, heat the goose fat, add the onion, and sauté until softened and translucent. Add the sauerkraut, wine, and bacon, cover, and place in the oven. Braise for one hour, remove from the oven, and add the goose liver. Cover, place in the oven, and continue to braise for an additional 40 minutes. Remove from the oven, season, and set aside, keeping warm.

For the truffle sauce, in a small saucepan, add the demi-glace and bring to a boil over medium-high heat. Reduce the heat and simmer until the mixture is reduced by one third. Incorporate the truffle essence, remove from the heat, and strain into a small saucepan. Add the diced truffle, season, and set aside, keeping warm.

To serve, spoon some of the sauerkraut onto a plate and place a piece of goose liver on top. Arrange some of the mushrooms beside the liver and garnish with pearl onions and potatoes.

Pasta Pouches with Fresh Seafood

(Serves 4)

For the filling:
2 tablespoons olive oil
4 large prawns, peeled and de-veined
4 oysters, shucked
8 clams, shucked
16 periwinkles*, shelled and steamed
8 mussels, shucked and steamed
¼ cup dry white wine
2 sprigs basil, stemmed and chopped
1 scallion, trimmed and chopped
1 tablespoon butter

For the dish:
4 9-inch rounds fresh pasta dough
4 blanched scallions
1 cup beurre blanc

For the garnish:
Chervil sprigs
Peeled and seeded Roma tomato slices

*Periwinkles, also called sea snails or winkles are found along the Atlantic coasts of Europe and north America. It grows to about 1-inch in size and is gray to dark olive with reddish brown bands.

recipe continued on next page

For the filling, in a large sauté pan, heat the oil, add the prawns and sauté for two minutes. Add oysters and clams and sauté for another minute. Incorporate the periwinkles and mussels, deglaze the pan with wine, and remove from heat. Place the seafood in a medium bowl leaving as much of the cooking liquid remaining in the pan as possible, and set aside. Place the pan over medium heat and bring the liquid to a boil. Reduce the heat and simmer until the liquid is reduced by three-fourths. Incorporate the butter, basil, and green onion, remove from the heat, and add to the seafood mixture, setting the filling aside to cool.

To assemble the pouches, prepare a steamer. Blanch the pasta rounds in boiling salted water, drain, and arrange on a flat work surface. Divide the seafood between the four rounds, mounding the filling in the center, bring the edges of the pasta together to form a pouch, and tie with a scallion. Arrange the pouches in the bottom of the steamer, cover, and steam for five to six minutes, or to desired doneness. Remove the steamer from the heat and set aside, keeping warm.

To serve, spoon some of the beurre blanc onto a plate and set a pasta pouch on top of the sauce. Garnish the dish with chervil and tomato slices.

Herb Pasta with Crawfish

(Serves 6)

For the pasta:
1 cup bread flour
½ teaspoon salt
3 egg yolks
Flour for kneading
Small basil leaves
Cilantro sprigs
Oregano leaves
Tarragon sprigs
Dill sprigs
1 egg, lightly beaten

For the vinaigrette:
4 sprigs basil, stemmed and crushed
¼ cup red wine vinegar
1¼ cups olive oil
½ teaspoon sugar
¼ pound haricots verts, blanched
1 yellow bell pepper, stemmed, seeded and julienned
Salt and pepper to taste

For the dish:
60 cooked crawfish tails
6 whole crawfish, cooked

For the garnish:
Fresh herbs

For the pasta, place the flour on a board and mix with the salt. Break the egg yolks into the center, and using a fork, mix until all of the flour is incorporated. Flour your hands and knead the dough for ten minutes. Shape into a ball, cover with a damp towel, and set aside to rest for two hours. Roll the dough through a pasta machine until the sheets are as thin as possible. Lay one sheet of pasta on a flat work surface and arrange the herb leaves about 1-inch apart on the sheet. Brush a second sheet of pasta with egg, lay over the first sheet, and press to seal. Cut in between the herbs and roll once again through the pasta machine. Cut the noodles into circles with a 2-inch cookie cutter and repeat the procedure until all the dough is used.

For the vinaigrette, in a medium bowl , add the basil and vinegar and set aside to marinate for one hour. Place in the bowl of a food processor fitted with the metal blade attachment, and puree until smooth. Strain into a small saucepan, pressing to extract the basil juices, incorporate the olive oil and sugar, and bring to a simmer. Remove from the heat, add the haricot verts and peppers and reserve.

To serve, bring a large saucepan of salted water to a boil, add the pasta, and cook for one minute. Drain, and chill in an ice bath. Drain again and reserve. Spoon a mound of the vegetables and vinaigrette in the center of the plate and arrange the crawfish tails and pasta in a circle around it. Set a whole crawfish on top of the vegetables and garnish with herbs.

Lobster and Potato Terrine

(Serves 6)

For the terrine:

2 leeks, leaves separated and blanched
3 1½-pound live lobsters
3 medium potatoes, peeled and diced
4 eggs
2 cups heavy cream
Salt and pepper to taste
1 carrot, peeled, finely diced, and cooked
1 turnip, peeled, finely diced, and cooked
¼ pound haricot verts, finely diced, and cooked
1 black truffle, peeled and finely chopped
1 bunch chives, chopped
1 bunch basil, chopped

For the salad:

1 tablespoon champagne vinegar
1 tablespoon mixed fresh herbs
4 tablespoons olive oil
Salt and pepper to taste
Assorted salad greens

For the garnish:

Chives
Dill sprigs
Chervil sprigs
Red and yellow cherry tomatoes
Tomato ragoût
Minced vegetables

For the terrine, preheat the oven to 375 degrees. Line a terrine mold with plastic wrap, allowing approximately 2-inches to hang over the sides. Line the plastic wrap with the leek leaves allowing some of the leaves to hang over the sides, and set aside. In a large saucepan of boiling salted water or court bouillon, add the lobsters, and bring to boil. Cook the lobsters for four minutes, remove from the pan, and set aside. When cool enough to handle, remove the meat, reserving the coral, one tail, and two claws. Place the remaining lobster meat in the bowl of a food processor fitted with a metal blade and add the potatoes, lobster coral, eggs, cream, and purée until smooth. Transfer to a medium bowl, fold in the vegetables and herbs, season, and reserve. Fill half of the terrine with the lobster purée and press the reserved lobster meat into the mixture. Finish with the remaining purée and enclose with the overhanging leek leaves and plastic wrap. Wrap in a double layer of aluminum foil, enclose with a terrine lid, and place in a shallow pan. Fill the pan with enough water to come half way up the sides of the pan, place in the oven, and bake for one hour. Remove from the oven and set aside to chill in the refrigerator.

For the salad, in a medium bowl, whisk together the vinegar, herbs, oil, season, and set aside. Toss with the salad greens and reserve.

To serve, unmold the terrine and slice into ½-inch pieces. Place a slice in the center of a plate and arrange some of the salad greens beside it. Spoon some of the minced vegetables and tomato ragoût next to the terrine and garnish the plate with chives, dill, chervil, and tomatoes.

Feuilleté of Pasta with Tuna and Caviar

(Serves 6)

For the pasta:

Peanut oil for frying
1 recipe for tomato, parsley, squid ink, and egg pasta
8 ounces tuna fillet, thinly sliced
6 ounces osetra caviar

For the sauce:

3 tablespoons raw lobster coral
6 ounces unsalted butter
⅓ cup lobster or fish stock
3 ounces osetra caviar
Salt and pepper to taste

For the feuilleté, in a large saucepan, heat the oil to 375 degrees. Roll each pasta as thinly as possible through a pasta machine. Place on a lightly floured work surface, cut into 3-inch circles, and set aside. Add the pasta to the oil in batches and fry for five seconds, or until crisp. Remove with a slotted spoon, drain on paper towels, and set aside. Repeat the procedure with the remaining pasta and keep warm. To assemble the feuilleté, alternate layers of pasta, tuna, and caviar, ending with a round of squid pasta, and set aside.

For the sauce, in the bowl of a food processor fitted with the metal blade attachment, add the lobster coral and butter, and purée until smooth. Transfer to a small saucepan, add the stock, and bring to a boil. Remove from the heat and strain into a small bowl. Incorporate the caviar, season, and keep warm.

To serve, place one feuilleté on a plate and spoon some of the sauce beside it.

Salmon Medallion in Shiitake Shell

(Serves 2)

For the medallions:

7 ounces salmon fillet, pin-boned, skinned and sliced into 2-inch in diameter rounds

4 large shiitake mushrooms, trimmed and stemmed

1 egg, lightly beaten

¾ cup breadcrumbs

3 ounces clarified butter

For the sauce:

Juice of ½ small lemon

2 tablespoons olive oil

2 sprigs fresh rosemary, stemmed and chopped

½ small tomato, peeled, seeded, and diced

Salt and pepper to taste

Salmon caviar

Rosemary sprigs

For the medallions, place the salmon rounds in between two of the shiitake caps, season, and brush with the beaten egg. Dust with the breadcrumbs, shaking off any excess, and set aside. Repeat the breading process and reserve. In a large sauté pan, heat the butter, add the mushrooms, and sauté until the crust is golden brown and the salmon is medium-rare. Remove from the heat and keep warm.

For the sauce, in a small saucepan, warm the lemon juice and olive oil. Remove from the heat, incorporate the rosemary and tomato, season, and keep warm.

To serve, spoon some of the sauce on a plate, slice a medallion in half and place over the sauce. Garnish the plate with salmon caviar and a sprig of fresh rosemary.

Medley of Mushrooms

Serves 3

For the mushroom mousse:

1 tablespoon butter

1 shallot, peeled and chopped

4 ounces button mushrooms, cleaned and sliced

½ cup white wine

½ cup heavy cream, whipped

Salt and pepper to taste

For the marinated mushrooms:

1 tablespoon olive oil

4 ounces button mushrooms, trimmed and quartered

2 tablespoons white wine

1 teaspoon coriander seeds

Salt and pepper to taste

For the mushroom chips:

¼ pound button mushrooms, stems removed and thinly sliced

1 quart frying oil

Salt

For the mushrooms with vinaigrette:

Juice of ½ small lemon

1 tablespoon olive oil

Salt and pepper

1 sprig thyme, stemmed and chopped

4 ounces button mushrooms, thinly sliced

For the jellied mushroom consommé:

2 cups chicken broth

4 ounces button mushrooms, sliced

¼ ounce unflavored gelatin, softened

Medley of Mushrooms

For the mushroom mousse, in a medium sauté pan, heat the butter, add the shallot, and sauté until translucent. Add the mushrooms and wine and cook until all of the liquid has evaporated. Place in the bowl of a food processor fitted with the blade attachment and purée. Transfer to a medium bowl, season, and set aside to cool. Fold in the cream and set aside in the refrigerator.

For the marinated mushrooms, in a medium sauté pan, heat the oil, add the mushrooms, and sauté until softened. Add the wine and coriander and reduce the heat to a simmer. Cover and continue to simmer for ten minutes. Remove from the heat and set aside for one hour.

For the mushroom chips, in a large saucepan, heat the oil to 350 degrees. Add the mushrooms in batches and fry until golden brown. Remove from the pan with a slotted spoon and drain on paper towels. Sprinkle with salt and keep warm.

For the mushrooms with vinaigrette, in a small bowl, whisk together the lemon juice and the olive oil, season, and set aside.

For the jellied mushroom consommé, in a small saucepan, add the chicken stock and bring to a boil. Add the mushrooms and simmer for ten minutes. Incorporate the gelatin, strain into a small bowl, and set aside in the refrigerator until set. Remove from the refrigerator, slice into small cubes and set aside.

To serve, spoon a quenelle of the mousse on the plate and garnish with a parsley leaf. Arrange some mushroom slices beside it, drizzle with the reserved vinaigrette, and sprinkle with thyme. Spoon some marinated mushrooms next to the quenelle and garnish with chervil. Scatter some the mushroom chips and jellied consommé around the plate.

Glazed Sea Urchin

(Serves 2)

For the sea urchins:
8 to 10 sea urchins
8 medium spinach leaves, trimmed and blanched
½ cup hollandaise sauce
2 tablespoons heavy cream, whipped to soft peaks
2 teaspoons sturgeon caviar

For the glazed sea urchin, using scissors or a sharp knife, make an incision in the bottom or mouth of the sea urchin. Cut away part of the bottom and remove the viscera, shaking the sea urchin if necessary. On the top of the shell, there will be five clumps of roe which can be removed with a small spoon. Place the roe in a small bowl and reserve. Repeat the procedure with the remaining sea urchin and set aside. On a flat work surface, overlap four of the spinach leaves and place half of the reserved roe in he center of the leaves. Bring the edges of the leaves toward the center enclosing the roe and fold to make a small package. Place in a small ramekin and set aside. Repeat the procedure with the remaining spinach and roe and reserve. Preheat the broiler. In a medium bowl, add the hollandaise and fold in the whipped cream. Spoon some of the hollandaise mixture into the ramekins, place on a parchment-lined sheet pan, and set aside.

To serve, place the sheet pan in the oven, and broil until the sauce begins to turn golden brown. Remove from the oven and top with some of the caviar.

Gratin of Asparagus

(Serves 4)

For the asparagus:
1 1/4 pounds asparagus, trimmed and sliced into 3-inch stalks
2 tablespoons lemon juice
Salt and pepper to taste

For the mushrooms:
½ pound fresh morels, cleaned and stemmed (if unavailable, substitute fresh shiitake or chanterelle mushrooms, do not use dried morels)
3 tablespoons unsalted butter
1 teaspoon fresh tarragon leaves, chopped (1/4 teaspoon dried)

For the dish:
½ pound country ham, finely julienned
½ pound Jarlsburg cheese, shredded
2 cups hollandaise sauce (recipe found in any French cookbook)
Salt and pepper to taste

For the asparagus, in a large saucepan of boiling salted water, add the asparagus spears and blanch in salted boiling water until the stalks are cooked but still crisp. Drain and plunge into ice water to stop the cooking action. Place in a large bowl, sprinkle with lemon juice, salt, and pepper, and set aside.

In a large sauté pan, heat the butter, add the morels, and sauté over medium high heat until they are cooked, about four minutes. Remove from the heat add the tarragon and season with salt and pepper.

To assemble the gratin, preheat the broiler. Divide the asparagus between four gratin dishes, and top with the morels, ham, and cheese. Spoon some of the hollandaise over the gratin and place in the oven approximately 6-inches from the broiler. Broil for one minute or until the surface is glazed and brown, remove from the oven, and serve immediately.

Frogs' Legs with Grapefruit

(Serves 4)

For the stock:

1 tablespoon unsalted butter
1 carrot, peeled and chopped
1 leek, trimmed, washed and sliced
4 mushrooms, trimmed and sliced
24 frogs' legs, top bone removed and reserved
2 cups water
1 cup chicken stock
Reserved frogs' leg bones

For the dish:

2 tablespoons grapefruit zest, finely julienned
1-inch piece ginger, peeled and minced
1 cup Sauternes
4 ounces unsalted butter, room temperature and diced
1 cup reserved stock
Salt and pepper to taste

For the stock, in a large saucepan, heat the butter, add the carrot, leek, and mushrooms, and sauté over low heat for five minutes. Place the frogs' legs on top of the mixture, cover, and continue to cook for eight minutes. Remove the frogs' legs and reserve, keeping warm. Add the bones, water, and stock to the pan and bring to a boil. Reduce the heat and simmer for 20 minutes. Increase the heat to just below a boil and reduce by half. Remove from the heat, strain, and reserve.

For the dish, in a small sauté pan, heat the butter, add the zest and ginger, and sauté over low heat for 30 seconds. Add the Sauternes, increase the heat, and simmer until all but one tablespoon of the liquid has evaporated. Remove from heat and whisk in the butter. Incorporate the stock, season, and set aside.

To serve, arrange the frogs' legs on a plate and top with some of the sauce.

Wild Mushroom Gratin

(Serves 6)

For the crust

½ cup fresh white bread crumbs
½ cup grated Parmesan cheese
½ cup grated Gruyère cheese
3 sprigs parsley, stemmed and minced
1 sprig basil, stemmed and chopped
1 sprig thyme, stemmed and chopped

For the filling:

2 tablespoons unsalted butter
1½ cups chanterelles, trimmed stems removed, and quartered
2 cups shiitake mushrooms, trimmed, stems removed, and quartered
½ cup oyster mushrooms, stems removed
1 shallot, peeled and minced
1 clove garlic, peeled and minced
¼ cup Madeira
1¾ cups heavy cream
½ teaspoon ground white pepper
1 tablespoon kosher salt
¾ cup Dry Sack Sherry

For the crust, in a medium bowl, combine all the ingredients and set aside.

For the filling, preheat the broiler. In a large sauté pan, heat the butter over medium heat, add the mushrooms, and sauté for five minutes. Add the shallots and continue to sauté for an additional two minutes, or until translucent. Add the garlic and sauté two more minutes. Incorporate the Madeira and cream and bring to a boil. Reduce the heat and simmer for five minutes. Remove the mushrooms with a slotted spoon, shaking the spoon over the pan to drain well, and reserve. Bring the sauce to a simmer and reduce until it is thick enough to coat the back of a spoon. Return the mushrooms to the sauce, season, and divide between six 8-ounce oven-proof dishes. Sprinkle each dish with, and top with the crust mixture. Brown under a preheated broiler until top is brown, remove from the oven, and serve immediately.

Curried Oysters with Cucumber Sauce

66

(Serves 6)

For the sauce:
1 medium English cucumber
⅓ to ½ cup rice wine vinegar
Salt and freshly ground white pepper to taste
2 egg yolks
¼ cup vegetable oil
¼ cup almond oil

For the oysters:
1 tablespoon curry powder
2 tablespoons flour
24 oysters, shucked and bottom shells reserved
¼ cup peanut oil
¼ cup butter

For the garnish:
Watercress
Salmon caviar
Orchid flowers

For the cucumber sauce, peel the cucumber with ½-inch of the flesh and chop coarsely. Place in the bowl of a food processor fitted with the metal blade attachment, add the rice vinegar, and purée until smooth. In a medium bowl, add the egg yolks and lightly whisk. Gradually add the oils in a steady stream, whisking to incorporate. Add enough of the puréed cucumber to the yolks to give the sauce the consistency of very lightly whipped cream, adjust seasoning with salt, pepper, and vinegar if necessary, and set aside.

For the oysters, in a small bowl, mix the curry and flour and lightly coat the oysters, dusting off any excess. In a large sauté pan, heat the oil and butter, add the oysters, and sauté over high heat for 15 seconds on each side. Remove from the pan, place on a paper towel-lined sheet pan to drain, and keep warm.

To serve, place a bed of watercress on a plate and arrange 6 oyster shells in a circle on top of the watercress. Spoon some of the cucumber sauce and set an oyster in each of the shells and garnish with caviar and orchid flowers.

Marinated Tuna with Maui Onions and Avocado

67

(Serves 4)

For the marinade:
3 tablespoon soy sauce
Juice of 2 limes
4 tablespoons olive oil
½-inch piece ginger, peeled and minced
Salt and freshly ground white pepper to taste

For the dish:
8 ounces sushi quality tuna, thinly sliced
1 small Maui onion, peeled halved and sliced into ¼-inch semi-circles
1 large ripe avocado, peeled, pitted, quartered, and sliced
2 teaspoons golden caviar
2 teaspoons Sevruga caviar

For the garnish:
Salad greens
Radish sprouts
Diced tomato

For the marinade, in a small bowl, whisk together the soy sauce, lime juice, olive oil, and ginger, season and set aside.

To assemble the dish, place some of the greens in the center of a plate. Arrange some of the tuna slices on top and drizzle with some of the vinaigrette. Place one-fourth of the avocado slices beside the tuna and garnish with radish sprouts, caviar, and tomato.

American Foie Gras with Country Ham

68

(Serves 4)

For the black-eyed pea vinaigrette:

4 ounces fat back

4 bay leaves

½ onion, peeled and chopped

6 sprigs parsley

3 sprigs thyme

1 teaspoon black peppercorns

4 ounces dried black-eyed peas, soaked overnight and drained

2 cloves garlic, peeled

3 cups water

2 tablespoons balsamic vinegar

Salt to taste

¼ cup vinaigrette

Salt and pepper to taste

For the salad:

8 sprigs watercress, cleaned

8 spears Belgian endive

4 leaves radicchio or red leaf lettuce, roughly chopped

2 teaspoons olive oil

8 slices country ham, cut into strips

For the dish:

4 ½-inch slices fresh foie gras

½ small shallot, peeled and minced

½ cup balsamic vinegar

2 tablespoons crème de cassis

1 small clove garlic, peeled and minced

For the garnish:

Minced chives

Chive blossoms

For the black-eyed pea vinaigrette, tie the fat back, bay leaves, onion, herbs, and peppercorns in a cheesecloth and place in a medium saucepan with the peas, garlic, water, vinegar, and salt. Bring to a boil, reduce the heat, and simmer covered for 12 to 15 minutes, or until the peas are tender. Drain peas and immediately toss with vinaigrette. Season and set aside to cool to room temperature.

For the salad, toss the watercress, endive, and radicchio with the olive oil and set aside. Divide the black eyed peas between four serving plates, top with some of the greens and ham, and reserve.

For the dish, heat a medium sauté pan over high heat, add the foie gras, and sear for 20 seconds on each side. Remove with a slotted spatula and keep warm. Pour half of the grease from the sauté pan, add the shallots, and sauté until softened. Add the vinegar and reduce slightly, incorporate the cassis and garlic, and reduce to syrup consistency. Remove from the heat and keep warm.

To serve, place slices of foie gras on top of the greens, spoon the sauce over the plate, and garnish with chives and chive blossoms.

Ricotta Cheese and Wasabi Pizza

69

(Makes 6 pizzas)

For the pizza:

1 pound ricotta cheese, softened

14 ounces cream cheese, softened

¼ cup wasabi powder

½ cup mirin

½ cup rice wine vinegar

2 tablespoons white wine vinegar

2½ tablespoons lime juice

6 thin 6 ½-inch rounds of unbaked pizza dough

6 teaspoons black sesame seeds

For the marinated vegetables:

¼ cup soy sauce

½ cup rice wine vinegar

1 tablespoon sake

For the dish:

4 large carrots, julienned

1 large daikon radish, peeled and thinly sliced

12 ounces sushi quality tuna, thinly sliced

For the garnish:

Chopped chives

Toasted black sesame seeds

recipe continued on next page

Ricotta Cheese and
Wasabi Pizza

continued from previous page

For the pizza, preheat the oven to 450 degrees. In the bowl of an electric mixer fitted with the paddle attachment, add the ricotta and cream cheese, wasabi powder, and the liquid ingredients. Mix on medium speed until the mixture is smooth and creamy, remove from the mixer, and divide into six equal parts. Arrange the rounds of dough on a parchment-lined sheet pan and spread ⅔ of the cheese mixture on each of the rounds, leaving a ½-inch edge around each pizza. Place in the oven and bake for six minutes. Remove from the oven and spoon the remaining cheese over the pizza. Sprinkle each with one teaspoon of sesame seeds, return to the oven, and bake for another two minutes. Remove from the oven and keep warm.

For the marinated vegetables, in a large bowl, whisk together the soy sauce, vinegar, and sake, add the vegetables, and set aside for one minute. Drain and reserve.

To serve, arrange some of the vegetables and tuna slices on each pizza and sprinkle with chives and sesame seeds.

Belgian Endive with Marinated Salmon

70

(Serves 4)

For the salmon:
Juice of 1 lemon
Juice of 1 lime
3 tablespoons olive oil
2 sprigs dill, stemmed and chopped
2 sprigs parsley, stemmed and chopped
½ teaspoon salt
1½ teaspoons sugar
¼ teaspoon freshly ground black pepper
½ teaspoon crushed pink peppercorns
1 pound salmon fillet, skinned and pin-boned

For the Belgian endive:
¼ cup olive oil
4 Belgian endive, trimmed and leaves separated
Pinch of salt
Pinch of sugar

For the garnish:
Salmon caviar
Sevruga caviar
Dill sprigs

For the salmon, place the fillet in a shallow pan and set aside. In a small bowl, whisk together the juices, olive oil, dill, parsley, salt, sugar, and peppers. Pour the mixture over the salmon and set aside in the refrigerator for 24 hours, turning occasionally.

For the endive, in a large sauté pan, heat the oil, add the endive, salt, and sugar, and sauté until lightly caramelized. Remove from the heat and keep warm.

To finish the salmon, remove from the marinade and pat dry. Slice the salmon into thin slices on the diagonal, wrap the slices in a circle to form four rosettes, and set aside.

To serve, arrange the endive in a circle in the center of a plate and place a salmon rosette on top. Garnish with caviar and sprinkle with dill.

Garlic Custard with Mushrooms

(Serves 1)

For the garlic custard:
1 cup heavy cream
4 cloves garlic, peeled
2 egg yolks
Salt, white pepper and nutmeg to taste

For the sauce:
1 teaspoon butter
½ teaspoon minced garlic
½ cup sliced shiitake and chanterelle mushrooms
4 tablespoons chicken stock
2 tablespoons seasoned walnuts
½ tablespoon butter
Salt and white pepper to taste

For the garnish:
Minced chives

For the custard, bring cream and garlic to a boil and reduce until this coats a spoon. Watch so that cream doesn't boil over. Measure total volume and run through food mill. Per cup of liquid, add two egg yolks. Combine well and season with salt, pepper and nutmeg. Pour into desired size molds and bake covered in a water bath at 250 degrees until set. You can reheat the custard to order in a sauté pan with water as the sauce is being made.

For mushroom sauce, sauté garlic and mushrooms in butter. Add stock and reduce by half. Add walnuts and butter and season to taste with salt and white pepper.

To serve, place custard on plate. Pour sauce around and garnish with minced chives.

Pasilla Chiles with Avocado Salsa

(Serves 32)

For the salsa:
16 ripe, but firm, avocados, peeled, seeded and diced
2 jalapeño peppers, roasted, peeled and minced
2 large red onions, minced
5 bunches cilantro, minced
1 cup rice vinegar
3 cups olive oil
Salt and white pepper to taste
2 bunches green onions, minced

For the chilies:
32 pasilla chile peppers, cored with stem and seed base removed
1 pound shredded Fontina cheese
1 pound shredded Monterey Jack cheese
1 pound shredded Jarlsberg cheese
1 pound shredded white cheddar cheese
1 pound grated Asiago cheese
Olive oil

For garnish:
Cilantro sprigs

For the salsa, combine avocados, chile peppers, onions, cilantro, vinegar, oil, salt, pepper and onions. Be careful not to mash avocado. Set aside.

For the peppers, remove any membranes after they are seeded. Blanch two minutes in boiling, lightly salted water. Refresh in ice water and drain. Combine shredded cheeses. Stuff each pepper with cheese mixture. Replace stem top. Lightly oil and grill over medium wood or charcoal fire until cheeses have melted and there are nice grill marks on both sides of the peppers.

To serve, spoon avocado salsa onto serving plates and top with a pepper. Garnish with cilantro sprigs.

Oysters Trufant

(Serves 6)

For the seafood seasoning:
2 tablespoons dried oregano
⅓ cup salt
¼ cup granulated garlic
¼ cup ground black pepper *
2 tablespoons ground cayenne pepper
2 tablespoons dried thyme
⅓ cup paprika
3 tablespoons granulated onion

For the dish:
1 quart heavy cream
5 dozen freshly shucked oysters (reserve all liquor)
1½ tablespoons seafood seasoning
Salt and pepper to taste

For the garnish:
Caviar
Chives

For the seafood seasoning, in a medium bowl, combine all of the ingredients, and mix thoroughly. Pour into a large glass jar and tightly seal. This recipe yields two cups of seasoning and will keep indefinitely.

For the dish, in a medium saucepan, add the cream and all of the oyster liquor and bring to a boil over medium high heat. Lower the heat and gently simmer until the liquid is reduced to one-and-a-half cups. Add half of the oysters and one tablespoon of seasoning, and cook for five minutes. Remove from the heat, remove the oysters from the pan, and reserve the liquid. In a large sauté pan, add the remaining oysters and seasoning, and sauté over high heat for five minutes, or until the oysters are heated through. Remove from the heat, drain the oysters on paper towels, and set aside.

To serve, arrange some of the oysters on a plate, and cover with some of the sauce. Place a spoon of caviar on top of each oyster and garnish the plate with chives.

Marinated Halibut

(Serves 12)

For the halibut:
3 cups salt
3 cups sugar
2 tablespoons cracked white peppercorns
3 teaspoons cracked mustard seeds
1 teaspoon ground allspice
1 side halibut
4 bunches fresh dill

For the garnish:
Chopped herbs
Cornichons and capers
Minced red onion

For the halibut, combine salt, sugar, peppercorns, mustard and allspice. Spread halibut with mixture and cover with dill. Let cure in refrigerator for 48 hours.
To serve, remove from curing mixture and pat dry. Slice thin and serve with garnishes of herbs, cornichons, capers and onion.

Oysters Maras

(Serves 2)

For the dish:
1 small shallot, peeled and minced
2 cloves garlic, peeled and minced
1 small Roma tomato, diced
2 tablespoons white wine
Pinch Creole seafood seasoning
Pinch fresh tarragon, basil, thyme, and crushed red pepper
12 large oysters
1 teaspoon Dijon mustard
1 scallion, minced
5 tablespoons cold unsalted butter
Salt and pepper to taste

For the garnish:
Fresh basil leaves

For the dish, in a large sauté pan over high heat, add the shallots, garlic, tomatoes, wine, seasoning, tarragon, basil, thyme, red pepper and oysters, and bring to a boil. Remove the oysters from the pan and set aside. Add mustard and scallions to pan and bring to a boil. Reduce the heat and simmer until the liquid is reduced by half. Increase the heat, whisk in butter, and bring to a boil. Remove from the heat, incorporate the oysters, and season.

To serve, arrange a few of the oysters on plate and cover with some of the sauce. Garnish the plate with a sprig of basil.

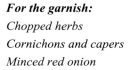

Aquavit's Herring Plate

(Serves 1)

For the matjes herring:
1 matjes herring
Crème fraîche
Chives

For the cured Islandic herring:
Islandic herring
Red onion
Allspice

For the fresh Baltic herring:
Fresh Baltic herring
Tomato sauce
Aspic
Heavy cream
Cod roe

For the Swedish anchovy:
Swedish anchovies
Hard-cooked eggs

For the bleak roe:
Imported bleak roe, a white fish roe

For the Gentleman's Delight:
2 eggs
1 tablespoon cod roe
4 anchovy fillets
Chopped parsley, dill and chives

For the salmon fins:
Belly part and fins from one Norwegian salmon
1 quart water
1 carrot, chopped
½ onion, minced
2 tablespoons salt
2 bay leaves
½ tablespoon white peppercorns
1 bunch dill sprigs
1 lemon, halved
3 gelatin leaves

For the matjes herring, garnish with crème fraîche and chives. For the cured Islandic herring, garnish with red onion and allspice. For the Baltic herring, roll some and cook in tomato sauce. Roll another portion and cook in aspic. Roll a third portion and cook in cream with cod roe. For the Swedish anchovy, garnish with egg. For the bleak roe, serve as is. For the Gentleman's Delight, combine eggs, cod roe, chopped anchovy fillets, and herbs.

For the salmon fins, rinse salmon well. Combine water, carrot, onion, salt, bay leaves, peppercorns, dill and lemon in pot and bring to a boil. Add gelatin leaves and pour over salmon fins. Let simmer for a few minutes. Cool.

To serve, place assortment of fish on plate. Serve with crisp bread and aquavit.

Tuna Carpaccio with Pesto

(Serves 10)

For the tuna:
1½ pounds No. 1 sushi-grade tuna

For the basil pesto:
¼ cup chopped fresh sweet basil
2 teaspoons chopped fresh garlic
2 tablespoons grated Parmesan cheese
1 tablespoon lightly toasted pine nuts
1 teaspoon Dijon mustard
1 cup extra virgin olive oil

For the red pepper pesto:
2 large, meaty red bell peppers
2 teaspoons chopped fresh garlic
1 tablespoon chopped fresh basil
2 tablespoons grated Parmesan cheese
1 tablespoon lightly toasted pine nuts
1 teaspoon chopped fresh cilantro

For the garnish:
1 piece Parmesan cheese
20 cracked black peppercorns

For the tuna, with a very sharp knife or an electric slicer, slice very thin 2-ounce pieces of tuna.

For the basil pesto, in a blender add basil, garlic, cheese, pine nuts, mustard, and purée. While blender is running add olive oil in a steady stream until all is incorporated and mixture is smooth. Season to taste with salt and white pepper.

For the red pepper pesto, broil red peppers over an open flame until skin begins to bubble and turn black all over. Put in metal bowl and cover tightly with plastic wrap. Let sit ten minutes. Peel, seed and chop red peppers. Use same method for basil pesto.

For garnish, run vegetable peeler over a piece of Parmesan cheese to form cheese curl.

To assemble, lay 2-ounce piece of tuna flat on chilled plate. Put each pesto into plastic squirt bottles. Squirt pestos randomly over tuna. Sprinkle on cracked black pepper and place cheese curls around plate.

Gravlax with Mustard Sauce

(Serves 12)

For the gravlax:
1 4-pound side Norwegian salmon
3 cups salt
3 cups sugar
2 tablespoons cracked white peppercorns
4 bunches fresh dill

For the mustard sauce:
4 tablespoons mustard
2 tablespoons red wine vinegar
¾ to 1 cup vegetable oil
Chopped dill to taste

For the gravlax, mix salt, sugar and peppercorns in a bowl. Rub onto both sides of the salmon very well. Cover with dill. Place in refrigerator to cure for 48 hours.

For the sauce, whisk mustard into vinegar and then whisk in oil. Add dill to taste.

To serve, remove salmon from cure. Rub off curing solution and pat dry. Slice into thin slices. On a hot surface, blacken skin side to crisp it. Arrange on plate with sauce.

Tempura Sashimi

(Serves 4)

2 pounds tuna fillet
4 asparagus, blanched and quartered
4 pieces sushi seaweed
2 shallots, finely chopped
1 teaspoon butter
½ cup champagne
½ cup heavy cream
3 ounces uni (sea urchin), about 12 pieces
½ teaspoon wasabi, mixed with enough cold water to make a paste
½ teaspoon red pepper flakes
½ teaspoon imported soy sauce
4 eggs
1 cup milk
¼ cup sake
1 tablespoon ground fresh ginger
1 scallion, finely chopped
1 cup flour, sifted
Peanut oil for deep frying
Seaweed for garnish, presoaked in in cold water

Using a wet knife, cut the tuna into thin strips (about 2 X 7 inches). Cover about half the seaweed piece with 2 to 3 tuna strips, making the tuna layer thicker at the top. Lay a row of asparagus pieces across the center of the tuna. Roll seaweed tuna tightly around the asparagus, wetting the other half of the seaweed to seal the roll before continuing.

Sauté shallots in butter over medium heat until clear. Add champagne and reduce liquid to about one-fourth. Add cream, cook to reduce by half. Remove from heat and pour into blender. Add uni, wasabi, red pepper flakes and soy sauce. Blend until mixed and add salt and pepper to taste.

Whisk together the eggs, milk, sake, ginger and scallion. Add flour slowly and mix until batter is slightly thick.

Prepare the plate in advance. Warm in oven for a few minutes and cover with uni sauce while the oil is heating in a wok or deep saucepan.

When the oil is hot enough that a drop of batter will sizzle and float to the surface almost immediately, cut the rolls in half and dip each into the batter and deep fry for about 15 seconds. Do not over-cook, and heat the oil for a few seconds before adding the next roll so it will regain the proper temperature. The rolls should be golden brown but the fish should not be cooked.

Slice each roll into about six pieces and place on the prepared plate. Garnish with seaweed, if desired.

Louisiana Seafood Fantasy

(Serves 8)

For the shrimp-onion bread:(see note)

¼ cup beef or veal fat

3 cups thinly sliced onions

½ teaspoon minced garlic

1¾ ounce package of dried shrimp, finely ground

1½ tablespoons black pepper

7½ cups all-purpose flour

6 tablespoons sugar

1½ teaspoons salt

2½ packages dry yeast

2¼ cups hot water (105 to 115 degrees)

1 tablespoon unsalted butter, melted

For the oysters in brie sauce:

1 cup cold water

4 cups shucked oysters, drained (about 80 medium oysters)

Seasoning mix for the oysters:

1 teaspoon salt

1 teaspoon paprika

¾ teaspoon white pepper

½ teaspoon onion powder

½ teaspoon garlic powder

½ teaspoon dry mustard

½ teaspoon cayenne pepper

½ teaspoon dried thyme

¼ teaspoon ground nutmeg

¼ teaspoon dried sweet basil leaves

For the garnish:

Blanched vegetables cut into fish shapes

For the crawfish and tasso in cream sauce:

3 tablespoons unsalted butter

2½ teaspoons Louisiana Cajun Magic Seafood mix

5 tablespoons finely chopped green onions

¼ teaspoon chopped garlic

¼ cup julienned tasso or any good lean smoked ham

⅔ cup seafood stock

2 cups peeled crawfish tails

1½ cups heavy cream

Cooked pasta or rice

For the brie sauce:

9 tablespoons unsalted butter

¾ finely diced onions

1 cup finely diced celery

1½ cups fresh ripe tomatoes, peeled and chopped

1 cup finely chopped green onions

5 tablespoons all-purpose flour

1 quart heavy cream (with 40 percent butterfat)

4 ounces brie cheese, trimmed of rind and cut into chunks

For the shrimp etouffée seasoning mix:

2 teaspoons salt

2 teaspoons ground red pepper (preferably cayenne)

1 teaspoon white pepper

1 teaspoon black pepper

1 teaspoon dried sweet basil

½ teaspoon dried thyme leaves

For the shrimp:

¼ cup chopped onions

¼ cup chopped celery

¼ cup chopped green bell peppers

7 tablespoons vegetable oil

¾ cup all-purpose flour

3 cups seafood stock

½ pound unsalted butter

2 pounds peeled medium shrimp

1 cup very finely chopped green onions

4 cups hot cooked rice

Note: We have provided you with the recipe for shrimp-onion bread that can be made into rolls or loaves in place of the skiff motif. In honor of the occasion of the Children's Hospital of Pittsburgh gala, Chef Paul had an architect specially design and build a boat mold which was used for the baking of the shrimp-onion bread. The same final taste for this recipe can be accomplished by ladling a portion of the sauce of the shrimp etouffée onto each serving plate and then topping with the bread. Surround the shrimp-onion bread with individual portions of 1) oysters and brie sauce, 2) crawfish and tasso in cream sauce, and 3) shrimp etouffée.

For the shrimp-onion bread, place fat and onions in a heavy 8-inch skillet over medium-high heat and cook, stirring constantly, until onions are caramelized, about 5 to 7 minutes. If onions start to get too dark at any point during caramelization, lower the heat. When onions are caramelized, stir in the garlic and cook about one minute, Add the shrimp and black pepper, stir to mix well and remove from heat. Scraping the skillet well, transfer mixture to a separate container and set aside. In a large bowl mix 6½ cups of the flour, 5 tablespoons of the sugar and the salt. In a separate bowl combine the yeast and the remaining 1 tablespoon sugar with the hot water. Let sit 5 to 10 minutes; stir until yeast granules thoroughly dissolve. Add reserved caramelized onion and shrimp mixture to bowl containing dissolved yeast mixture, stirring until well combined. Add half of onion-yeast mixture to flour. Mix with hands to moisten flour as much as possible. Add remainder of onion-yeast mixture to dough and mix until flour is thoroughly incorporated. Turn onto a lightly floured surface and knead by hand until smooth and elastic to the touch, about 15 minutes, gradually adding about ½ to 1 cup additional flour. Place in a large greased bowl and invert dough so top is greased; cover with dry towel and let stand in a warm place until doubled in size. Punch down dough. To make the bread, divide dough into 3 equal portions. Form each into a ball, then shape each into a loaf, stretching top and tucking edges under to form as smooth a surface as possible; pop any large air bubbles by pinching them. Place in 3 greased 8½ x 4½ inch loaf pans. Cover with the towel and let rise until almost doubled in size. Bake at 325 degrees until lightly browned about 45 to 50 minutes, rotating the pans after 25 minutes for more even browning;

recipe continued on next page

continued from previous page

brush tips with melted butter and bake until done, about 5 to 10 minutes more. Cool 5 to 10 minutes before removing from pan. Let cool about 1 hour more before slicing. To make rolls, pinch off enough dough to make about 1-½ inch balls. Roll dough into smooth balls with hands. Pop any large air bubbles by pinching them. Place in a greased 13 x 9-inch baking pan with rolls fitted snugly against each other and sides of pan. Cover and let rise until doubled in size, about 35 to 45 minutes. Bake as for bread.

For the oysters in brie sauce, to make oyster water, add 1 cup cold water to the oysters: stir and refrigerate for 1 hour. Strain and reserve oysters and 1 cup oyster water in the refrigerator until ready to use. In a small bowl, thoroughly combine seasoning mix ingredients and set aside. In a heavy 12-inch skillet over high heat, melt 4 tablespoons of the butter. Add ½ cup of onions and cook, stirring constantly, just until onions start to brown, about 3 minutes. Stir in ½ cup of the celery and the seasoning mix and cook about 2 minutes, scraping pan bottom as seasoning begins to crust. Add 1 cup of the tomatoes and cook, stirring frequently, about 3 minutes. Add to oyster water and cook, stirring occasionally about 4 minutes. Add the remaining ¼ cup onions and ½ cup celery and continue cooking, stirring often, about 2 minutes. Stir in 2 tablespoons more butter and cook until melted, about 1 minute. Add the remaining ½ cup tomatoes, and cook until mixture begins sticking to pan bottom, about 5 minutes Stir in the remaining 3 tablespoons butter and green onions. Add the flour, 1 tablespoon at a time until all flour is added, stirring well after each addition and continue cooking, scraping pan bottom constantly, about 4 minutes. Whisk in the cream and continue to simmer, whisking frequently, until mixture reaches a boil. Add the cheese and oysters and return mixture to a boil, stirring occasionally, Remove from heat and keep warm.

For the shrimp etouffée, thoroughly combine the seasoning mix ingredients in a small bowl and set aside. In a separate bowl combine the onions, celery and bell peppers. In a large heavy skillet, heat the oil over high heat until it begins to smoke. With a long-handled metal whisk, gradually mix in the flour, stirring until smooth. Continue cooking, whisking constantly, until roux is dark red-brown, about 3 to 5 minutes. Remove from heat and immediately stir in the vegetables and 1 tablespoon of the seasoning mix with a wooden spoon; continue stirring until cooled, about 5 minutes. In a 2 quart saucepan bring 2 cups of the stock to a boil over high heat. Gradually add the roux and whisk until thoroughly dissolved. Reduce heat to low and cook until flour taste is gone, about 2 minutes, whisking almost constantly (if any of the mixture scorches, don't continue to scrape that part of the pan bottom). Remove from heat and set aside. In a 4 quart saucepan melt 1 stick of the butter over medium heat. Stir in the shrimp and the green onion; sauté about 1 minute, stirring almost constantly. Add the remaining stick of butter, the stock mixture and the remaining 1 cup of stock; cook until butter melts and is mixed into the sauce, about 4 to 6 minutes, constantly shaking the pan in a back-and-forth motion. Add the remaining seasoning mixture; stir well and remove from heat. Keep warm with rice.

Tips on making roux:
1) Cooked roux is called Cajun napalm in my restaurant's kitchen because it is extremely hot and sticks to your skin; so be very careful to avoid splashing it on you; it's best to use a long-handled metal whisk or wooden spoon.

2) Always begin with a very clean skillet or pot- preferably one that is heavy. If possible, use a skillet with flared sides because this makes stirring easier and thus makes it less likely the roux will burn. In addition, use a large enough skillet so that the oil does not fill it by more than one-fourth of its capacity.

3) The oil should be smoking hot before the flour is added.

4) Once the oil is heated, stir in the flour gradually and stir or whisk quickly and constantly to avoid burning the mixture.

5) If black specks appear in the roux as it cooked, it has burned; discard it, then start the roux over again-c'est la vie!

6) As soon as the roux reaches the desired color, remove it from the heat; stir in the vegetables, which stop the browning process and enhance the taste of the finished dish, and continue stirring until the roux stops getting darker (at least 3 to 5 minutes)

7) While cooking roux (bringing it to the desired color) if you feel it is darkening too fast, immediately remove it from the heat and continue whisking constantly until you have control of it.

8) Care and concentration are essential for you to be successful with this fast method of method of making roux.

Especially the first few times you make a roux, be certain that any possible distractions are under control. In addition, have all cooking utensils and required vegetables or seasoning mixtures prepared ahead of time and near at hand before you begin cooking.

For the crawfish and tasso in cream sauce, in a heavy skillet over high heat, melt butter. Add Seafood Magic, green onions, garlic, and tasso and sauté until tasso is browned and a crust begins forming on pan bottom. Stir and scrape well. Pour in ½ cup of the seafood stock and stir well, scraping up all browned bits from pan bottom. Add crawfish and cream and stir to mix well. Reduce heat to medium-high and continue cooking until mixture comes to a boil. Add remaining 3 tablespoon stock and again let mixture come to a boil, stirring occasionally. Remove from heat.

Garnish the dish with blanched vegetables cut in fish shapes.

Is there another group of food that offers such variety in terms of flavor and preparation? Undoubtedly, there is not. In terms of treasures from the sea, these foods permit us much variety in preparation and pleasure on the palate. As with all foods, our memories are marked with concepts based on history and prior impressions. Some of us knew fish that was fresh from the sea, eaten hours after being caught as a part of a day at the beach. Others remember frozen, breaded mystery fish sticks, soggy and flavorless, even hot out of the oven. Then there were those of us who were fortunate enough to have our lives centered around the ocean. Despite our past notions of seafood, as chefs, we've learned to embrace it in another fashion.

Seasonality and species availability play a big part in the fish we are able to secure and serve to our guests daily. We devote time to finding the right product, which we offer to our guests at a price reasonable for them yet profitable for us. We secure fish for our staple menu items, and any specials that we offer. Of course, we prefer to know exactly what we are going to do with the product we've just purchased, but sometimes we purchase knowing that we will "find something to do with it." Our next step becomes maximizing the product. The first instinct may be to pair the fish with something "extraordinary" or visually appealing. Yet our primary concern should be how to emphasize the natural fish flavor while enhancing its unique species' qualities, a task accomplished by picking the appropriate cooking method.

Fish is delicate in nature, and it is important to remember that the cooking method must respect the individual structure of the fish. While there are many ways of preparing the same fish, the individual fish may not withstand each cooking method. Capture the essence of the fish and appreciate its unique personality.

Method:	Type of fish:	Sauce:	Special considerations:
Roasting	Any round or flat fish, whole or fillets. Preserves delicate flavor of fish.	Extra virgin olive oil, compound butter, beurre blanc.	Roasting means cooking in the open air on a spit, while baking means to cook in an enclosed space such as an oven (Peterson 13). Roasted and baked fish have nearly the same qualities. However, fish is often baked with aromatics and vegetables that render liquid when cooked, producing the steam that actually cooks the fish. This method cooks the product with dry, direct heat.
Poaching	Any firm fish, round or flat. Poach whole, as fillets or as tranches.	Sauce made from shallow-poaching liquid or, in the case of deep-poaching, an emulsion-based sauce prepared separately.	Shallow poach by buttering a pan, preparing a natural rack with shallots, seasoning fish, and covering fish one-third of the way with half wine/half fish fumet. Bring to a simmer, cover with buttered parchment, and finish on stove or in moderate oven until done. Strain liquid and prepare a sauce by finishing with butter, cream, and garnish. Deep poach by first preparing an aromatic poaching liquid. Strain liquid and submerge fish in 165°F liquid, maintaining a bare simmer. Cook fish to desired doneness. Prepare a sauce separately.
Deep-Frying	Any white-fleshed fish. Whole, fillets, or finger-size pieces.	An emulsion sauce garnished and served on the side.	Deep-frying, when done properly, produces a crisp and moist product which actually absorbs very little oil. Coat the product in a flour or breadcrumb batter to protect the fish, then deep-fry until golden in color. Patties, cakes, or croquettes can also be prepared by combining fish with a binder, shaping, coating, and frying. The fish can also be wrapped in rice paper, brik, or a rolled flour product and then fried. Drain on paper towels before serving.
Grilling and Broiling	Any firm-fleshed fish, whole, fillets, or tranches.	Compound butter or extra virgin olive oil.	Although the words are used interchangeably, grilling means cooking over the heat source, while broiling means cooking under the heat source.
Pan-frying	Any fish, any cut.	Sauce prepared separately, particularly lemon brown butter.	Pan-frying requires more fat than sautéeing, but far less than deep-frying. Coat fish in milk and flour before pan-frying, blot dry. Garnish with lemon brown butter. Do not prepare a sauce from the *fond* of pan-fried fish.

Grilled John Dory with Basil Vinaigrette

88

(Serves 6)

For the vinaigrette:
4 sprigs basil, stemmed and minced
6 Roma tomatoes, peeled, seeded and finely diced
2 shallots, peeled minced
3 tablespoons red wine vinegar
Salt and pepper to taste

For the fish:
6-6 ounce John Dory fillets, pin-boned
⅓ cup extra virgin olive oil
Salt and pepper to taste

For the garnish:
Arugula leaves
Thyme blossoms
Grilled onion rounds
Minced basil

For the vinaigrette, in a medium bowl, add the basil leaves, tomatoes, shallots, vinegar, and olive oil. Whisk to combine, season, and set aside.

For the fish, prepare a hot grill. Brush the fillets with olive oil and sprinkle with salt and pepper. Grill to desired doneness, remove from the heat, and keep warm.

To serve, arrange some of the arugula and thyme around a plate and place four onion rounds in each corner. Place an oval ring mold in the center of the plate and fill with some of the vinaigrette. Remove the ring mold, place a fillet on top and sprinkle with basil.

Lobster with Ginger Sauce

89

(Serves 2)

For the ginger reduction:
2 ounces fresh ginger
4 cloves garlic, peeled and minced
1½ cups plum wine (or port wine)
4 tablespoons rice wine vinegar

For the lobster:
4 tablespoons peanut oil
2 1½-pound live lobsters
4 tablespoons unsalted butter

For the ginger sauce:
8 scallions, peeled and sliced
2 to 3 tablespoons curry powder
½ cup dry white wine
1 cup fish stock
¼ teaspoon hot chili flakes
2 tablespoons Chinese black vinegar or balsamic vinegar
1 cup heavy cream
Reserved ginger reduction
Salt and pepper to taste

For the garnish:
Fried young spinach leaves
Chive sprigs
Julienned ginger

For the ginger reduction, peel and finely julienne the ginger, reserving the peel for the sauce. In a small saucepan, add the ginger, garlic, one cup of the plum wine or port, and the rice wine vinegar and bring to a boil. Reduce the heat and simmer until the mixture is reduced to two tablespoons. Remove from heat and reserve.

For the lobster, preheat the oven to 500 degrees. In a large sauté pan, heat the oil almost to the smoking point, add two of the lobster halves, and sauté for three minutes. Turn lobster over and add two tablespoons of the butter. Continue to sauté until the lobster shells begin to turn red and the butter begins to brown. Place in the oven for ten minutes, or until the lobster is just cooked. Remove from oven and keep warm. In another large sauté pan, repeat the procedure with the remaining lobster halves and set aside.

For the ginger sauce, combine the fat from the two sauté pans and place over medium high heat. Add the scallions, ginger peels, and curry powder and sauté until the scallions are soft. Incorporate the remaining plum wine, white wine, stock, chili flakes, and vinegar and bring to a boil. Reduce the heat and simmer until the liquid is reduced to one cup, add the cream, and reduce by half. Strain into small saucepan, bring to a boil, and whisk in the remaining butter. Add the ginger reduction, season, remove from the heat, and keep warm.

To serve, place two of the lobster halves on a warm platter, and pour some of the sauce over the plate. Arrange some spinach leaves around the lobster and garnish with chive sprigs and ginger.

King Crab Pasta with Italian Parsley

90

(Serves 4)

For the pasta:

10 ounces all-purpose flour, sifted
3 eggs
1 tablespoon olive oil
1 teaspoon salt
Flour for rolling
1 bunch Italian flat-leaf parsley, leaves only

For the dish:

Legs of 1 king crab
3 tablespoons olive oil
6 shallots, peeled and dice
6 cloves garlic, peeled and finely minced
6 Italian plum tomatoes, peeled, seeded and diced
2 tablespoons fresh tarragon
1 teaspoon fresh thyme
1 cup white wine
1 cup fish stock (or bottled clam juice)
Salt and pepper to taste
1 cup heavy cream
3 tablespoons butter
Cayenne pepper

For the garnish:

Italian parsley leaves
Chives
Chive blossoms

For the pasta, in the bowl of a food processor fitted with the metal blade attachment, combine the flour, eggs, olive oil and salt and process until the dough resembles a coarse meal. Remove from the bowl, gather into a ball, and wrap in plastic wrap. Set aside to rest for two hours. Unwrap the dough and shape in a flattened rough oval or rectangle. Roll through a pasta machine set at the widest setting, fold into thirds, and repeat this step, rolling and folding at this setting three more times. Sprinkle the dough with the parsley, set the rollers at the next narrowest setting, and roll the dough through the machine Repeat this procedure, decreasing the opening after each rolling and dusting the dough lightly with flour if necessary, until desired thinness is reached. Cut into 1-inch wide strips and place on a parchment-lined sheet pan to dry slightly, cover with plastic wrap, and set aside.

For the dish, cut crab legs into 3-inch long pieces. Heat olive oil in a large sauté pan, add the crab and sauté until shells turn red. Add shallots, garlic, tomatoes, tarragon, and thyme and sauté for two minutes, stirring constantly. Deglaze the pan with the white wine and reduce over high heat for five minutes. Add the fish stock, salt and pepper to taste and cook over medium high heat for ten minutes. Remove crab and set aside. Add cream to sauce and reduce until the sauce is thick enough to coat the back of a wooden spoon. Purée the sauce in a blender or food processor fitted with a steel blade. Strain through a sieve into a pan, return to the heat, and whisk in the butter and cayenne pepper. To finish the pasta, cook pasta in boiling salted water until just al dente, no more than one minute. Drain well and add to sauce. Halve the crab legs lengthwise with a sharp knife and reserve.

To serve, place pasta on a warm plate and arrange some of the crab legs on top. Pour some of the sauce over the pasta and garnish the plate with parsley, chives, and chive blossoms.

White Alaskan Salmon with Spicy Pecan Butter

91

(Serves 4)

For the spicy pecan butter:

1 jalapeño pepper, stemmed, seeded, and chopped
½ cup toasted pecans
6 sprigs parsley, stemmed and chopped
6 sprigs cilantro, stemmed and chopped
Juice of 1 lemon
1 cup white wine
3 shallots, peeled and finely chopped
1 teaspoon tequila
¼ cup heavy cream
6 ounces butter, softened

For the salmon:

Salt and freshly ground pepper to taste
4 8-ounce salmon filets
2 tablespoons olive oil

For the garnish:

Grilled leek halves
English peas
Grilled eggplant halves
Toasted pecan halves
Diced tomato
Cilantro sprigs

For the spicy pecan butter, in the bowl of an electric mixer fitted with the metal blade attachment, add the jalapeño, pecans, parsley,cilantro, butter and lemon and purée until smooth. Transfer to a small bowl and reserve. In a medium saucepan, add the white wine,shallots, and tequila, bring to a boil. Reduce the heat and simmer until the mixture id reduced by half, incorporate the cream and continue to simmer until the mixture is thick enough to coat the back of a wooden spoon. Whisk in the reserved pecan butter and strain into a small saucepan. Season and set aside, keeping warm.

recipe continued on next page

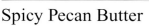

For the salmon, prepare a hot grill. Season salmon steaks and brush with olive oil. Place on a hot grill and cook until medium rare in the center, or to desired doneness.

To serve; divide sauce between four plates. Set the salmon on top and place the grilled vegetables beside it. Arrange the pecan halves on the sauce and garnish the salmon with tomatoes and cilantro.

Steamed Salmon with Lemon-Hazelnut Butter

92

(Serves 4)

For the salmon:
4 6-ounce salmon fillets, skin on and pin-boned
2 tablespoons butter, softened
Salt and pepper to taste

For the sauce:
9 ounces butter
1 small shallot, peeled and minced
½ cup dry white wine
4 tablespoons hazelnut liqueur
Juice of 1 small lemon
⅛ cup hazelnuts, toasted and finely ground
Salt and pepper to taste

For the garnish:
Flower petals
Tarragon leaves
Blueberries
Toasted chopped hazelnuts
Whole scallions

For the salmon, rub the skin of the fillets with butter, season, and set aside. Bring a large saucepan filled with 2-inches of water to a simmer and place a wire rack over the water. Set the salmon fillets on the rack, cover, and steam to desired doneness. Remove from the heat and keep warm.

For the sauce, in a medium saucepan, heat two tablespoons of the butter, add the shallots, and sauté until softened. Add the wine, three tablespoons of the hazelnut liqueur, and the lemon juice, and bring to a boil. Reduce the heat and simmer until the liquid is reduced to three tablespoons. Incorporate the remaining butter, liqueur, and hazelnuts, remove from the heat, season, and set aside.

To serve, spoon some of the sauce on a plate and place a salmon fillet in the center of the plate. Garnish with flower petals, tarragon, blueberries, hazelnuts, and scallions.

Roasted Monkfish with Vegetables

93

(Serves 4)

For the dish:
2 tablespoons vegetable oil
1½ pounds monkfish fillets, skinned and pin-boned
2 ounces bacon, minced
3/4 cup dry white wine
1 cup fish stock
2 carrots, peeled, sliced into small ovals, and blanched
2 turnips, peeled, sliced into small ovals, and blanched
8 small new potatoes, peeled, sliced into small ovals, and blanched
8 red cherry tomatoes
8 yellow cherry tomatoes
16 asparagus tips, blanched
5 ounces unsalted butter, softened

For the garnish:
Parsley sprigs

For the monkfish, preheat the oven to 450 degrees. In a large sauté pan, heat the oil, add the monkfish, and sear until browned on all sides. Remove from the pan, season, and set aside. Add the bacon to the sauté pan and sauté until crisp. Deglaze the pan with wine and stock and bring to a boil. Reduce the heat and simmer for five minutes. Return the monkfish to the pan and add the carrots, turnips, potatoes and tomatoes. Cover and bring to a boil over high heat. Place in the oven and bake for seven minutes. Remove from the oven, transfer the fish to a cutting board and add the asparagus to the sauté pan. Return to the heat and simmer until all of the vegetables are tender. Whisk in the butter, season, and keep warm.

To serve, slice the fish into ½-inch slices and arrange on a plate. Spoon some of the vegetables around the plate, pour some of the sauce over the fish, and garnish with parsley.

Steamed Salmon with Black Bean Sauce

(Serves 4)

For the dish:

4 4-ounce salmon fillets, no more than ½-inch thick, skinned and
  pin-boned
2 red bell peppers, stemmed, seeded, and julienned
2 green bell peppers, stemmed, seeded, and julienned
¼ cup shredded fresh bamboo shoots
1 tablespoon fermented black beans
1-inch piece ginger, peeled and minced
2 scallions ,white part only, trimmed and minced
¼ cup soy sauce
2 tablespoons chicken stock
⅛ teaspoon freshly ground white pepper
1 tablespoon vegetable oil
1 teaspoon sesame oil

For the salmon, prepare a steamer and place over a large saucepan of simmering water. Season the salmon and place on a plate that will fit inside of the steamer. Place the fillets on the plate and arrange the peppers in a single layer on top of the fillets Scatter bamboo shoots over fish and sprinkle with black beans, ginger, and scallion. Mix the remaining ingredients in a small bowl and pour over the fish. Steam in a covered steamer for five to eight minutes, or until just cooked through and opaque.

To serve, divide salmon on plates and sprinkle with vegetables and sauce.

Fricassee of Cod

(Serves 4)

For the cod:

1 6-to 8-pound cod, including tongue, liver and roe
3 tablespoons white wine
1 shallot, minced
Salt and pepper

For the cod roe:

Reserved cod roe
Salt and white pepper
2 tablespoons bread crumbs
2 tablespoons clarified butter

For the sauce:

6 to 7 tablespoons strong fish stock
3 tablespoons white wine
6 tablespoons cream
1 cup cooked seasonal vegetables

For the cod, place all parts except for roe in a buttered pan. Add wine, shallots, and salt and pepper to taste. Cover with foil and set aside.

For the roe, season with salt and pepper and dip in breadcrumbs. Sauté in butter. Reduce fish stock with wine. Add cream and cooked vegetables. Place cod in a 350-degree oven and cook until done. Slice sautéed roe.

To serve, arrange all on plate with cream sauce and vegetables.

Roulade of Yellowfin Grouper

(Serves 4)

For the dish:

4 6-ounce fillets yellowfin grouper
Salt and pepper
Fines herbes
2 tablespoons bread crumbs
2 carrots, sliced paper-thin and blanched and shocked
½ cup bread crumbs
Fresh spinach leaves, blanched and shocked
4 large potatoes, peeled and sliced thinly
Olive oil for sautéing
1 cup olive oil
½ cup red wine vinegar

For the garnish:

Chives
Chervil
Thyme sprigs
1 cup tomato concasse
Swiss chard

Roulade of
Yellowfin Grouper
continued from previous page

For the fish, season fillets with salt, pepper, fines herbes and bread crumbs. Pat the carrot strips dry and place on half the fish. Fold fish over and season outside with salt and pepper and bread crumbs. Wrap spinach leaves around outside of fish. Wrap potato slices around spinach. Season with salt and pepper and sauté in olive oil until golden brown all over.

To serve, cut fish fillet portions into three pieces on the bias. Place on plate and sprinkle border with olive oil and vinegar. Garnish with herbs, tomato concasse and pieces of Swiss chard.

Crawfish and
Fettuccine

(Serves 2)

For the crawfish sauce:
1 tablespoon butter
½ small red bell pepper, stemmed, seeded and diced
½ small green pepper, stemmed seeded, and diced
½ small onion, peeled and diced
1 cup cooked and peeled crawfish tails
½ teaspoon Creole seasoning
Crushed red pepper flakes to taste
1 tomato, diced
1 scallion, trimmed and diced
3 ounces unsalted butter, cubed and softened

For the garnish:
Minced parsley

For the crawfish sauce, in a large sauté pan, heat the oil, add the peppers and onions, and sauté until softened. Incorporate the crawfish and Creole seasoning and continue to sauté for two minutes. Add the tomatoes and scallions, sauté for one minute and incorporate the butter. Remove from the heat, season, and keep warm.

For the fettuccine, bring a large saucepan of salted water to a boil, add the fettuccine and cook to desired doneness, Drain, toss with the olive oil, and set aside.

To serve, mound some of the pasta on a plate and pour some of the sauce over the pasta. Place some more of the pasta on top of the sauce and garnish with parsley.

Seared Codfish

(Serves 4)

For the mushroom consomme:
4 cups chicken stock
1 pound ground chicken
½ cup finely chopped carrot
1 cup chopped onion
½ cup chopped celery
1 pound egg whites
Salt and white pepper to taste

For the fish:
4 7-ounce fillets of cod
Salt and pepper
Mushroom dust (made by grinding mushroom stems that have been
*   left to dry overnight)*
Butter for sautéing
4 tablespoons parisienne cut carrots
4 tablespoons haricot verts
4 tablespoons green onions, cut on the bias
½ cup enoki mushrooms
½ cup morels
1 pound fresh scallion pasta bow ties, cooked to al dente
4 tablespoons foie gras butter

recipe continued on next page

Seared Codfish

continued from previous page

For the consommé, place stock in pot. Add chicken, carrot, onion, celery and egg whites. Heat and cook over low heat until clarified. Remove from heat. Gently break a whole in top of raft and ladle consommé into a fine sieve double lined with cheesecloth. Adjust seasoning.

For the fish, season cod with salt and pepper. Dredge in mushroom dust. Sear cod on both sides in pan until cooked to firm. In a separate pan heat carrots, haricot verts, green onions, and mushrooms with 2 cups mushroom consommé.

To serve, line deep dinner plates with bow ties. Ladle mushroom consommé into bottom of plates and spoon vegetables around sides. Place cooked cod in center and place disk of foie gras butter on top.

Sea Robin Tails

(Serves 4)

For the artichokes:
2 artichoke hearts
1 cup olive oil
2 minced shallots
3 tablespoons mint vinegar
1 tablespoon chopped parsley

For the tomato vinaigrette:
2 cups tomato juice, reduced to ½ cup
⅔ cup olive oil
4 tablespoons mint vinegar
Salt and pepper to taste

For the fish:
8 sea robin tails
Salt and pepper to taste
½ pound thinly sliced pancetta
3 zucchini, sliced lengthwise into strips, salted and allow to drain
All-purpose flour
Salt and pepper to taste
Safflower oil

For the garnish:
Julienned jicama

For the artichoke, marinate hearts in a mixture of olive oil, shallots, vinegar and parsley. Set aside.

For the tomato vinaigrette, blend tomato juice, olive oil, vinegar and salt and pepper. Set aside.

For the fish, pat tails dry with towel. Season with salt and pepper. Place a piece of pancetta across top of tail. Wrap tail in zucchini strips. Dust with flour and season with salt and pepper. Sauté in a hot pan with safflower oil.

To serve, slice and fan out artichokes on plates. Place searobin tails on plate and add sauce. Garnish with jicama strips.

Langouste with Thai Herbs

(Serves 1)

For the langouste*:
1 1½-pound langouste

For the sauce:
1 tablespoon butter
1 tablespoon Thai green curry paste
1 stalk lemon grass
1 cup white port
½ small carrot, peeled and finely julienned
½ small Granny Smith apple, peeled and julienned
1 tablespoon ground turmeric
½ cup heavy cream, lightly whipped
Salt and pepper to taste

recipe continued on next page

Langouste with Thai Herbs

continued from previous page

For the garnish:

Chervil sprigs

*If langouste is not available, rock or Maine lobster may be substituted.

For the langouste, bring a large saucepan of salted water or court bouillon to a boil and add the langouste. Once the liquid returns to a boil, cook the langouste for five minutes. Remove from the pan and set aside to cool slightly. Halve transversely, remove the meat from the tail, and keep warm. Save the shells and set aside.

For the sauce, in a large sauté pan, heat the butter, add the curry and lemon grass, and sauté for two minutes. Deglaze the pan with the port and add the carrots and apples. Bring to a boil, reduce the heat, and simmer until the liquid is almost completely reduced. Add the turmeric and cream and bring to a simmer. Remove from the heat, discard the lemon grass, season, and keep warm.

To serve, place the reserved shell on a plate. Slice the tail meat into medallions and place back into the shell. Pour the sauce over the langouste, arrange the julienned fruit and vegetables over the lobster, and garnish with chervil.

Monkfish with Fennel and Star Anise

(Serves 4)

For the sauce:

6 shallots, minced
1 bulb fennel, chopped
12 peppercorns
2 sprigs thyme
Pinch fennel seeds
2 star anise
Oil for sautéing
2 cups white wine
2½ cups veal stock reduced by half
Salt and pepper to taste

For the vegetables:

4 carrots, cut into 2-inch cylinders just ¼-inch in diameter
4 bulbs fennel
Butter
Salt and pepper to taste

For the fish:

4 8-ounce portions of monkfish, bone-in and tied with butcher's twine
2 tablespoons chopped chervil
Potato crisps
Salt and pepper to taste

For the sauce, sauté shallots and fennel in oil with peppercorns, thyme, fennel seeds and star anise. Deglaze the pan with white wine. Add veal stock. Reduce. Season to taste. Cook carrots and set aside. Place fennel in cold pan with butter. Cook over moderate heat until golden. Season with salt and pepper and finish cooking in the oven until fork tender. In separate pan, sauté monkfish in butter, searing on all sides. Reheat carrots in butter.

To serve, place crisp potato chips on plate, and top with the monkfish. Drizzle with the sauce and garnish with the carrots and chervil. Serve with fennel.

Sautéed Sea Robin with Chanterelles

99

(Serves 4)

For the fish:
6 whole sea robin
Salt and pepper
All-purpose flour
Extra virgin olive oil
2 cups cleaned, chopped chanterelles
4 cups chicken stock that has reduced by half to 2 cups
12 reconstituted, sun-dried tomatoes
12 cloves garlic, roasted
Salt and pepper to taste

For the garnish:
Fresh chives and parsley

For the fish, fillet sea robins. Season each fillet with salt and pepper and dredge in flour. Sauté in a hot pan with olive oil, skin side down and then turn and sauté on other side. Set aside. Sauté chanterelles in olive oil. Remove. Deglaze pan with reduced chicken stock. Add tomatoes, cut into ¼-inch wide strips, garlic cloves and salt and pepper to taste. Reduce sauce with four tablespoons more olive oil.

To serve, place chanterelles in center of plate. Place overlapping fish fillets on top, skin side up. Spoon sauce around fish and garnish with garlic cloves and herbs.

Black Bass with Port Wine Sauce

100

(Serves 6)

For the sauce:
2¼ cups port
4 cups red wine
2½ cups fish stock
7 ounces unsalted butter
Salt and pepper to taste

For the dish:
¼ cup olive oil
6 6-ounce black bass fillets
2 tablespoons unsalted butter
½ pound snow peas, stemmed, sliced, and blanched
6 ounces scallions, trimmed, sliced, and blanched
1 bunch watercress, stemmed
Salt and pepper to taste

For the sauce, in a medium saucepan, add the port, wine, and fish stock and bring to a boil. Reduce the heat and simmer until the sauce has syrup consistency. Remove from the heat and incorporate the butter. Season and keep warm.

For the dish, in a medium sauté pan, heat the oil, add the fillets, and sauté to desired doneness. Remove from the heat, season and keep warm. In a large sauté pan, heat the butter, add the blanched vegetables and watercress, and sauté until the watercress has wilted. Remove from the heat, season, and set aside.

To serve, spoon some of the sauce on the plate, top with a fillet, and spoon some of the salad beside it.

Striped Bass with Thyme Flowers

(Serves 4)

For the sauce:
4 tablespoons unsalted butter
½ cup shopped shallots
1 cup champagne
1½ cups fish stock
1 cup heavy cream
¼ small fennel bulb, blanched and finely chopped

½ small leek, white part only, finely chopped
1 mushroom, finely chopped
½ small zucchini, finely chopped
½ small tomato, peeled, seeded, and finely chopped
1 thyme, stemmed
Salt and pepper to taste

recipe continued on next page

Striped Bass with

Thyme Flowers

continued from previous page

For the dish:

6 tablespoons olive oil

4 4 to 6-ounce fillets sea bass, pin-boned

Salt and freshly ground pepper to taste

For the garnish:

Thyme sprigs and flowers

For the sauce, in a small saucepan, heat two tablespoons of the butter, add the shallots, and sauté until softened. Add the champagne, bring to a boil, and reduce by three-fourths. Add the fish stock, bring to a boil, and reduce by three-fourths. Incorporate the cream, bring to a boil, and reduce until the sauce coats the back of a spoon. Remove from the heat and reserve. In a medium sauté pan, heat the remaining butter, add the vegetables and thyme, and sauté until softened. Combine with the cream sauce, season, and reserve.

For the dish, in a large sauté pan, heat the oil, add the fillets, and sauté until cooked but still slightly translucent in the center. Remove from the heat, season, and set aside.

To serve, spoon some of the sauce on a plate, place a fillet in the center, and garnish with thyme flowers.

Seared Bluefish with
Melon Relish

(Serves 6)

For the bluefish:

⅓ cup rice wine vinegar

1 tablespoon chopped rosemary

1 tablespoon chopped oregano

2 tablespoons honey

2 tablespoons balsamic vinegar

Salt and pepper to taste

4 tablespoons clarified butter

6 7-ounce portions boneless bluefish fillets, skin-on

For the dressing:

⅝ cup extra virgin olive oil

2 tablespoons hazelnut oil

¼ cup balsamic vinegar

2 tablespoons sherry vinegar

Juice of 1 lemon

Salt and pepper to taste

For the relish:

2 tablespoons clarified butter

1 cup peeled, seeded, and diced tomato

2 cups assorted melon balls (cantaloupe, honeydew, casaba)

2 tablespoons chopped basil

2 tablespoons chopped dill

Wash the fillets and pat dry. In a shallow pan, whisk together the vinegar, rosemary, oregano, honey, balsamic vinegar, salt, and pepper. Add the fillets and set aside to marinate for two hours.

For the dressing, in a small bowl, combine all of the ingredients, and reserve.

For the relish, in a large sauté pan, heat the butter, add the tomatoes, and sauté over medium high heat for one minute. Add the melon balls and sauté for one minute. Remove from the heat, mix in the herbs, and remove from heat. Incorporate the reserved dressing and set aside.

To finish the bluefish, preheat the oven to 375 degrees. In a large sauté pan over high heat, heat the butter, add the bluefish and sear the fillets on both sides. Place in the oven and finish baking to desired doneness.

To serve, spoon some of the relish onto a plate. Place a fillet on top and garnish with elderflowers.

Pike with Sauvignon Blanc Sauce

102

(Serves 2)

For the sauce:
1 cup celery juice
Clarified butter
3 stalks celery, trimmed and julienned and trimmings reserved
3 stalks celery, trimmed, cut into small diamonds, and blanched and trimmings reserved
2 tablespoons whipped cream
½ cup Sauvignon Blanc
Celery salt

For the fish:
2 7-ounce pike fillets
2 ounces wine
Caviar

For the sauce, in a medium saucepan, place all of the celery trimmings, cover with water and bring to a boil over high heat. Reduce the heat and simmer until the liquid is reduced to a half cup. Fry julienne of celery and leaves in clarified butter until crisp. Blanch celery diamonds. Combine one cup celery juice and the reduction in the pot. Bring to a boil, reduce heat and reduce mixture by half. Add whipped cream, wine, season with celery salt, and set aside.

For the fish, season pike with celery salt and place in a baking pan with wine. Bake at 400 degrees for three minutes. Put fish on plate and pour sauce over. Garnish with julienne and leaves. Arrange celery diamonds around fish and place a bit of caviar on each diamond.

Scallops in Leek and Champagne Sauce

103

(Serves 2)

For the scallops:
8 ounces sea scallops (for appetizer) or 1 pound (for main course)
Sparkling wine such as Ironhorse Brut
½ onion, peeled and stuck with 5 cloves

For the leeks and mushrooms:
1 leek
1 tablespoon flour
Clarified butter
4 tablespoons butter
8 ounces sparkling wine
8 ounces wild mushrooms
Clarified butter for sauteing
Salt and pepper

For the scallops, remove the roe, place in a small saucepan, and cover with sparkling wine. Add onion with cloves, bring this to a boil, remove from the heat and set aside. Halve the scallops transversely and set aside in the refrigerator.

For the leek basket, cut leek into thirds. Julienne the light green section, add flour and fry in butter in a basket shape. Make two. For the leek butter, roughly chop remaining leek and cook in salted water until tender. Place this in blender or food processor with four tablespoons butter and purée. To finish the scallops, in a large sauté pan, sauté scallops for 20 seconds per side in butter. Strain reserved broth and bring liquid to a boil. Whisk in leek butter, salt and pepper. Add sparkling wine and set aside. Clean mushrooms and sauté in clarified butter. Season with salt and pepper. Set aside.

To serve, spoon sauce onto plates. Place mushrooms in leek baskets on plates and arrange scallops on top of sauce.

Lobster and St. Pierre with Zinfandel Sauce

104

(Serves 6)

For the fish stock:
1 teaspoon olive oil
4 leeks, white part only, trimmed, washed, and sliced
3 shallots, peeled and thinly sliced
2 mushrooms, cleaned and thinly sliced

1 sprig thyme
5 pounds fish bones and skin
2 quarts water
1 cup white wine

recipe continued on next page

Lobster and St. Pierre with Zinfandel Sauce

continued from previous page

For the sauce:

2 cups zinfandel

2 shallots, peeled and sliced

3 peppercorns

8 tablespoons unsalted butter

1 sprig thyme, stemmed

3 cloves garlic, peeled and minced

Salt and pepper to taste

For the dish:

3 St. Pierre or John Dory fillets, skinned and boned

6 lobster claws

1 tablespoon olive oil

24 pearl onions

1 cup chicken stock

3 tablespoons unsalted butter

1 sprig thyme

3 tomatoes, peeled, seeded and finely diced

Salt and pepper to taste

2 sprigs thyme, stemmed

For the stock, in a large sauté pan, sauté the leeks, shallots, mushrooms, and thyme in olive oil for five minutes over medium heat. Add the fish bones and skin, water and wine. Bring to a boil and simmer, uncovered, for three hours. Strain and reserve.

For the sauce, in a small saucepan, bring the wine, shallots, and peppercorns to a boil over medium heat, reduce the heat and simmer until only two tablespoons of liquid remain. Remove from the heat, gradually incorporate the butter, and add the thyme and garlic. Strain, season, and keep warm.

For the dish, preheat the oven to 500 degrees. In a large sauté pan, sauté the lobster claws in olive oil over high heat. Place in the oven for remove from the oven and set aside for five minutes. Crack the claws, remove the meat, and set aside. In a small sauté pan, add the pearl onions, chicken stock, one tablespoon of the butter and thyme and cook for five minutes. Remove the onions from the pan, peel, and set aside. In a large saucepan, add the reserved stock and bring to just below a simmer. Add the fish and poach to desired doneness. Remove from the pan and set aside.

To serve, slice the lobster and fillets into large pieces and set aside. In a large saucepan, heat the remaining butter, add the lobster pieces and fish fillets, and sauté until heated through. Arrange on a plate, sprinkle with chopped tomato, onions, and herbs, and spoon a few tablespoons of the sauce around the plate.

Shrimp with Carrot-Sauvignon Blanc Sauce

(Serves 2)

For the sauce:

3 carrots

2 tablespoons butter

Pinch of cinnamon, nutmeg, clove, salt and cayenne pepper

2 ounces Sauvignon Blanc wine

For the spiced shrimp:

16 medium shrimp

Clarified butter for sauteing

For the garnish:

Deep-fried carrot shavings

Flat-leaf parsley or chervil

For the sauce, extract juice from two carrots. You should have one cup. Make carrot balls from third carrot and blanch in salted boiling water and cool in an ice bath. In a saucepot, place carrot juice, butter, spices and carrot balls. Add wine. Bring to a boil and set aside.

For the spiced shrimp, peel and devein shrimp, leaving tail intact. Sauté shrimp in clarified butter to desired doneness. Remove from the pan and keep warm.

To serve, arrange shrimp on plates and pour sauce over. Garnish with fried carrot shavings and either flat-leaf parsley or chervil.

Shrimp Balls with Matsutake Mushrooms

(Serves 4)

For the simmering broth:
2 ½ cups dashi
½ cup sake
⅓ cup mirin
2 tablespoons light soy sauce

For the dish:
12 ounces ground raw shrimp
1 egg, lightly beaten
1 teaspoon salt
2 tablespoons sake
1 tablespoon soy sauce
1 tablespoon fresh ginger juice
1 bunch mitsuba, chopped and blanched
3 or 4 matsutake mushrooms, cleaned and halved

For the garnish:
Lemon zest

For the simmering broth, in a large saucepan, add all of the ingredients, bring to a boil, and set aside.

For the dish, in a medium bowl, add the shrimp and gradually incorporate the egg, salt, sake, soy sauce, and ginger juice. Mix thoroughly, form into 12 balls, and set aside. In a large saucepan of boiling salted water, place the balls in the pan and cook for approximately five minutes, or until the balls rise to the surface. Drain and set aside. Bring the simmering broth to a boil, add the shrimp balls, and reduce the heat to low. Cover and simmer for five minutes. Uncover, add the mitsuba and mushrooms, and remove from the heat.

To serve, arrange a shrimp ball and some of the mushrooms and mitsuba in a bowl. Add some of the broth and garnish with lemon peel.

Steamed Sea Bass with Mussels and Ponzu Sauce

(Serves 4 to 6)

For the ponzu sauce:
3 scallions, peeled and sliced
¼ cup soy sauce
¼ cup white wine vinegar
1 tablespoon plum wine
¼ teaspoon chili oil

For the sea bass:
1 bunch scallions, trimmed and chopped
2 cloves garlic, peeled
2-inch piece ginger, peeled and julienned, peels reserved for steaming liquid
1 pound young spinach leaves
1 3-pound sea bass, gutted and scaled
10-12 black mussels, cleaned and de-bearded
½ bunch scallions, peeled and julienned

For the garnish:
Julienned red bell pepper
Julienned yellow bell pepper
Scallions
Cilantro sprigs

For the sauce, in a small bowl, whisk together all of the ingredients and set aside.

For the sea bass, in a large saucepan, add the scallions, garlic, and ginger peels, cover with water and bring to just below a simmer. Prepare a bamboo steamer, arranging a layer of spinach leaves on the bottom of the tray and setting a plate large enough to hold the fish on top. Place the fish on the plate and arrange the mussels around the fish. Sprinkle with ginger and scallions and drizzle one teaspoon of the sauce over the fish. Place the tray over the saucepan, cover, and poach the fish to desired doneness.

Remove the tray from the saucepan, garnish with peppers, scallions, and cilantro, and serve with the remaining sauce.

Grilled Butterfish
Yuan Style

107

(Serves 4)

For the grilled butterfish:
4 4-ounce butterfish fillets, skin on
Salt to taste
½ cup soy sauce
½ cup sake
½ cup mirin

For the garnish:
Japanese maple leaves

For the grilled butterfish, sprinkle the fillets with salt, and set aside for one hour. In a medium bowl, whisk together the soy sauce, sake, and mirin and reserve. Rinse the fillets and place in the bowl to marinate for 30 minutes. Preheat the broiler. Remove the fillets from the marinade, pat dry, and with a sharp knife, slice shallow incisions 1½-inches wide and ½-inch apart into the surface of the skin. Place the fish skin side down on an oiled sheet pan and set in the oven. Broil for five minutes, turn, brush with mirin, and broil for an additional five minutes, or to desired doneness. Remove from the oven and set aside.

To serve, arrange a few maple leaves on a plate and place the fillets on top.

Spiny Lobster

(Serves 2)

For the court bouillon:
1½ quarts water
1½ quarts white wine
1 large onion, peeled and chopped
4 stalks celery, chopped
1 leek, cleaned and chopped
2 carrots, peeled and chopped
5 mushrooms chopped
2 sprigs fennel fronds
2 sprigs tarragon, stemmed and chopped
2 sprigs thyme. stemmed and chopped
2 sprigs parsley, stemmed and chopped
2 1½-pound Spiny lobsters (Maine lobsters may be substituted)

For the dish:
1 medium carrot, cut into small cubes
1 medium turnip, cut into small cubes
1 shallot, peeled and finely diced
½ cup dry white wine
2 ounces unsalted butter
½ cup heavy cream
Reserved lobster meat
1 truffle, diced
Salt and pepper to taste

For the garnish:
Reserved long tentacles

For the court bouillon, in a large saucepan, add all of the ingredients and bring to a boil. Reduce the heat and simmer for 25 minutes. Remove form the heat and reserve.

For the dish, bring the court bouillon to a boil and add the lobsters. When the liquid returns to a boil, cover the pan and cook for eight minutes. Remove the lobsters and set aside to cool. Crack the tails and remove the meat. Halve the tail lengthwise and set aside and reserve the long tentacles for garnish. In a medium saucepan, add the shallots, carrot, turnips, and white wine and bring to a boil. Reduce the heat and simmer until the mixture is reduced by half. Add the cream and bring to a boil. Reduce the heat and simmer until the mixture is reduced by half. Remove from the heat, incorporate the butter, and season. Return to the heat, add the lobster and truffle and bring to a light boil over medium heat. Remove from the heat and set aside.

To serve, arrange a lobster tail on a plate and spoon some of the sauce and vegetables around the lobster. Garnish with lobster tentacles.

Crisp Szechuan Fish

(Serves 6)

For the dish:
Vegetable oil for frying
1 2-pound whole grouper, rockfish or sea bass, cleaned and gutted
2 cups cornstarch
2 cups chicken broth
2 tablespoons oyster sauce
1 tablespoon Chinese black vinegar, or balsamic vinegar
1 teaspoon sugar
1 tablespoon dry sherry
1 tablespoon red szechwan chile paste with garlic
1 tablespoon sesame oil
2 tablespoons oil
½ teaspoon finely minced fresh ginger
½ teaspoon finely minced garlic
⅓ cup chopped onion
⅓ cup chopped straw mushrooms
⅓ cup chopped water chestnuts
4 dried shiitake mushrooms, soaked in hot water for 20 minutes, then stemmed and shredded
2 tablespoons cornstarch, mixed with 1/4 cup cold water

For the garnish:
Minced scallions

For the dish, in a large wok or saucepan deep enough to hold the fish, heat the oil to 375 degrees. Score either side of the fish, making incisions approximately 1-inch deep and 1-inch apart. Coat with cornstarch, rubbing the cornstarch into the incisions. In a medium bowl, combine the chicken broth, oyster sauce, vinegar, sugar, sherry, and chile paste, and set aside. Add the fish to the hot oil and fry until golden brown and crispy. Gently remove from the oil, drain on paper towels, and keep warm. Pour the oil from the pan, heat the remaining oils, add the ginger and garlic, and stir fry for 30 seconds, or until fragrant. Follow with the onion, straw mushrooms, water chestnuts, and shiitake and stir fry for three minutes. Add the reserved chicken broth mixture and bring to a boil. Reduce the heat and simmer for three minutes. Incorporate the cornstarch and water mixture and bring back to a boil until lightly thickened. Remove from the heat and reserve.

To serve, place the fish on a platter. Pour the sauce over the fish and sprinkle with scallions.

Soft-Shell Crab in Red Pepper Sauce

(Serves 8)

For the sauce:
4 red bell peppers, stemmed, seeded and chopped
1 cup fish stock
2 shallots, peeled and halved
Salt and pepper to taste

For the crabs:
Vegetable oil for frying
8 medium soft shell crabs
Milk
Flour seasoned with salt and red pepper

For the garnish:
Diced red bell pepper
Diced green bell pepper
Lemon grass slices
Thyme sprigs
Jalapeño chile pepper halves

For the sauce, in a large saucepan over high heat, add the red peppers, fish stock, and shallots, and bring to a boil. Reduce the heat and simmer for 25 minutes. Transfer the mixture to the bowl of a food processor fitted with the metal blade attachment, and purée until smooth. Return to the saucepan, season, and keep warm.

For the crabs, in a large sauté pan, heat the oil to 365 degrees. Dip the crabs in milk and then dredge in seasoned flour. Add to the pan and fry until golden brown and crisp. Remove from the pan, transfer to a paper towel-lined sheet pan to drain, and keep warm.

To serve, spoon some of the sauce onto a plate and place a crab in the center of the plate. Garnish the sauce with the bell peppers, lemon grass, and chervil, and arrange a jalapeño pepper on the rim of the plate.

Grilled Tuna with Red Pepper Sauce

(Serves 4)

For the red pepper sauce:

8 red peppers, stemmed
1 onion, peeled and chopped
2 ribs celery, chopped
1 carrot, peeled and chopped
4 cups chicken stock
1 teaspoon paprika
Salt, cayenne, and white pepper to taste
2 cups heavy cream

For the tuna:

4 tablespoons olive oil
1 red bell pepper, stemmed, seeded, and julienned
1 green bell pepper, stemmed, seeded, and julienned
1 yellow bell pepper, stemmed, seeded, and julienned
1 stalk celery, julienned
1 red onion, julienned
4 6-ounce yellowfin tuna steaks
2 teaspoons seafood seasoning
4 tablespoons clarified butter

For the garnish:

Basil sprigs

For the red pepper sauce, preheat the oven to 375 degrees. In a large roasting pan, add the peppers, onion, celery, and carrot, and place in the oven to roast until blackened. Remove from the oven and transfer to a large saucepan. Add the stock and bring to a boil over high heat. Reduce the heat and simmer until the liquid is reduced by half. Strain through a chinois into a medium saucepan, add the cream and bring to a boil. Remove from the heat, season, and keep warm.

For the tuna, prepare a hot grill. In a large sauté pan, heat the oil, add the julienned vegetables, and sauté until just softened. Rub the seasoning on both sides of the tuna and brush with melted butter. Place the steaks on the grill and grill for three to four minutes on each side. Remove from the grill and keep warm.

To serve, spoon a pool of sauce on a plate and arrange some of the julienned vegetable on the sauce. Place a tuna steak over the vegetables and garnish with a sprig of basil.

Barbecued Shrimp

(Serves 2)

For the dish:

7 large shrimp, with heads on
3 tablespoons unsalted butter
1½ teaspoons black pepper
1 teaspoon cracked fresh black pepper
½ teaspoon Creole seasoning
1½ tablespoons Worcestershire sauce
½ lemon, juice only
½ teaspoon minced garlic

For the preparation, place shrimp and rest of ingredients in a 10-inch frying pan, just large enough to hold shrimp in one layer. Place in a 450-degree F oven for two minutes. Turn shrimp and cook another 2 to 3 minutes. Remove shrimp from frying pan to a serving bowl. Pour sauce over shrimp and serve with French bread for dipping.

Steamed Bok Choy with Seafood

112

(Serves 6)

For the hot and sour sauce:
1 cup plus 2 tablespoons fish stock
2 tablespoons rice wine vinegar
2 drops Tabasco sauce
¼ teaspoon soy sauce
¼ teaspoon minced ginger
¼ teaspoon Thai fish sauce
1 teaspoon arrowroot
3 tablespoons sherry
6 baby bok choy, steamed and sliced lengthwise
6 ounces Dungeness crab meat
6 ounces ahi (red) tuna, sliced and rolled into rosettes
6 shrimp, poached
6 mussels, steamed

For the garnish:
2 tablespoons cubed tofu
1 tablespoon red and yellow peppers, cut into diamonds
1 small bunch enoki mushrooms

For the hot and sour sauce, heat fish stock. Add vinegar, Tabasco, soy sauce, ginger and Thai fish sauce. Bring to a boil. Combine arrowroot and sherry and pour into heated liquid. Allow to simmer several minutes, then remove from heat.

To assemble, pour three tablespoons sauce onto each plate. Place two halves baby bok choy in center of plate, arranging seafood at base of bok choy. Garnish plate with tofu, peppers and enoki mushrooms.

Fillet of Sea Bass with Fennel

113

(Serves 6)

For the dish:
3 tablespoons olive oil
6 cloves garlic, peeled
3 bulbs fennel, each sliced into six wedges
6 9-ounce sea bass fillets, pin-boned and sliced into 3-ounce pieces
¾ cup dry white wine
3 sprigs Italian parsley, stemmed and chopped
Salt and pepper to taste

For the garnish:
Dill sprigs
Minced parsley
Reserved garlic cloves

For the dish, preheat oven to 350 degrees. In a large sauté pan over medium heat, add the oil and sauté the garlic until lightly golden. Remove from the pan with a slotted spoon and reserve. Add the fennel and sauté for one minute on each side. Place the sea bass on top of the fennel, add the white wine, salt and pepper, and cover the pan with aluminum foil. Place in the oven and bake for eight minutes. Remove from the oven, set aside the fennel and sea bass, and return the sauté pan to medium high heat. Bring the cooking liquids to a boil and reduce by half. Remove from the heat, incorporate the parsley, season, and set aside.

To serve, place three pieces of fennel on a plate and lay three pieces of sea bass on top. Garnish the plate with dill sprigs, parsley, and reserved garlic cloves.

Skate with Fennel

113

(Serves 4)

For the shrimp oil:
10 ounces shrimp shells
2 tablespoons olive oil
½ cup sliced shallots
2 tablespoons minced garlic
1 tablespoons crushed white peppercorns
2 tablespoons tomato paste
1 cup brandy
1½ cups white wine
2 cups olive oil
2 cups corn oil

For the shrimp vinaigrette:
4 tablespoons sliced shallots
1½ teaspoons white peppercorns
1 tablespoon shrimp oil
12 parsley stems
1 cup white wine
½ tarragon vinegar
2 tablespoons Dijon mustard
3 cups shrimp oil
Salt, white pepper, cayenne pepper and sugar to taste

recipe continued on next page

Skate with Fennel

continued from previous page

For the skate:

2½ pounds skate wing

1 fennel bulb, halved

1½ cups fish stock

Salt and pepper

For the garnish:

Chives

Fennel sprigs

Parisienne scoops of colored peppers

For the shrimp oil, sauté shrimp shells in olive oil. Add shallots, garlic and white pepper. Cook until light brown. Add tomato paste and cook about three minutes. Deglaze with brandy and white wine and let reduce until almost dry. Add olive oil and corn oil. Bring to a boil and lower heat to simmer. Let cook 20 to 25 minutes. Strain and keep warm.

For the shrimp vinaigrette, lightly sauté shallots and peppercorns in one tablespoon shrimp oil. Add parsley stems, white wine, tarragon vinegar and bring to a boil. Stir in Dijon mustard. Reduce mixture to half. Strain reduction and place in a mixing bowl. Heat shrimp oil and slowly incorporate about two cups of the oil into the reduction. More may be added for taste. Season with salt, peppers and sugar.

For the skate, remove skin and bones of the skate wing. Use the bones to make fish stock. Portion skate wings into four 4-ounce portions and set aside. Strain the fish stock and keep hot. Cut fennel bulb in half and remove core. Slice remaining fennel stalks. Place fennel in the bottom of a saucepan with one and a half cups fish stock. Cook about one to two minutes or until fennel is slightly tender. Season skate wings with salt and pepper and place in saucepan on top of fennel and cover pan. Steam skate for five minutes or until firm to the touch.

To serve, ladle shrimp vinaigrette onto plates. Remove skate and fennel separately from pan. Arrange skate on top of vinaigrette and fennel on skate. Garnish with chives, fennel sprigs and parisienne peppers.

Choucroute of Seafood

(Serves 4)

For the sausage:

1 tablespoon butter

1 shallot, peeled and minced

2 chives, minced

2 sprigs parsley, stemmed and minced

1 tablespoon chopped pistachios

8 ounces lobster meat

8 ounces scallops

1 small egg white

1 cup cream

Juice of 1 lemon

Salt and pepper to taste

Small sausage casings

For the dish:

1½ pounds sauerkraut, blanched

12 ounces salmon fillets, skinned and pin-boned

12 ounces monkfish fillets, boned

12 ounces sea scallops

4 medium shrimp

2 tablespoons juniper berries

Salt and pepper to taste

For the vegetables:

16 snow peas blanched

8 Yukon gold potatoes, peeled and cooked

For the garnish:

Chervil sprigs

For the sausage, in a small saucepan over medium heat, heat the butter, add the shallots, and sauté until softened and translucent. Remove from the heat, incorporate the chives and pistachios, and set aside to cool. In the bowl of a food processor fitted with the metal blade attachment, combine the lobster, scallops, and egg white and purée until smooth. Add the lemon juice and cream and briefly mix to combine. Transfer to a medium bowl, incorporate the reserved shallot mixture, season, and set aside. Stuff the casings with the filling and tie into 2-ounce links. Arrange on a parchment-lined sheet pan and set aside in the refrigerator. Fill a large saucepan with 2-inches of water and bring to just below a simmer. Add the sausage, cover, and poach to desired doneness. Remove from the heat and set aside, keeping warm.

To assemble the choucroute, preheat the oven to 375 degrees. Line the bottom of a shallow roasting pan with half of the sauerkraut, sprinkle with juniper berries, and arrange the seafood on top. Cover with the remaining sauerkraut, season, and place in the oven. Bake for ten minutes, remove from the oven and set aside.

To serve, spoon some of the sauerkraut onto a plate and place a piece of each variety of seafood on top. Arrange a few of the snow peas and potatoes beside the choucroute and garnish with a sprig of chervil.

Pan-Fried Gulf Red Snapper

(Serves 4)

For the black bean relish:
1 1-pound smoked ham bone
1 small onion, peeled and chopped
1 stalk celery, chopped
1 carrot, peeled and chopped
1 bay leaf
1 tablespoon black peppercorns
3 serrano chili peppers, stemmed, seeded, and chopped
2 jalapeño chili peppers, stemmed, seeded, and chopped
3 cloves garlic, peeled and minced
½ small bunch cilantro, stemmed and chopped
2½ cups chicken stock
¾ cup dried black beans, rinsed
1 small red bell pepper, stemmed, seeded, and diced
1 small yellow bell pepper, stemmed, seeded, and diced
2 tablespoons white wine vinegar
1 tablespoon balsamic vinegar
1 tablespoon virgin olive oil
Juice of 1 lemon
Juice of 1 lime
Salt to taste

For the serrano chili-cilantro sauce:
3 small serrano chili peppers, stemmed, seeded, and sliced
2 shallots, peeled and minced
3 garlic cloves, peeled and minced
2 cups chicken stock
2 cups heavy cream
½ bunch cilantro, stemmed and chopped
4 medium spinach leaves
Juice of a ½ lime
Salt to taste

For the fish:
4 6-ounce red snapper fillets, skinned and pin-boned
Salt to taste
6 tablespoons peanut oil

For the garnish:
Fried oysters
Cilantro sprigs

For the black bean relish, in a large saucepan, add the ham bone, onion, celery, carrot, bay leaf, peppercorns, serrano chilies, 1 of the jalapeño peppers, two garlic cloves, half of the cilantro, and chicken stock, and bring to a boil. Reduce the heat and simmer for one hour, skimming the surface of any residue that rises. Remove from the heat, strain, and set aside, reserving the liquid. In a medium saucepan, add the beans and cover with two cups of the reserved ham stock. Bring to a boil, reduce the heat, and simmer for 45 minutes or until the beans are just tender. Strain, and while the beans are still hot place in a large bowl and toss together with the peppers, remaining cilantro, vinegars, and oil. Add the remaining jalapeño and garlic, the citrus juice, and season. Set aside to cool to room temperature.

For the serrano chile sauce, in a medium saucepan, add the serrano chilies, shallots, garlic, chicken stock and cream and bring to a boil. Reduce the heat and simmer for 20 to 25 minutes or until liquid is reduced by half. Pour into the bowl of a food processor fitted with the metal blade attachment, add the cilantro and spinach, and purée until smooth. Strain through a fine sieve, add the lime juice, and season, keeping warm.

For the fish, season the fillets with salt and set aside. In a large sauté pan over medium heat, add the fillets, presentation side down, and brown slowly for two to three minutes. Turn and finish cooking for an additional two minutes, carefully remove from pan, and drain on paper towels.

To serve, spoon some of the black bean relish on a plate, and place a fillet on top. Arrange a couple of the oysters around the relish and garnish with cilantro sprigs.

Wood-Grilled Swordfish

(Serves 6)

For the black bean sauce:
1 tablespoon peanut oil
2 shallots, peeled and chopped
1 clove garlic, peeled and chopped
1 serrano chili, stemmed, seeded, and chopped
½ cup cooked black beans
1 cup reserved chicken stock
Salt and pepper to taste

For the red chili sauce:
1 tablespoon peanut oil
3 red bell peppers, stemmed, seeded, and chopped
2 shallots, peeled ad chopped
1 clove garlic, peeled and chopped
1 serrano chili, stemmed, seeded, and chopped
1 cup chicken stock
Salt and pepper to taste

recipe continued on next page

Wood-Grilled Swordfish

continued from previous page

For the mango sauce:
1 tablespoon peanut oil
1 large ripe mango, peeled and seed removed
1 shallot, peeled and chopped
½ clove garlic, peeled and chopped
½-inch piece ginger, peeled and minced
1 cup chicken stock
Salt and pepper to taste

For the swordfish:
6 7-ounce center cut swordfish fillets
3 tablespoons peanut oil
Salt and pepper to taste

For the garnish:
Black bean and jicama salad
Cilantro sprigs

For the black bean sauce, in a large sauté pan over high heat, heat the oil, add the shallots, garlic, serrano chili, and black beans and sauté until softened. Add the chicken stock and bring to a boil. Reduce the heat and simmer until the liquid is reduced by half. Transfer to the bowl of a food processor fitted with the metal blade attachment and purée until smooth. Strain through a cheesecloth, season and set aside, keeping warm.

For the chili sauce, in a large sauté pan over medium high heat, heat the oil, add the red peppers, shallots, garlic, and serrano chili, and sauté until softened. Add the chicken stock and bring to a boil. Reduce the heat and simmer until the liquid is reduced by half. Transfer to the bowl of a food processor fitted with the metal blade attachment and purée until smooth. Strain through a cheesecloth, season and set aside, keeping warm.

For the mango sauce, in a large sauté pan over medium high heat, heat the oil, add the mango, shallot, garlic, and ginger, and sauté until softened. Add the chicken stock and bring to a boil. Reduce the heat and simmer until the liquid is reduced by half. Transfer to the bowl of a food processor fitted with the metal blade attachment and purée until smooth. Strain through a cheesecloth, season and set aside, keeping warm.

For the swordfish, prepare a hot grill. Brush the fillets with peanut oil and season with salt and pepper. Place on the grill sear for approximately two and a half minutes on each side, being careful not to over-cook. Remove from the grill and keep warm.

To serve, decoratively drizzle the three sauces on a plate and place a swordfish fillet on top of the sauces. Spoon some of the black bean salad beside the fish and garnish with cilantro.

Red Mullet with Fava Beans and Basil

(Serves 4)

For the red mullet:
6 whole red mullets, scaled and filleted
Salt and pepper to taste
1 cup shelled fava beans
3 sprigs basil, stemmed and minced
1 ripe, firm tomato, peeled and chopped
4 tablespoons olive oil
2 tablespoons white wine

For the garnish:
Young zucchini with flowers attached
Steamed asparagus bundles wrapped with carrot

For the red mullet, preheat the oven to 325 degrees. Cut four pieces of aluminum, 12-inches square and set aside. Lay a sheet of aluminum on a flat work surface and arrange three fillets in the center. Season the fish and spoon some of the fava beans, basil, and tomato on top. Sprinkle with olive oil, and white wine and wrap tightly into a pouch. Repeat the procedure with the remaining wrappers and ingredients to make four pouches and arrange on a sheet pan. Place in the oven and bake for four minutes. Remove from the oven and set aside.

To serve, unwrap a pouch and place the fillets on a plate. Spoon some of the fava beans, tomatoes and sauce over the fish and garnish with a zucchini and an asparagus bundle.

Poached Turbot with Brown Butter

(Serves 4)

For the turbot:
1 large, fresh turbot
Salted water for poaching
½ cup butter
1 piece fresh horseradish, sliced
Boiled, peeled potatoes, seasoned with butter and dill

For the turbot, fillet into four pieces. Poach in salted water.

For the sauce, brown butter.

To serve, place turbot on plate with browned butter, horseradish and potatoes.

Monkfish Wrapped in Bacon

(Serves 4)

For the monkfish:
1 loin monkfish
Salt and pepper
10 thin slices bacon
Oil or clarified butter for sautéing

For the asparagus:
1 pound pencil-thin asparagus

For the lemon vinaigrette:
Juice from ½ lemon
3 to 4 tablespoons olive oil
Fresh minced herbs
Salt and freshly ground white pepper

For the monkfish, season loin with salt and pepper and wrap in bacon. Sauté quickly on all sides, so that the bacon gets crisp but the fish remains moist inside.

For the asparagus, cook in boiling water until crisp and bright green. Set aside.

For the lemon vinaigrette, whisk together lemon juice and oil. Add herbs and salt and pepper to taste.

To serve, place asparagus on plate and drizzle with vinaigrette. Slice monkfish and arrange on plate.

Grilled Butterfish with Vegetable Tempura

(Serves 4)

For the simmered potatoes:
1 cup dashi
3 tablespoons granulated sugar
¼ teaspoon salt
1 tablespoon soy sauce
1 8-ounce eel fillet
8 small taro roots or new potatoes, peeled, and blanched
1 bunch spinach, cleaned, blanched, and roughly chopped

For the grilled butterfish:
4 4-ounce butterfish fillets, skin on
Salt to taste
½ cup soy sauce
½ cup sake
½ cup mirin
Mirin for brushing

For the tempura batter:
1 egg
1 cup ice water
1 cup all-purpose flour

For the tempura:
Oil for frying
8 small green bell peppers
12 small cauliflower florets
12 sardines, cleaned

recipe continued on next page

Grilled Butterfish with Tempura

continued from previous page

For for the simmered taro, in a medium saucepan over high heat, add the dashi, sugar, salt, and soy sauce and bring to a boil. Add the eel, reduce the heat, and return the liquid to a simmer. Place a plate over the eel to prevent it from floating to the top, without completely covering the pan, and simmer for ten minutes, or until the liquid is almost evaporated. Remove the plate, add the taro and spinach, and continue to cook until the vegetables are tender. Remove from the heat and set aside. Slice the eel and taro into 2-inch pieces, return to the pan, and keep warm.

For the grilled butterfish, sprinkle the fillets with salt, and set aside for one hour. In a medium bowl, whisk together the soy sauce, sake, and mirin and reserve. Rinse the fillets and place in the bowl to marinate for 30 minutes. Preheat the broiler. Remove the fillets from the marinade, pat dry, and with a sharp knife, slice shallow incisions 1½-inches wide and ½-inch apart into the surface of the skin. Place the fish skin side down on an oiled sheet pan and set in the oven. Broil for five minutes, turn, brush with mirin, and broil for an additional five minutes, or to desired doneness. Remove from the oven and set aside.

For the tempura batter, in a medium bowl, combine the egg and ice water. Add the flour and stir briefly with chopsticks or a fork. The batter should be thin and lumpy. In a large saucepan, add the oil and heat to 375 degrees. Holding the fish by the tail, dip into the batter, draining off any excess, and add to the oil. Fry the fish for approximately one minute, remove from the pan and drain on paper towels. Repeat the procedure with the remaining fish and vegetables and keep warm. Make sure the coating remains thin, lacy, and light in color.

To serve, place some of the eel, taro, and spinach in a small bowl and cover with some of the cooking liquid. In a small basket, arrange pieces of sardine, cauliflower, and pepper and set beside the simmered taro. Place a butterfish fillet on a plate and serve with the tempura and simmered taro. Serve with soy sauce.

Multi-Colored Stracci with Grilled Scampi

(Serves 6)

For the shrimp:
18 large shrimp, head and tail left on
¼ cup olive oil
2 cloves garlic, peeled minced
1 sprig thyme
6 leaves basil

For the pasta:
1 cup semolina flour
1 cup all-purpose flour
2 eggs
2 teaspoons olive oil
Salt to taste
1 tablespoon fresh beet purée
1 tablespoon semolina flour
8 spinach leaves, puréed
5 basil leaves, puréed
¼ cup Italian parsley, puréed
1 egg
¼ teaspoon squid ink

For the sauce:
1 shallot, peeled minced
⅜ cup dry white wine
Salt and pepper to taste
2 egg yolks
2 ripe tomatoes, peeled, seeded, puréed and strained
1½ pounds porcini, cleaned and sliced

For the garnish:
Basil leaves
Thyme sprigs

For the shrimp, in a large bowl, add the shrimp, olive oil, garlic, thyme and basil, and set aside in the refrigerator to marinate for 24 hours.

For the pasta, in the bowl of a food processor fitted with the metal blade attachment, add the flours, eggs, olive oil, and salt and process until the dough comes together into a ball. Transfer to a lightly floured work surface and knead by hand. Cover with plastic wrap and set aside to rest for 30 minutes. Divide the dough into four pieces. Incorporate the beet purée and semolina into one piece, the purée of the spinach, basil, parsley, and egg to another piece; add the squid ink to the third piece. Roll the dough through the pasta machine into long strips, and cut the strips into large triangles.

For the sauce, in a medium bowl, add the yolks, and set aside. Bring a medium saucepan filled with 2-inches of water to a simmer. In a small saucepan, add the shallot and wine and bring to a boil. Reduce the heat and simmer until the liquid is reduced by half. Strain the reduced mixture over the yolks, place over the bowl of simmering water and whisk until light and frothy. Add the purée, season, and set aside. To finish the dish, prepare a hot grill. Season the shrimp and mushrooms with salt and pepper, place on the grill, and cook to desired doneness. In a large saucepan, add one tablespoon of oil and salt and cook the pasta until al dente. Drain and set aside.

To serve, spoon some of the sauce on a platter and arrange the triangles of pasta in alternating colors. Place the shrimp and mushrooms on the pasta and garnish with basil leaves and thyme sprigs.

Trout Ravioli with Onion Sauce

(Serves 4)

For the pasta dough:
2½ cups flour
1 egg
6 tablespoons water

For the trout:
2 tablespoons butter
10 ounces trout fillets, skinned and pin-boned
½ onion, peeled and chopped
1 tablespoon chopped parsley
1 egg yolk
Salt and pepper

For the sauce:
1½ onions, chopped
2 tablespoons butter
Few pink peppercorns
½ cup white wine
2 cups heavy cream
2 tablespoons butter

For the garnish:
Sautéed diced eggplant
Diced tomato

For the pasta dough, in the bowl of a food processor fitted with the meal blade attachment, combine the flour, egg, and water and process until the dough comes together to form a ball. Remove the dough from the bowl, place on a lightly floured work surface, and knead for ten minutes, or until the dough is elastic and smooth. Form the dough into a flattened disk, wrap in plastic wrap, and set aside in the refrigerator for at least 30 minutes.

For the trout, in a medium sauté pan over medium-high heat, heat the butter, add the trout, onion, and parsley, and sauté until the onions are softened and translucent and the trout is cooked to desired doneness. Remove from the heat and pass through a food grinder using a medium die. Place the trout in a medium bowl, add the egg, and mix until well combined. Season and set aside.

To finish the pasta, divide the dough in half and roll each piece into a sheet as thinly as possible. Lay one of the sheets on a lightly floured flat work surface and place 24 teaspoons of the filling one-inch apart on the pasta. Moisten the area surrounding the filling with water and place the second sheet of pasta on top. Using a 1½-inch round cookie cutter with a decorative edge, cut the pasta into 24 ravioli. Press the edges of the ravioli to seal expelling any air that may have been trapped. Arrange the ravioli on a parchment-lined sheet pan and set aside in the refrigerator.

For the sauce, in a small saucepan over medium-high heat, heat the butter, add the onion, and sauté until lightly caramelized. Add the peppercorns and wine and bring to a boil. Reduce the heat and simmer until the mixture is reduced by half. Incorporate the cream and bring to a simmer. Remove from the heat and strain into a medium saucepan. Bring the mixture to a simmer over medium heat, incorporate the butter, and season. Remove from the heat and set aside, keeping warm.

To finish the ravioli, bring a large saucepan of boiling salted water to a boil, add the ravioli, and cook to desired doneness. Drain and set aside, keeping warm. To serve, arrange six of the ravioli in the bottom of a bowl, spoon some of the sauce on top, and garnish with tomato and eggplant.

Grilled Abalone

(Serves 1)

For the abalone:
1 10 ounces-abalone
1 quart herb flavored court bouillon
Salt and pepper to taste
1 ounce unsalted butter
1 teaspoon meat drippings

For the abalone, crack open the abalone and remove the steak. Discard the viscera and trim off the dark mantle along the edges. Remove the dark skin from the lower part of the foot and place the trimmed abalone on a wooden board. Gently pound the abalone with a rolling pin or mallet. The pounding should be gentle, just enough to release the white juices. In a large saucepan, bring the court bouillon to a boil, add the abalone, and blanch for no more than six minutes, being careful not to over-cook. Remove from the pan, season, and set aside. Prepare a hot grill, place the abalone on the grill and grill for two minutes on each side. Remove from the grill and keep warm. In a medium sauté pan, add the butter, and cook until golden brown and nutty tasting. Remove from the heat, add the meat drippings, and set aside.

To serve, place the abalone on a plate and spoon some of the sauce around the plate.

Lobster with Red Pepper Sauce

120

(Serves 4)

For the lobster:
2 1½-pound lobsters

For the sauce:
4 tablespoons olive oil
1 onion, peeled and sliced
12 red bell peppers, stemmed, seeded and chopped
1 clove garlic, peeled and minced
1 large tomato, seeded and chopped
Salt and pepper to taste
1¼ cups water
½ cup cream

For the lobster, place the lobsters in a large saucepan of boiling salted water and cook for seven to eight minutes. Remove the lobsters from the pan and set aside to cool slightly. Discard the head, and remove the meat from the tail and claws. Halve the tail lengthwise and reserve with the claw meat.

For the sauce, in a large saucepan over medium-high heat, heat the oil, add the onion, and sauté until softened and translucent. Add peppers, garlic, tomato, and water, and bring to a boil. Reduce the heat and simmer covered for 30 minutes. Remove from the heat, strain, and place in a medium saucepan. Incorporate the cream and bring to a boil over medium-high heat. Remove from the heat, season, and set aside, keeping warm.

To serve, spoon some of the sauce onto a plate and arrange a piece of lobster tail and a claw in the center.

Open Ravioli

(Serves 4)

For the pasta:
1 pound fresh egg pasta dough
4 leaves fresh Italian parsley
4 large squares spinach pasta dough

For the topping:
14 ounces fresh sea scallops
2 tablespoons butter
¼ cup white wine
1 teaspoons ginger juice
6 tablespoons butter
Salt and pepper

For the pasta, cut eight large lasagna squares from pasta dough. Place a parsley leaf in the middle of four of them and place other four egg pasta squares on top. Pass squares through a pasta machine and the leaf should come out printed in the lasagna. Set spinach squares aside.

For the topping, cut scallops lengthwise, season, and sauté in two tablespoons butter for a few seconds. Add wine and then remove scallops from the pan. Reduce pan juices and add ginger juice. Add the remaining butter. Season to taste.

To serve, cook pasta squares in boiling salted water until al dente. Place scallops back in sauce. Place green lasagna square on plate, add scallops and cover with egg pasta square. Pour sauce around and serve.

Steamed Halibut in Cardamom Sauce

 122

(Serves 2)

For the sauce:
2 cups rich chicken stock
4 cardamom pods
7 tablespoons butter
Juice of ½ lemon
2 tablespoons dry sherry
Salt and pepper to taste
1 zucchini, julienned and blanched
1 mango, peeled, pitted, and julienned

For the halibut:
4 4-ounce halibut fillets, boned and skinned
Salt and pepper to taste

For the garnish:
Caviar

For the sauce, in a small bowl, add the chicken stock, and bring to a boil. Reduce the heat and simmer until the liquid is reduced to ¼ cup. Add the cardamom, gradually whisk in the butter, and remove from the heat. Incorporate the lemon juice and sherry and strain into a small saucepan. Season, add the zucchini and mango, and set aside, keeping warm.

For the halibut, prepare a steamer. Season the fillets and place in the bottom of the steamer. Cover and steam to desired doneness. Remove from the steamer and set aside, keeping warm.

To serve, spoon some of the sauce onto a plate, place a fillet in the center, and garnish the fish with caviar.

Crispy Salmon with Herb Sauce

123

(Serves 1)

For the salmon:
6 ounces salmon fillet
Salt and pepper to taste
Butter for sautéing

For the garnish:
5 very thin slices celery root

For the sauce:
½ cup broccoli florets
¼ cup heavy cream
1 sprig parsley
5 sprigs chervil
5 tarragon leaves
1 sprig cilantro
10 chives
1 cup spinach leaves
Butter
Salt and pepper to taste

For the garnish:
Chives

For the salmon, season with salt and pepper and pan-fry in butter on skin-side only. Finish cooking in oven until middle of the fish is rare and exterior is crisp.

For garnish, fry celery root slices in butter until blond in color.

For sauce, blanch broccoli and blend to a purée. Strain. Set aside. Place cream, herbs and spinach leaves in pan and simmer. Blend and strain again. Mix with broccoli purée and butter to taste. Season with salt and pepper.

To serve, spoon herb sauce on plate. Insert chives in salmon, place atop herb sauce, and garnish with celery root.

Sea Bass with Red Beet Sauce

(Serves 4)

For the sauce:
1 carrot
1 rib celery
2 shallots, minced
2 cloves garlic, minced
Butter for sautéing
½ cup white wine
1 cup plus 2 tablespoons chicken stock
Pepper to taste
1 sprig fresh thyme
5 leaves marjoram
1 cooked, chopped beet root

For the fish:
Butter for sautéing
4 sea bass fillets, skin on

For the garnish:
4 miniature eggplants
Butter for sautéing

For the sauce, slice carrot and celery and sauté in butter along with shallots and garlic. When soft, add wine and reduce liquid to nearly dry. Add chicken stock, pepper, thyme, marjoram and a beet root. Cook mixture ten minutes and then purée in blender. Strain, set aside and keep warm.

For the fish, in a large sauté pan, heat the butter, add the fish and sauté on the skin-side only until skin is very crisp. Finish cooking fish in a medium oven for five minutes. Remove from the oven and keep warm.

For garnish, slice eggplant in half lengthwise and sauté in butter.

To serve, place sauce on plates and fish in middle. Garnish with eggplant.

Sturgeon Scallopine with Shrimp Sausage

(Serves 8)

For the scallopini:
8 2-ounce pieces white sturgeon scallopini
Salt and pepper to taste

For the herb mixture:
2 tablespoons chopped parsley
¾ tablespoon chopped dill

For the mousse:
5 ounces raw shrimp, peeled and de-veined
¾ cup heavy cream
Salt, pepper and cayenne pepper to taste
3 tablespoons smoked and diced yellow and red bell peppers
Lamb casings

For the assembly:
1 cup white wine
3 parsley stems
5 peppercorns, crushed
1 shallot, diced
3 cups heavy cream
4 tablespoons soft butter
1½ tablespoons sturgeon caviar
1½ tablespoons white fish caviar
1 tablespoon chives, cut short
2 tablespoons peanut oil
Salt and pepper to taste
Fleurons of puff pastry

For the scallopini, season sturgeon with salt and pepper. For the herb mixture, combine parsley and dill. Dip one side of scallopini into mixture and set aside.

For the mousse, using a food processor, make mousse with shrimp and heavy cream. Season with salt and pepper. Fold peppers into mousse. Fill into lamb casings, shape small sausages 3-inches long and reserve.

To assemble, combine white wine, parsley stems, peppercorns and shallots in saucepan over low heat and reduce until almost dry. Reduce cream to one half in separate skillet at same time. Add to wine reduction. Strain. Mount with butter. Add caviar and chives. Reserve. Poach sausage for five minutes at 140 degrees. Grill sturgeon scallopini quickly in non-stick skillet with peanut oil, putting herbed side down first.

To serve, arrange everything on plate. and top with small fleuron.

Salmon with Julienne of Vegetables

(Serves 4)

For the vegetables:

¼ cup olive oil
2 tablespoons lemon juice
1 tablespoon mustard
2 cucumbers, peeled, seeded, and finely julienned
2 leeks, white part only, trimmed and finely julienned
1 yellow bell pepper, stemmed, seeded, and finely julienned
½ cup Kalamata olives, pitted and sliced
1 cup Pousse Pierre
Salt and pepper to taste

For the salmon:

1 tablespoon olive oil
4 6-ounce salmon fillets, skinned and pin-boned
Salt and pepper to taste

For the vegetables, in a large bowl, whisk together the olive oil, lemon juice, and mustard. Toss the vegetables with the dressing, season, and allow to sit for ten minutes before serving.

For the salmon, in a large sauté pan, heat the oil, season the fillets and place in the pan. Sauté the salmon on both sides cooking to desired doneness, remove from the heat, and keep warm.

To serve, spoon some of the vegetables on a plate and place a salmon fillet on top.

Red Snapper with Carrots

125

(Serves 4)

For the red snapper:

2 tablespoons olive oil
6 tablespoons butter
4 6-ounce red snapper fillets, skin on
2 lemons, peeled, sectioned, and membrane discarded
Salt and pepper to taste

For the carrots:

4 medium carrots, peeled, sliced into rounds, and blanched
Juice of 1 lemon
1 clove garlic, peeled and minced
4 tablespoons chopped parsley
Salt and white pepper to taste

For the garnish:

Julienned blanched carrot
Julienned blanched lemon zest
Basil leaves
Dill sprigs

For the red snapper, in a large sauce pan, heat the oil and a half tablespoon of the butter, add the fillets, and sauté for two minutes on each side. Remove the fillets from the pan and set aside.

For the carrots, in a large sauté pan, heat two tablespoons of the butter, add the carrots, and sauté for one minute. Add the garlic and parsley and sauté for two minutes. Remove from the heat, season and keep warm.

To finish the snapper, melt the remaining butter, add the lemon juice and sections, and sauté to desired doneness. Remove from the heat, season and set aside.

To serve, arrange some of carrots on a plate and place a fillet on top. Spoon some of the sauce over the fish and garnish with julienned carrots and zest, basil leaves, and dill sprigs.

Grilled Marinated Quail

133

(Serves 6)

For the marinade:

4 tablespoons pure maple syrup

2 tablespoons lemon juice

1 tablespoon chopped fresh herbs (thyme and tarragon)

1 tablespoon peanut oil

12 boneless quail, either whole or butterflied

For the harvest cakes:

4 tablespoons unsalted butter

2 tablespoons minced onions

¼ teaspoon minced garlic

2 tablespoons minced red bell pepper

2 tablespoons minced Anaheim pepper

¼ cup diced wild mushrooms

3 tablespoons chopped wild hickory nut meat

3 tablespoons chopped wild pecan meat

6 tablespoons flour

¼ cup heavy cream

1 cup cooked wild rice

Salt and freshly ground black pepper

¼ cup fresh white bread crumbs

2 tablespoons sliced chives

For the sauce:

2 tablespoons cracked black pepper

1½ cups fresh wild huckleberries

1 tablespoon sugar

4 tablespoons red wine vinegar

2 cups rich quail or poultry sauce

2 tablespoons unsalted butter

For the chestnuts:

24 fresh American chestnuts (approximately 1¼ pound, shelled and peeled)

4 tablespoons unsalted butter

2 tablespoons water

For the marinade, mix together the maple syrup, lemon juice, herbs and oil and pour over the boneless quail one hour before cooking.

For the harvest cakes, in a heavy skillet, melt the butter and sauté the onions, garlic, and peppers until tender. Add the wild mushrooms and chopped nuts and continue to sauté for another few minutes. Sprinkle the mushroom mixture with flour and stir over a medium heat for a few minutes, being careful not to brown the flour. Add the heavy cream and stir in until smooth. Let simmer and stir in the cooked wild rice. Season with salt and freshly ground black pepper. Continue to cook the mixture over a low heat for two to three more minutes. Remove from the heat and stir in the fresh bread crumbs and chives. Pour the mixture into a shallow glass or non-corrosive pan. Cover with parchment paper and allow to cool to room temperature. When cooled, refrigerate for at least two to three hours (the mixture can be made the day before and refrigerated). When the mixture is completely cold, shape 12 oval cakes and set on a tray. Dust each cake lightly in flour and sauté in melted butter until lightly browned on both sides. With a spatula, remove the cakes to an absorbent towel.

For the sauce, place the cracked black pepper, ¼ cup of the huckleberries and sugar in a heavy bottomed saucepan. Over medium heat cook the huckleberries until they begin to caramelize. Deglaze the pan with the vinegar and cook for a minute or two. Add the rich quail sauce and simmer eight to ten minutes. Strain the sauce into a second pan and add the remaining huckleberries. Simmer the sauce for three to four minutes and stir in the butter. Set aside and keep warm.

For the chestnuts, place the shelled, peeled chestnut meat in a sauté pan with the butter and water. Bring the water and butter to a simmer and cook the chestnuts until they are well coated with butter and water has evaporated. Set aside in a warm place.

For the dish, remove the quail from the marinade and pat dry. Brush each quail lightly with oil and season with salt and freshly ground black pepper. Grill the quail over a medium-hot charcoal fire 2-3 minutes per side.

Arrange two harvest cakes on each plate with two quail. Spoon the wild huckleberry sauce over each of the quail and arrange the chestnuts on each and serve.

Chicken with Eggplant Ravioli and Foie Gras

134

(Serves 6)

For the chicken:

3 tablespoons olive oil
1 onion, peeled and thinly sliced
4 red bell peppers, stemmed, seeded, and, and sliced into thin strips
3 cloves garlic, peeled and minced
1 sprig thyme, stemmed and chopped
2 tablespoons clarified butter
12 chicken legs, trimmed
Salt and pepper to taste
1 quart chicken stock

For the chicken mousse:

1 boneless, skinless breast of chicken, chilled
1 boneless, skinless breast of squab, chilled
1 juniper berry
3 tablespoons fresh foie gras, chilled
½ cup cream, chilled
Salt and pepper to taste

For the eggplant:

2 tablespoons butter
1 eggplant, peeled and diced
½ small onion, peeled and diced
1 small tomato, peeled, seeded, and diced
¼ pound wild mushrooms, cleaned and sliced
1 strip bacon, cooked and crumbled
1 clove garlic, peeled and minced
Salt and pepper to taste

For the ravioli dough:

2 cups bread flour
6 egg yolks
1 teaspoon salt
2 ounces fresh foie gras, sliced into 1-inch squares
1 egg, lightly beaten

For the garnish:

Sage leaves

For the chicken, in a large sauté pan, heat the olive oil, add the onion and peppers, and sauté over medium high heat for ten minutes. Remove from the heat and incorporate the garlic and thyme. In a large sauté pan, heat the butter, add the drumsticks, and sauté the until golden brown. Season and set aside. In a large saucepan, add the stock, vegetables, and chicken and bring to a boil. Reduce the heat and simmer covered for 25 minutes. Remove from the heat and set aside.

For the chicken mousse, in the bowl of an electric mixer fitted with the metal blade attachment, add the chicken, squab, juniper berry, and foie gras, and purée until smooth. Slowly add the cream to incorporate, season, and set aside.

For the eggplant purée, in a large sauté pan, heat the butter, add the eggplant, onion, tomato, and wild mushrooms, and sauté over low heat until the vegetables are very soft and caramelized. Add the bacon and garlic, place in the bowl of a food processor fitted with the metal blade attachment, and purée until smooth. Transfer to a large bowl, season, and reserve.

For the ravioli, place the flour on a board and incorporate the egg yolks and salt, forming a ball. Knead the dough for ten minutes, cover with plastic wrap, and set aside to rest for two hours. Divide the dough in half and roll into two sheets through a pasta machine, ending at the thinnest possible setting. Place the sheets on a lightly floured work surface and set aside. To assemble the ravioli, add the chicken mousse to the eggplant purée and set aside. Line one sheet of pasta with foie gras squares placing them about 3-inches apart, and top each with half tablespoon of the purée. Brush the second sheet with egg, lay over the first sheet, and press to seal. Cut the ravioli into desired shapes and crimp the edges. Prepare a cold smoker and smoke the ravioli for five minutes. In a large saucepan of boiling salted water, add the ravioli and cook for one minute. Remove with a slotted spoon and set aside.

To serve, place one chicken leg and a few ravioli in a soup bowl, ladle some of the sauce over the top, and garnish with sage leaves.

Roast Quail with Bean Ragoût

136

(Serves 4)

For the lima bean ragout:

2 tablespoons butter
4 shallots, peeled and minced
3 cloves garlic, peeled and minced
2 cups cooked lima beans

½ cup heavy cream
½ pound venison sausage, browned and sliced
2 tablespoons sour cream
Salt and pepper to taste

recipe continued on next page

291

Bean Ragoût

continued from previous page

For the thyme flower sauce:
2 tablespoons butter
6 shallots, peeled and minced
2 cloves garlic, peeled and minced
2 tomatoes, quartered
1 bunch fresh thyme, stemmed and chopped and flowers reserved
2 cups white wine
1½ quarts chicken stock
Salt and pepper
Reserved thyme flowers
½ cup cooked pinquinto beans
¼ cup cooked yellow split peas
¼ cup cooked green split peas

For the quail:
8 quail, butterflied and back and rib bones removed
Salt and pepper
2 ounces vegetable oil

For the garnish:
Thyme sprigs

For the ragoût, in a large sauté pan over medium high heat, heat the butter, add the shallots and garlic, and sauté until softened. Incorporate the beans and heavy cream and bring to a boil. Reduce the heat and simmer until the sauce has thickened and coats the beans. Add sausage, and sour cream, and continue to simmer until heated through. Remove from the heat, season, and set aside, keeping warm.

For the thyme sauce, in large saucepan over medium high heat, heat the butter, add the shallots and garlic and sauté until softened. Add the tomatoes, thyme, and wine and bring to a boil. Reduce the heat and simmer until reduce by two-thirds. Add chicken stock. Bring to a boil, lower heat and simmer until reduced to desired consistency. Remove form the heat, strain and season. Add the thyme flowers, beans and peas, and set aside, keeping warm.

For the quail, preheat the oven to 375 degrees, and season the quail with salt and pepper. In a large sauté pan over high heat, heat the oil, add the quail, and sear on both sides until the skin is golden brown and crisp. Place in the oven and roast to desired doneness, remove form the oven, and set aside.

To serve, spoon some of the sauce on a plate and spoon some of the ragoût to the side of the plate. Set a quail on top of the ragoût, and garnish the plate with thyme.

Crépinette of Grouse

137

(Serves 4)

For the grouse:
4 grouse legs, thigh bone removed
Salt and pepper to taste
2 tablespoons Armagnac

For the stock:
2 grouse carcasses
5 juniper berries
2 shallots, peeled and minced
4 tablespoons black currants
1 sprig rosemary, stemmed and minced
1 cinnamon stick
¾ cup red wine
1 tablespoon butter
Salt and pepper to taste

To finish:
1 pound sauerkraut rinsed and blanched
7 ounces caul fat

For the dish:
Blanched green beans
Baby corn
Purple Brussels's sprouts
Herb spätzle

recipe continued on next page

Crépinette of
Grouse
continued from previous page

For the grouse, place the legs in a medium bowl, season, and sprinkle with the Armagnac. Cover with plastic wrap and set aside in the refrigerator to marinate for two hours.

For the stock, in large saucepan, combine the grouse bones, juniper berries, shallots, currants, rosemary, cinnamon and red wine, and cover with water. Bring to a boil over high heat, reduce the heat and simmer for 30 minutes, or until the mixture is slightly reduced. Remove from the heat and strain into a medium saucepan. Place the pan over medium high heat and bring to a boil. Reduce the heat and simmer until the mixture is reduced to three-fourths cup. Gradually incorporate the butter and whisk to combine. Remove from the heat, season, and set aside, keeping warm.

To finish the grouse, preheat the oven to 350 degrees. Lay a piece of caul fat on a flat work surface, coat with a layer of sauerkraut, and place a grouse leg on top. Tightly wrap the caul fat around the grouse leg and place in a roasting pan. Repeat the procedure with the remaining caul fat, sauerkraut, and grouse and place in the oven. Roast for 20 minutes or to desired doneness, remove from the oven and set aside.

To serve, spoon some of the sauce onto a plate, slice the grouse leg, and arrange on top of the sauce. Spoon some of the spätzle beside the grouse and serve with corn, Brussels sprouts, and green beans.

Rabbit Loin with Tartelette of Mousseron Mushrooms

(Serves 2)

For the poached pear:
½ cup red wine
1 cinnamon stick
2 whole cloves
1 tablespoon granulated sugar
1 pear, peeled, cored, and halved

For the dish:
1 saddle of rabbit
Salt and pepper to taste
1 tablespoon vegetable oil
½ cup white wine
1 cup heavy cream
1 teaspoon fresh thyme
1 tablespoon butter
1 pound mousseron mushrooms
2-2-inch tartlet shells, pre-baked
1 medium zucchini, sliced into ¼-inch thick rounds and blanched

For the garnish:
Minced thyme

For the poached pear, in a small saucepan, add the red wine, cinnamon, cloves, and sugar, and bring to a boil. Add the pears, bring to a low simmer, and poach until the fruit is tender. Remove from the heat and set aside to cool in the poaching liquid. Remove the pears from the liquid, slice thinly, and reserve.

For the dish, season the saddle of rabbit with salt and pepper. In a large sauté pan, heat the oil, add the rabbit, and sauté over medium heat for ten minutes. Remove from the heat and set aside for ten minutes. Cut the rabbit loins off of the bone and keep warm. Preheat the oven to 350 degrees. Chop the bones and place them in a shallow pan. Place the pan in the oven and roast until the bones are golden brown. Remove from the oven and deglaze the pan with white wine. Strain into a small saucepan and bring to a boil. Lower the heat to medium and reduce the liquid by half. Incorporate the cream and reduce again by one-third. Remove from the heat and add the thyme. Season and keep warm. In a medium sauté pan, heat the butter, add the mushrooms, and sauté until all of the liquid has evaporated. Place the mushrooms in heated tartlet shells and keep warm.

To serve, place a pool of the sauce on a plate. Alternate slices of pear and zucchini in a circle around the outer rim of the plate. Slice the rabbit loin into ⅛-inch thick pieces and arrange within the pear and cucumber circle. Place a tartlet in the center of the circle and garnish the plate with thyme.

Roast Squab with Woodcock Mousse

(Serves 6)

For the dish:
3 tablespoons olive oil
6 tablespoons butter
Salt and pepper to taste
6 squab breasts, deboned
1 medium onion, peeled and chopped
2 cups Italian arborio rice
1 cup dry white wine
4 cups squab broth (or rich chicken stock)
1 teaspoon saffron threads, crushed
1 black truffle, thinly sliced
6 tablespoons grated Parmesan cheese
Salt and pepper to taste

For the dish, in a large saucepan, heat the oil and one tablespoon of the butter over medium high heat. Season the squab, add to the pan, and sear on all sides. Remove from the pan and set aside. Reduce the heat to medium, add the onions, and sauté until softened. Incorporate the rice and continue to sauté for one minute. Add the wine, increase the heat to high, and cook until the wine is almost evaporated, stirring occasionally. In a small saucepan, bring the stock to a boil. Place one cup of the stock in a small bowl, add the saffron threads, and set aside. Start adding the boiled stock to the rice, one cup at a time, stirring until incorporated. Add the saffron stock last, reduce the heat to low, and cook slowly for 15 minutes. Remove from heat and stir in the truffle, cheese, and remaining butter. Season and keep warm. Slice the squab into ½-inch medallions and set aside.

To serve, spoon some risotto in a wide soup bowl and arrange some of the squab pieces on top.

Ragoût of Rabbit with Artichoke

(Serves 4)

For the dish:
3 tablespoons butter
2 rabbit loins, boned and cubed
Salt and pepper to taste
1 clove garlic, peeled and minced
1 teaspoon white wine vinegar
1 teaspoon brown veal stock
2 teaspoons rabbit stock
1 tablespoon butter
16 small potatoes, peeled and blanched
4 cooked artichoke bottoms, quartered

For the garnish:
Minced parsley
Halved rabbit kidneys

For the dish, in a large sauté pan over medium-high heat, heat one tablespoon of the butter, add the rabbit, and sauté to desired doneness. Remove the rabbit from the pan and set aside. Remove as much of the grease from the sauté pan as possible and place over medium-high heat. Deglaze the pan with vinegar and bring to a boil. Slightly reduce the liquid, incorporate the stocks, and bring to a boil. Reduce the heat and simmer until the liquid is reduced by one-fourth. Remove from the heat, incorporate one tablespoon of the butter, and reserve, keeping warm. In a large sauté pan, heat the remaining butter, add the potatoes, and sauté until lightly caramelized. Incorporate the artichoke bottoms and reserved rabbit and continue to sauté until heated through. Remove from the heat, add to the reserved sauce and set aside, keeping warm.

To serve, arrange some of the rabbit, potatoes, and artichokes in the bottom of a bowl and pour some of the sauce on top. Garnish the dish with minced parsley and a rabbit kidney.

Chicken Breast with Cèpes and Flageolet Beans

(Serves 2)

For the dish:
1 whole chicken
2 ounces fresh frozen cèpes
4 ounces flageolet beans
1 cup brown chicken stock
2 tablespoons butter
1 garlic clove, mashed
1 cup water
1 tablespoon Italian parsley, chopped
1 bouquet garni
½ leek stalk, julienned
1 tablespoon olive oil
½ cup white wine
Salt and pepper to taste
Pommes Macaire

Remove the two breasts from the chicken carcass leaving the wing bone and skin attached. Set aside.

Peel the flageolet beans. In a sauté pan, sweat the leek in 1 tablespoon of butter. Add the beans, one cup of water and the bouquet garni and simmer for 20 minutes. Drain and set aside.

Wash and slice the cèpes. Set aside. Season the chicken breast with salt and pepper. Sauté them in one tablespoon butter for eight to ten minutes over medium heat. Remove the chicken breasts and remove all grease from the pan. Deglaze the pan with white wine, add the chicken breast, chicken stock and simmer until half of the liquid has evaporated. Remove from heat and set aside and keep warm.

Heat the olive oil in a sauté pan. Add the cèpes and sauté until golden brown. Add the mashed garlic.

To serve: Place the chicken breasts on preheated plates and nap with the sauce. Garnish with the flageolet beans and cèpes and pommes Macaire.

Squab with Risotto

(Serves 6)

For the dish:
3 tablespoons olive oil
6 tablespoons butter
Salt and pepper to taste
6 squab breasts, deboned
1 medium onion, peeled and chopped
2 cups Italian arborio rice
1 cup dry white wine
4 cups squab broth (or rich chicken stock)
1 teaspoon saffron threads, crushed
1 black truffle, thinly sliced
6 tablespoons grated Parmesan cheese
Salt and pepper to taste

For the dish, in a large saucepan, heat the oil and one tablespoon of the butter over medium high heat. Season the squab, add to the pan, and sear on all sides. Remove from the pan and set aside. Reduce the heat to medium, add the onions, and saute until softened. Incorporate the rice and continue to sauté for one minute. Add the wine, increase the heat to high, and cook until the wine is almost evaporated, stirring occasionally. In a small saucepan, bring the stock to a boil. Place one cup of the stock in a small bowl, add the saffron threads, and set aside. Start adding the boiled stock to the rice, one cup at a time, stirring until incorporated. Add the saffron stock last, reduce the heat to low, and cook slowly for 15 minutes. Remove from heat and stir in the truffle, cheese, and remaining butter. Season and keep warm. Slice the squab into ½-inch medallions and set aside.

To serve, spoon some risotto in a wide soup bowl and arrange some of the squab pieces on top.

Venison Loin with Peppercorn Crust

(Serves 10)

For the crust:
4 cups brioche bread crumbs
1 tablespoon chopped fresh parsley
1 tablespoon chopped fresh chervil
1 teaspoon chopped fresh rosemary
1 teaspoon chopped fresh thyme
2 tablespoons chopped green peppercorns
1 teaspoon chopped fresh garlic
1 teaspoon chopped fresh shallot

For the venison:
10 6-ounce loin cut pieces of venison
Salt and white pepper to taste
1 egg yolk
¾ cup Dijon mustard

For the sauce:
2 heads of garlic (cut in half)
2 tablespoons olive oil
10 freshly cracked black peppercorns
1 sprig chopped rosemary
½ cup Champagne vinegar
1 cup white wine
3 finely diced shallots
15 whole white peppercorns
½ bay leaf
4 cups game stock
Salt and white pepper to taste

For sweet potato wild rice cakes:
2 large eggs
½ cup all-purpose flour
¼ cup milk
1 cup julienned sweet potato
1 cup wild rice, cooked in chicken stock
1 tablespoon fresh chopped chives
Salt and white pepper to taste

For the garnish:
Steamed and seasoned sugar snap peas
Steamed and seasoned thin green beans
Steamed and seasoned diagonally cut carrot slices
Diced red bell pepper

For the crust, mix bread crumbs, herbs, green peppercorns, garlic and shallot.

For the venison, season venison loins with salt and white pepper and sear in a large hot skillet with olive oil two at a time. Mix egg yolk and Dijon mustard. Rub the venison loins generously with the mixture and then roll them in the crust mixture. Roast in a 375-degree F oven until the meat is rare to medium rare.

For the sauce, toss the garlic with the olive oil, black pepper and rosemary. Roast in a 325 degree oven for approximately 20 minutes or until soft and golden brown. Remove cloves from head and purée until smooth. Reduce vinegar by half, add white wine, shallots, peppercorns, bay leaf and thyme. Add game stock and reduce by a third. Strain, stir in garlic purée and season with salt and white pepper.

For the sweet potato wild rice cakes, mix eggs and flour together. Thin with milk, Add sweet potatoes, wild rice and chives. Season with salt and white pepper. Form mixture into little patties and sauté lightly on each side until done all the way through.

To serve, place venison atop sauce and garnish with wild rice cakes, pea pods, green beans, peppers and carrots.

Chicken Breast with Pinto Beans

146

(Serves 6)

For the beans:
2 cups pinto beans
1 small white onion, peeled
1 clove garlic, minced
4 cups chicken stock

⅛ teaspoon cumin
⅛ teaspoon chili powder
⅛ teaspoon chopped fresh oregano
1 cup tomato concasse
Salt and pepper to taste

recipe continued on next page

Chicken Breast with

Pinto Beans
continued from previous page

For the basil aîoli:
2 egg yolks

1 tablespoon chardonnay wine vinegar

Juice of ½ lemon

¼ teaspoon Dijon mustard

½ teaspoon minced garlic

½ cup olive oil

½ bunch basil leaves

½ bunch Italian parsley

2 tablespoons cold water

Salt, white and black pepper to taste

For the tomatillo sauce:
1 cup chopped red onions

1 pound quartered tomatillos

1 dried and reconstituted ancho chili

1 clove garlic

2 cups tomato concasse

1 jalopeño pepper, seeded

½ cup chicken stock

¼ teaspoon chili powder

¼ teaspoon oregano

Salt and pepper to taste

6 half chicken breasts, (4 ounces each) grilled

For the garnish:
6 rosemary sprigs

For the beans, soak beans in water overnight. Drain and place beans in pot with chicken stock. Sauté onion and garlic in beans. Cook beans until tender. Add cumin, chili powder and oregano. Add tomato concasse. Stir. Drain excess liquid and reduce to a sauce-like consistency. If beans need to be thickened, purée some and add back to beans. Adjust seasoning with salt and pepper. Set aside.

For the basil aîoli, combine egg yolks, vinegar, lemon juice, mustard and garlic in blender. Add olive oil, slowing, in order to make a mayonnaise. Mince leaves of basil and parsley. Fold into mayonnaise. Adjust consistency with cold water. Adjust seasoning with salt and peppers. Set aside.

For the tomatillo sauce, sauté red onions in a little oil until, clear. Add tomatillos, chili, garlic, tomato, jalapeño and chicken stock. Cook 15 to 20 minutes. Add chili powder, oregano and salt and pepper. Purée until smooth.

To serve, place tomatillo sauce on base of plate and spoon beans into center of sauce. Mount grilled chicken breast on beans and drizzle basil aîoli over chicken. Garnish with rosemary sprig.

Medallions of Veal with Sweetbread Terrine

(Serves 4)

For the veal stock:
5 pieces veal shank
Veal bones
1 carrot, peeled and sliced
3 shallots, peeled and sliced
1 sprig thyme
2 cups tomato purée
3 quarts water

For the terrine:
2 sweetbreads, soaked in water overnight
1 recipe chicken mousse (see recipe for Chicken with Eggplant Ravioli and Foie Gras)

For the sauce:
1 cup vermouth
½ cup white wine
2 shallots, peeled and sliced
6 black peppercorns
½ small tomato, peeled, seeded and finely diced
¼ cup glace de veau
1 cup heavy cream
5 cloves garlic, peeled, halved, and blanched in salted water
Salt and pepper to taste

For the dish:
4 tablespoons clarified butter
1 pound boneless veal loin, trimmed and sliced into 2-ounce medallions
Salt and pepper to taste
24 fresh morels, cleaned

For the garnish:
2 cups reserved veal stock
4 cloves garlic, blanched in salted water for 5 minutes, and slivered
1 tomato, peeled, seeded and finely chopped
Sprigs of fresh thyme

For the stock, preheat the oven to 450 degrees. In a roasting pan, add the veal shank, bones, carrot, and shallots, and place in the oven for one hour, or until browned. Remove from the oven, deglaze the pan with water, and transfer to a large saucepan. Add the thyme and tomato purée and bring to a boil. Reduce the heat and simmer, skimming any reside that rises to the surface, for four hours. Strain, remove any grease that rises to the surface, and cool in an ice bath. Remove any additional grease and pour into a medium saucepan. Bring to a boil over medium heat and reduce until two cups of stock remain. Remove from the heat and set aside.

For the terrine, preheat the oven to 350 degrees. Remove the connective tissue from the sweetbreads and place in a roasting pan. Place in the oven and roast for ten minutes. Remove from the oven and slice thinly. Heavily butter four 4-ounce molds. Alternate layers of sliced sweetbread and chicken mousse and place in a shallow pan. Fill the pan with enough water to reach half way up the sides of the molds and carefully place in the oven. Cover with aluminum foil and bake for 45 minutes. Remove from the oven and place a weight such as a board or a light brick on top.

For the sauce, in a small saucepan, add the vermouth, white wine, shallots, peppercorns, and tomato and bring to a boil. Reduce until only a few tablespoons of liquid remain, add the glace de veau and cream, and simmer over low heat for ten minutes. Add the garlic and simmer for five minutes. Place the sauce in the bowl of a food processor and purée until smooth. Strain into a small saucepan, season, and set aside.

For the dish, in a medium sauté pan, heat two tablespoons of the butter over high heat. Season the medallions, place in the pan, and sauté for 30 seconds on each side. Remove from the pan and keep warm. Add the remaining butter to the pan, add the morels, and sauté until cooked. Remove from the heat, season, and keep warm.

To serve, place two veal medallions and a terrine on a plate. Arrange a few morels and spoon some of the sauces around the plate. Garnish the plate with garlic, tomato, and thyme.

Medallions of Veal with Country Ham and Rosemary Cream

(Serves 4)

For the rosemary cream:
1 tablespoon unsalted butter
2 bunches fresh rosemary, stemmed and finely chopped
½ small shallot, peeled finely minced
2 cloves garlic, peeled and minced
6 mushrooms, cleaned and finely chopped
2 sprigs parsley, stemmed and chopped
3 bay leaves
1½ cups Sauternes
1/2 cup glace de veau
1 quart heavy cream

For the veal:
1½ pounds veal loin, bones and sliced into 12 medallions
2 tablespoons flour
¼ cup vegetable oil
1/2 cup dry white wine

recipe continued on next page

Medallions of Veal with Country Ham
and Rosemary Cream

continued from previous page

For the vegetables:
1 tablespoon olive oil
½ small shallot, peeled and minced
1 small clove garlic, peeled and minced
4 ounces haricot verts, trimmed and blanched
1 tablespoon unsalted butter
8 young carrots, peeled and blanched
2 sprigs mint, stemmed and chopped
2 tablespoons unsalted butter
4 ounces pearl onions, peeled and blanched
Sugar to taste
2 tablespoons unsalted butter
¼ pound morels, cleaned and sliced
Salt and pepper to taste

For the pasta:
6 ounces fresh fettuccini
4 tablespoons browned butter
1 tablespoon olive oil
Pinch of nutmeg
1 clove garlic, peeled and minced
2 ounces country ham, finely julienned

For the garnish:
Minced chives
Chive blossoms

For the rosemary cream sauce, in a large sauté pan, heat the butter, add the rosemary, shallots, garlic, mushrooms, parsley and bay leaves, and sauté over low heat for five minutes. Deglaze the pan with Sauternes, add the glace de veau, and bring to a boil. Reduce the heat and simmer until the mixture is syrup consistency. Add the cream and bring to a boil. Reduce the heat and simmer until the mixture is reduced by half. Strain into a small saucepan and keep warm.

For the veal, preheat oven to 425 degrees. Dust the veal medallions lightly with flour and set aside. In a large sauté pan, heat the oil add the medallions and brown on both sides. Remove from pan and deglaze the pan with white wine. Return the medallions to the pan, place in the oven, and roast to desired doneness. Remove from the oven and set aside.

For the vegetables, in a small saucepan, heat the olive oil, add the shallots and garlic, and sauté until softened. Add the haricots verts and continue to sauté until heated through. Remove from the heat and keep warm. In another small sauté pan, heat the butter, add the carrots, and sauté until tender. Incorporate the mint, remove from the heat, and keep warm. In a third small sauté pan, heat the butter, add the onions, and sauté until lightly caramelized. Add the sugar and sauté until the granules dissolve. Remove from the heat and keep warm. Season all the vegetables with salt and pepper and reserve.

For the pasta, in a large saucepan of boiling water, add the fettuccini and cook until al dente. Drain, combine with the browned butter, olive oil, nutmeg, garlic, and ham, and keep warm.

To serve, spoon some of the sauce in a shallow bowl and mound some of the vegetables and pasta in the center. Arrange three medallions around the plate and garnish with minced chives and chive blossoms.

Grilled Veal Loin
with Beans

(Serves 4)

For the sauce:
1 tablespoon vegetable oil
2 shallots, peeled and minced
1 sprig thyme, stemmed and chopped
2 cups white wine
2 cups veal stock
1 cup white beans, soaked
Salt and pepper to taste

For the veal:
4 6-ounce veal loin filets
Salt and pepper to taste

For the garnish:
Diced red tomatoes
Diced yellow tomatoes
Cooked kidney beans
Cooked black beans
Sautéed sliced garlic
Thyme sprigs

recipe continued on next page

Grilled Veal Loin
with Beans
continued from previous page

For the sauce, in medium sauté pan over medium high heat, heat the oil, add the shallots and thyme, and sauté until the shallots are softened and translucent. Add the wine and bring to a boil. Reduce the heat and simmer until the mixture is reduced by half. Incorporate the stock and beans and simmer until beans are soft, about two hours. Strain, season, and set aside, keeping warm.

For the veal, prepare a hot grill. Season the filets and place on the grill to cook to desired doneness. Remove from the grill and set aside.

To serve, spoon some of the sauce onto plate, and place a filet on top of the sauce. Arrange the tomatoes and beans around the filet and garnish the plate with garlic and thyme sprigs.

Roasted Veal Shank
with Riesling

154

(Serves 2)

For the shank:
1 veal shank
Salt and pepper to taste
3 tablespoons clarified butter
4 shallots, minced
1 small carrot, peeled and diced
⅓ small leek, minced
½ rib celery, minced
White peppercorns
Fresh rosemary and thyme
1 clove garlic, minced
½ cup Riesling wine
2 cups veal stock
6 tablespoons veal glace
Salt and pepper to taste
3 tablespoons butter

For the stuffed kohlrabi:
2 medium kohlrabi
Chicken stock
Salt and pepper to taste
½ cup heavy cream
1 tablespoon small kohlrabi leaves, minced
1 tablespoon hollandaise sauce

For the remaining garnish:
Turned carrots, blanched and seasoned
Pan-fried breaded eggplant slices
Turnip balls, blanched and seasoned
Stuffed root vegetables
Red Onion Confit (see recipe)

For the shank, season with salt and pepper and brown in clarified butter. Add vegetables and let them cook until transparent. Add herbs and peppercorns and garlic and deglaze pan with wine. Place pan in 300 degree oven. Turn shank from time to time and deglaze pan with veal stock when shank is done and of good brown color. Remove shank from the pan and keep warm. Add veal glace to pan. Reduce until the sauce has thickened, strain, and season to taste. Mount with butter and set aside.

For the stuffed kohlrabi, remove outer large leaves of kohlrabi and keep small leaves for use later. Peel and cook kohlrabi in seasoned chicken stock until tender. Remove and let cool. Make a cavity with a melon ball scoop. Retain trim and chop it fine. Combine chopped trim with cream and reduce until thick. Add chopped small leaves. Season to taste and fill back into cavity. Nap kohlrabi with hollandaise and bake until golden.

To serve, place shank on serving platter with sauce. Arrange eggplant slices, carrots, turnips and stuffed kohlrabi and other vegetables around it. Serve with red onion confit.

Roasted Veal Tenderloin with Arugula and Grilled Wild Mushrooms

155

(Serves 10)

For the sauce:

1 cup white wine
10 whole white peppercorns
6 shallots, finely diced
1 sprig of fresh thyme
1 bay leaf
2 cups veal glace
Salt and white pepper to taste

For the mushrooms:

1 head fresh garlic (split in half)
1 cup extra virgin olive oil
1 teaspoon chopped fresh rosemary
1 teaspoon chopped fresh oregano
1 teaspoon chopped fresh thyme
10 shiitake mushrooms
10 white trumpet mushrooms
10 morel mushrooms
10 oyster mushrooms

For the veal:

4 tablespoons leftover garlic oil
10 veal tenderloins
Salt and white pepper to taste

For the arugula:

3 bunches arugula
6 shallots, finely diced
Salt and white pepper to taste

For the garnish:

Rosemary sprigs

For the sauce, bring white wine to a boil with peppercorns, shallots, thyme, and bay leaf. Reduce. Add veal glace and reduce. Strain and season with salt and white pepper.

For the mushrooms, make garlic oil by cutting head of garlic in half and pouring olive oil over it. Let stand 48 hours. Drain oil off and add chopped herbs. Lightly toss mushrooms with the herbed olive oil. Season with salt and pepper to taste. Drain the mushrooms and mark them lightly on the grill. Finish them in a 325 degree oven for approximately four to five minutes. For the veal, heat garlic oil in a large skillet. Season the veal tenderloins with salt and white pepper. Sear two at a time on all sides, place in oven and roast for 6-8 minutes or until medium-rare. Let rest three minutes, then slice thin and serve.

For the arugula, sauté arugula and shallots in hot olive oil for 10 seconds only. Season with salt and white pepper. To serve, place veal with sauce, arugula and mushrooms. Garnish with rosemary sprigs.

Grilled Veal Chop with Smoked Tomato Sauce

(Serves 4)

For the tomato sauce:

12 to 14 large tomatoes
Creole seasoning
Bouquet garni (3 bay leaves and 2 sprigs thyme)
2 splashes Tabasco
½ teaspoon Creole seasoning
2½ tablespoons paprika
1 clove garlic, peeled and minced
⅛ teaspoon crushed red pepper flakes
½ cup rich chicken or veal stock
⅓ cup rice wine vinegar
⅓ cup heavy cream
1½ pounds cold unsalted butter, cubed

For the veal chops:

4 10 to 12-ounce veal chops
Kosher salt and black pepper to taste

For the garnish:

Grilled hearts of fennel
Fresh sprigs of fennel

For the sauce, prepare a hot hickory smoker, place the tomatoes on the grill, and smoke until the tomatoes are softened. Remove from the smoker and set aside to cool. Peel and seed the tomatoes and place the flesh and any juice in a large saucepan with the bouquet garni, Creole seasoning, paprika, garlic, and red pepper. Bring to a boil over high heat, reduce the heat, and simmer until the sauce is slightly thickened. Remove from the heat and transfer to the bowl of a food processor fitted with the metal blade attachment, Purée, strain, and return the saucepan. Add the stock and vinegar and bring to a boil over high heat. Reduce the heat and simmer until the sauce is thickened. Incorporate the cream and butter, remove from the heat, and keep warm.

For the veal, prepare a hot grill with hickory chips. Season the veal, place on the grill, and grill on both sides to desired doneness. Remove form the grill and keep warm.

To serve, spoon some of the sauce on a plate and place a veal chop on top of the sauce. Arrange three pieces of the fennel heart next to the veal and garnish with fennel sprigs.

Noisettes of Veal with Chive Sauce and Vegetable Ravioli

(Serves 4)

For the vegetable ravioli:
¼ cup olive oil
½ red bell pepper, stemmed, seeded, and diced
½ green bell pepper, stemmed, seeded, and diced
½ small zucchini, stemmed and diced
½ small eggplant, stemmed, and diced
1 clove garlic, peeled and finely minced
10 fresh basil leaves, minced (or ½ teaspoon dried)
2 tablespoons plain bread crumbs
Salt and pepper to taste
12 round wonton wrappers

For the veal noisettes:
3 tablespoons clarified butter
1½-pounds veal tenderloin, sliced into 16 rounds and lightly pounded to ½-inch thickness
½ cup white wine
¼ cup white Vermouth
1 cup heavy cream
¼ cup glace de viande (or reduce 2 cups of unsalted veal stock to ¼ cup)
2 tablespoons unsalted butter

For the dish:
2 tomatoes, peeled, seeded, and diced
12 asparagus spears, steamed and kept warm

For the garnish:
4 tablespoons minced fresh chives

For the vegetable ravioli, in a large sauté pan, heat the oil, add the vegetables, garlic and basil and sauté until cooked but still slightly crisp. Add the bread crumbs and season. Form ravioli by placing a few teaspoons of the filling in the center of each wrapper. Brush the edges with water, fold in half to form a crescent, and crimp the edges to seal. Bring a large sauté pan filled with 2-inches of water to just below a simmer, add the ravioli, and poach for three minutes. Remove with a slotted spoon and drain well. Place on a parchment-lined sheet pan and keep warm.

For the veal noisettes, in a large sauté pan, heat butter over high heat, add the veal, and sauté for two minutes on each side. Remove from pan and set aside. Add the wine, Vermouth, cream, and glace de viande and bring to a boil. Reduce the heat and simmer until the mixture is thick enough to coat the back of a spoon. Whisk in the butter, incorporate the tomato and chives, and remove from the heat. Season and set aside.

To serve, spoon some of the tomato to the side of a plate and place three vegetable ravioli on top. Place four noisettes of veal beside the ravioli, and arrange three asparagus spears in the center of the plate. Pour some of the sauce over the veal and garnish with minced chives.

Sautéed Veal with Basil and Mozzarella

(Serves 4)

For the veal:
4 tablespoons clarified butter
8 4-ounce veal loin medallions
Salt and freshly ground black pepper to taste
Flour and paprika for dusting
1 large ripe tomato, peeled, seeded, and diced
4 ounces mozzarella, diced
4 slices prosciutto, julienned

For the dish:
2 cups veal stock reduced by half
1 pound spinach fettuccine, cooked and sautéed in butter

For the garnish:
Basil sprigs

For the veal, preheat the oven to 375 degrees. Season the medallions, dust in flour, sprinkle with paprika and set aside. In a large sauté pan over high heat, heat the butter, add the veal, and briefly sear on each side. Spoon some of the tomato, mozzarella and prosciutto on each medallion and bake for ten minutes, or until the cheese begins to melt. Remove from the oven and set aside.

To serve, season the reduced stock, spoon onto a plate and arrange two medallions on top. Mound some of the spinach pasta beside the medallions and garnish the dish with basil leaves.

Veal Noisettes
with Citrus

(Serves 2)

For the sauce:

Zest of 1 orange
Zest of 1 lemon
Zest of 1 lime
1 cup water
Veal stock

For the veal:

8 2-ounce noisettes of veal
1 medium zucchini, cut into julienne slices

For the garnish:

Reserved fruit of orange, lemon and lime, cut into segments
Reserved fruit zest

For the sauce, blanch zest in boiling water for two minutes. Remove and drain zest. Set aside. Reduce blanching liquid to a third. Add veal stock and reduce by half. Keep sauce warm.

For the veal, heat Teflon pan and sear noisettes for two minutes per side. Set aside to keep warm. Steam zucchini julienne until just tender.

To serve, place a mound of zucchini in the center of the plates. Place three medallions on each plate. Ladle sauce over veal and garnish with zest and reserved fruit segments.

Loin of Lamb Centennial

164

(Serves 4)

For the lamb:
2 racks of lamb
Salt and pepper
6 tablespoons olive oil
8 lamb sweetbreads
Juice of ¼ lemon
3 tablespoons bread crumbs
2 tablespoons butter
1 garlic clove, chopped
2 tablespoons parsley, chopped
1 tablespoon mustard
1 egg yolk for wash

For the sauce:
Bones and trimmings from lamb loin
6 shallots peeled
1 carrot, peeled and diced
2 onions, peeled and diced
2 stalks celery, diced
3 cloves garlic
1 bottle red wine
2 cups lamb stock
Salt and pepper to taste
2 tablespoons olive oil

For the basil oil:
20 medium basil leaves
2 tablespoons olive oil
Salt and pepper

For the garnish:
Deep-fried basil leaves

For the mashed potatoes:
4 medium Idaho potatoes, peeled
3 tablespoons basil oil
3 tablespoons butter
3 tablespoons olive oil
Salt and pepper

For the sauce, preheat the oven to 400 degrees. Place the lamb bones and trimmings, shallots, carrot, onion, celery and garlic in a roasting pan, and roast for one hour, stirring occasionally, until nicely browned. Pour in half of the bottle of red wine, and roast one hour longer. Transfer the mixture into a saucepan, add the remaining wine, and cook until only one cup remains. Strain, add the lamb stock, and season with salt and pepper to taste. Set aside and keep warm. Just before serving, slowly add the olive oil.

For the lamb, blanch the sweetbreads in water with the lemon juice for ten minutes. In a blender, combine sweetbreads, bread crumbs, butter, garlic, parsley and mustard. Blend until you reach a dough-like consistency. Roll out with a rolling pin to a thickness of ⅛-inch. Cut out strips to cover the lamb racks and set aside. Season the lamb racks with salt and pepper and sear in hot olive oil until browned and still rare. Let the racks cool, and cover with the bread crumb strips. Brush with the egg wash and place in a preheated oven of 350 degrees for ten minutes. Set aside and keep warm.

To make the basil oil, bring water to a boil, and add the basil leaves. Blanch for ten seconds and remove, shock in ice water, and drain well. In a food processor, purée the basil leaves with the olive oil. Season to taste with salt and pepper.

For the mashed potatoes, cut the potatoes into six pieces each and cook in boiling salted water for 20 minutes, or until tender. Drain and place on a sheet pan. Place in a 250 degree oven until all traces of water are gone, stirring occasionally. Mash the potatoes with a potato masher and add the butter, olive oil, basil oil and salt and pepper. With large soup spoons dipped in warm water, form two potato quenelles per plate.

To assemble, pour a small amount of sauce on each preheated plate, and place three lamb chops on top. Place the potato quenelles off to the side, and garnish with deep-fried basil leaves.

Rack of Lamb with Cannelloni

166

(Serves 2)

For the eggplant and lamb filling:
1 medium eggplant
½ green bell pepper
½ red bell pepper
2 anchovies
3 button mushrooms

Olive oil
Salt and pepper to taste
1 rack of lamb
Olive oil
2 wonton wrappers

recipe continued on next page

304

Rack of Lamb with

Cannelloni

continued from previous page

For the garlic wine:

1 quart cabernet sauvignon

½ pound garlic, peeled and cut in two

3 bunches thyme

3 bunches tarragon

3 bunches parsley

10 black peppercorns

2 zucchini

1 tablespoon garlic wine

Thyme leaves

3 tablespoons olive oil

For the garnish:

Thyme and gaufrette potatoes

For the filling, roast eggplant in 400 degree oven for 30 minutes. Peel peppers and cut into small dice. Dice anchovies and mushrooms. Cut eggplant in half and scrape out pulp into bowl. Sauté diced vegetables in olive oil until tender. Add to eggplant, along with salt and pepper to taste. Trim rack of lamb to obtain loin. Sauté trimmings in olive oil and season. Add this to eggplant mixture. Blanch wonton wrappers in salted boiling water. Stuff with mixture and roll up. Set aside.

For the garlic wine, heat together wine, garlic, thyme, tarragon, parsley and peppercorns. Turn off heat and let rest for 30 minutes. Strain.

For the sauce, extract juice from zucchini to make one cup. Place juice, wine, thyme and olive oil in saucepot. Bring to a boil and keep warm.

For lamb, sauté loin in olive oil on top of stove. Finish cooking in 400 degree oven for six minutes. Bake cannelloni in oven for five minutes to crisp.

To serve, slice loin and place on serving plate. Nap with sauce and place

Glazed Pork

Shanks

167

(Serves 4)

For the pork shanks:

4 6-ounce pork shanks

1 clove garlic, peeled and minced

1 teaspoon caraway seeds

Salt and pepper to taste

4 tablespoons vegetable oil

4 shallots, peeled and minced

½ carrot, peeled and chopped

¼ rib celery, chopped

1 small leek, trimmed and chopped

1 sprig thyme

1 small bay leaf

1 teaspoon whole black peppercorns

4 cups chicken stock

Chicken stock as needed

¾ cup veal demi-glace

Salt and pepper to taste

For the gratin:

6 tablespoons butter

1 medium turnip, peeled and thinly sliced into rounds

1 medium potato, peeled and thinly sliced into rounds

¾ cup cream

Salt and pepper to taste

1 clove garlic, peeled and minced

For the garnish:

Cooked Brussels sprouts, leaves separated

For the shanks, preheat the oven to 300 degrees. Sprinkle the shanks with garlic and caraway seeds, season and set aside. In a large saucepan over medium-high heat, heat the oil, add the shanks, and sear until the skin is well caramelized. Set the shanks aside, add the vegetables, thyme, bay leaf, and peppercorns and sauté until the vegetables have softened. Deglaze the pan with chicken stock, add the reserved shanks, cover, and place in the oven. Braise the shanks for approximately one hour or until the meat is very tender, adding additional stock as needed. Remove from the oven and set the shanks aside. Place the saucepan over medium-high heat, incorporate the demi-glace, and bring to a boil. Reduce the heat and simmer until the sauce has thickened. Remove from the heat and strain into a medium saucepan. Season, add the reserved shanks, and set aside, keeping warm.

For the gratin, preheat the oven to 350 degrees. In a large sauté pan over medium-high heat, heat the butter, add the turnip, and sauté until slightly softened. Add the potato and continue to sauté for five minutes. Incorporate the cream, season, and remove from the heat. Sprinkle the bottom of a ceramic gratin dish with garlic and fill with the turnip mixture. Place in the oven and bake until the vegetables have softened and the top of the gratin begins to caramelize. Remove from the oven and set aside.

To serve, spoon some of the gratin onto a plate. Arrange the Brussels sprout leaves in the center of the gratin, place a shank on top, and brush with some of the sauce.

Lamb Loin with Black Trumpet Mushrooms

166

(Serves 2)

For the dish:
14 ounces lamb loin, de-boned and trimmed
1 egg, lightly beaten
Salt and pepper to taste
¼ pound black trumpet mushrooms, cleaned and finely chopped
10 ounces fresh fava beans, shelled
¼ cup heavy cream
2 tablespoons clarified butter
1 cup lamb jus
1 tablespoon unsalted butter

For the garnish:
Fava beans
Black trumpet mushrooms

For the dish, season the lamb loin with salt and pepper, and dip in the egg. Roll the loin in the mushrooms and set aside. In a large saucepan of boiling salted water, add the fava beans, and cook until tender. Remove with a slotted spoon, transfer to the bowl of a food processor fitted with the metal blade attachment, and purée until smooth. Incorporate the cream, season, and set aside. In a large sauté pan, heat the butter, add the lamb, and sauté over medium heat, turning frequently. Sauté for about 12 minutes or until just pink. Remove from pan and set aside for 15 minutes, keeping warm. In a small saucepan, add the lamb jus and bring to a boil. Reduce the heat and simmer until the liquid is reduced by half. Incorporate the butter and season. Remove from the heat and keep warm.

To serve, slice the lamb into ¾-inch thick rounds and reserve. Place a pool of the sauce in the center of the plate and spoon some of the fava bean purée in three points around the plate. Arrange slices of lamb on the purée and garnish with fava beans and mushrooms.

Steamed Loin of Lamb

168

(Serves 4)

For the lamb:
2 8-ounce pieces of lamb tenderloin, trimmed of all fat
¼ teaspoon ground coriander
¼ teaspoon ground cumin
1 clove garlic, minced
Juice of ½ lemon
Freshly ground black pepper
Savoy cabbage
4 scallions
2 cups lamb stock, reduced to ¾ cup
1 tablespoon unsalted butter

Rub each lamb fillet with half the coriander, cumin, garlic and lemon juice. Grind black pepper over all sides. Set aside for two to three hours at room temperature, or refrigerate overnight.

Bring a large pot of water to a boil. Pull off and discard the hard, very dark outer cabbage leaves. Cut out the core and pull the leaves off one by one. You will need about 12 (6 ounces). Put them in boiling water to soften, about 2 minutes. Drain them under cold running water. Put the scallions in the same water to blanch, about 2 minutes. Drain under cold water. Cut each in half crosswise. Cut away the roots.

Spread a kitchen towel on your work surface. Trim the center veins on the cabbage leaves so they lie flat (do not cut them out). Using the dark leaves first, arrange two leaves on the towel so the core ends meet in the middle and they slightly overlap. Place whole or half lighter leaves so you have a solid rectangle about ten inches long and nine inches wide. Put two blanched scallion greens on the cabbage going the long way.

Put one lamb fillet over the scallions to cover. Top with two scallion whites, going in the same direction. Fold the short ends of the cabbage over the lamb and roll up like an egg roll. Place on a 20-inch piece of good quality plastic wrap. Fold over to seal. Tuck in the ends and wrap in another piece of plastic in the other direction. (This is easiest if you have someone to help who can keep the plastic taut as you work.) Repeat with the other lamb fillet and remaining scallions and cabbage. Place the rolled lamb fillets on a steamer rack.

Bring some of the cabbage water to a boil in the bottom of a wok or steamer. Cover the steamer rack and place it over the boiling water. Steam for ten minutes. Let the lamb rest for five minutes, still covered.

Meanwhile, heat the stock and whisk in the butter. Season to taste with freshly ground black pepper.

Remove the plastic from the lamb rolls. Cut off the ends so they are even. Slice each roll into six pieces, about ¾-inch wide. Serve three slice per person on a plate with some of the sauce.

Grilled Lamb Sausage
with Cumin

(Serves 4)

For the sausage:
1 pound boneless lamb shoulder, medium ground
1 pound boneless pork butt, medium ground
¼ pound fresh fat back, medium ground
2 cloves garlic, peeled and minced
1½ tablespoons salt
Black pepper to taste
1 teaspoon sugar
¾ teaspoon ground cumin
¼ small bunch cilantro, stemmed and minced
1 tablespoon cold water
Small sausage casings

For the vinaigrette:
1 tablespoon Dijon mustard
3 tablespoons balsamic vinegar
¾ cup olive oil
Salt and pepper to taste

For the potato salad:
12 small potatoes
1 bunch chives, minced
1 small clove garlic, peeled and minced
1 small red onion, peeled and minced
Salt and pepper to taste

For the dish:
2 bunches watercress, stemmed
Reserved vinaigrette

For the garnish:
Mint sprigs
Pineapple sage blossoms

For the sausage, in a large bowl, combine the ground meats and fat back, garlic, salt, pepper, sugar, cumin, cilantro, and cold water and mix thoroughly. Stuff into sausage casings and tie into twelve 3-ounce links. Arrange on a parchment-lined sheet pan and set aside in the refrigerator.

For the vinaigrette, in a small bowl, combine all of the ingredients and whisk until incorporated. Season and set aside.

For the salad, in a large saucepan of boiling salted water, add the potatoes and cook until tender. Drain and while still warm, slice thinly and place in a large bowl with three tablespoons of the vinaigrette, the chives, garlic, and red onion. Season and set aside.

To finish the sausage, prepare a hot grill. Place the sausages on the grill and cook for 10 to 15 minutes, or to desired doneness. Remove from the grill and keep warm.

To serve, spoon some of the potato salad onto a plate and arrange two of the sausages beside it. Place some of the watercress onto the plate, drizzle with some of the vinaigrette, and garnish the dish with mint sprigs and pineapple sage blossoms.

Loin of Lamb
with Lentils

(Serves 8)

For the vegetables:

2 tablespoons diced carrots (brunoise)

2 tablespoons diced celery (brunoise)

2 tablespoons diced onions (brunoise)

2 tablespoons diced shallots (brunoise)

1 clove garlic, minced

1 tablespoon butter

1 cup lentils

1 tablespoon apple cider vinegar

4 cups chicken stock

1 sprig fresh thyme

1 bay leaf

1 cup heavy cream

For the lamb:

2½ pounds loin of lamb, completely trimmed

Salt and pepper to taste

1½ tablespoons mixed chopped rosemary, thyme and garlic

For the assembly:

1 pound French green beans, ends cut off and washed

24 pearl onions, peeled

1 cup chicken stock

2 tablespoons soft herb-seasoned butter

1 cup heavy cream

2 cups fresh spinach, cleaned washed and blanched

Salt and pepper to taste

For the vegetables, sauté diced vegetables with butter in saucepot. Add lentils, deglaze with vinegar. Add chicken stock, thyme and bay leaf. When lentils are almost cooked, add heavy cream, finish cooking and reserve.

For the lamb, season loin of lamb with salt, pepper and herb mixture. Stir quickly in skillet, roast in oven at 375 degrees for 12-15 minutes. (Should be medium-rare). Reserve. (Meat should set for at least 15 minutes before slicing).

For the assembly, cook French beans in salt water. When done, refresh and reserve. Sauté pearl onions until golden brown. Add some chicken stock and simmer until done. Add French beans and reheat with onions. When liquid has evaporated take away from heat and fold in herb butter. Reserve. Reduce one cup heavy cream by a third. Add blanched spinach, fold in cooked lentils, season with salt and pepper. Spoon on plate, add roasted sliced lamb loin, french beans and pearl onions. Serve.

Grilled Loin
of Lamb

(Serves 4)

For the green peppercorn sauce:

4 tablespoons Cognac

2 tablespoons Port

1 tablespoon green peppercorns

1 cup rich lamb stock

Salt and freshly ground white pepper

4 to 6 tablespoons butter

1 small tomato, diced

1 sprig tarragon, stemmed and minced

1 sprig chervil, stemmed and minced

1 sprig chive, minced

1 sprig thyme, stemmed and minced

Salt and pepper to taste

For the flageolet flan:

6 eggs

1¾ cups heavy cream

1¼ cups puréed cooked fresh flageolet beans

Salt and freshly ground white pepper to taste

For the lamb:

1 lamb loin, boned and trimmed

Olive oil

Salt and freshly ground black pepper to taste

For the dish:

2 cups assorted wild mushrooms, sautéed in butter

4 cups assorted young vegetables, blanched and sautéed in butter

For the garnish:

Fried potato slices

recipe continued on next page

For the peppercorn sauce, in a small saucepan over medium-high heat, combine the Cognac, port and green peppercorns and bring to a boil. Reduce the heat and simmer until the mixture is reduced by two-thirds. Add the lamb stock and bring to a boil. Reduce the heat and simmer until the mixture is slightly reduced. Remove from the heat and set aside.

For the flageolet flan, lightly butter four 4-ounce ramekins. Preheat the oven to 350 degrees. In a medium bowl, combine the eggs and cream and whisk until incorporated. Fold in the purée, season, and fill the prepared ramekins three-fourths full. Place the molds in a water bath, set in the oven, and bake for 10 to 15 minutes, or until set. Remove from the oven and set aside, keeping warm.

For the lamb, prepare a hot grill. Brush the loin with oil, season, and grill to desired doneness. Remove from the grill and set aside to rest for ten minutes before carving. Slice into eight medallions and set aside, keeping warm.

To finish the sauce, bring the sauce to a boil, reduce the heat to low, and gradually add the butter, whisking to combine. Remove from the heat incorporate the remaining ingredients, and season, keeping warm.

To serve, arrange some of the mushrooms onto a plate and arrange two slices of lamb on top. Unmold a flan and set beside the lamb slices. Spoon some of the sauce and arrange the vegetables around the plate and garnish with a fried potato slice.

Lamb Shank with Persillade

171

(Serves 6)

For the shanks:

5 tablespoons olive oil
Salt and pepper to taste
6 lamb shanks, trimmed
6 shallots, peeled and minced
½ carrot, peeled and chopped
½ rib celery, chopped
5 whole black peppercorns
1 sprig of thyme
1 clove garlic, peeled and minced
¾ cup dry white wine
½ teaspoon balsamic vinegar
2 cups lamb stock
Additional lamb stock as needed
½ cup Dijon mustard
½ cup persillade (½ cup bread crumbs and 1 tablespoon minced parsley)
¾ cup veal glace
3 tablespoons butter

For the garnish:

Vegetable gâteau (sautéed slices of eggplant, tomato concasse and
  sautéed zucchini)
Herbed potato cakes, sautéed in butter
Thyme sprigs
Basil sprigs

For the shanks, season the lamb and set aside. In a large saucepan over medium-high heat, heat the oil, add the shanks, and sear until the skin is well caramelized. Set the shanks aside, add the vegetables, herbs, peppercorns, and garlic, and sauté until the vegetables have softened. Return the shanks to the pan and deglaze with white wine, balsamic vinegar, and lamb stock. Cover, place in the oven, and braise for one hour or until the meat is very tender, turning the shanks occasionally and adding additional lamb stock as needed. Remove from oven and place the shanks on a parchment-lined sheet pan. Preheat the broiler, brush the shanks with mustard and coat with the persillade. Place the sheet pan under the broiler and bake until golden browned and crisp. Remove from the broiler and set aside, keeping warm.

For the sauce, place the saucepan over medium-high heat, add the veal glace, and bring to a boil. Reduce the heat and simmer until the sauce has thickened. Strain into a small saucepan, and bring to a simmer. Gradually add the butter, whisking to incorporate, season, and set aside keeping warm.

To serve, spoon some of the sauce onto a plate and set a lamb shank on top. Arrange a vegetable gâteau, three potato cake wedges, and a few garlic cloves on the plate and garnish with sprigs of thyme and basil.

Sukiyaki in a Seashell

(Serves 4)

For the rolled Napa cabbage:

6 leaves Napa (Chinese cabbage), halved lengthwise
1 small red bell pepper, stemmed, seeded, and sliced into thin rings
Soy sauce to taste

For the cooking liquid:

1 cup soy sauce
6 tablespoons sugar
½ cup mirin
1½ cups dashi

For the dish:

4 large mollusk shells
24 ounces beef loin, thinly sliced
8 dried shiitake mushrooms, reconstituted in water
12 1-inch square cubes tofu
16 ounces shungiku or spinach
Zest of two lemons
Reserved rolled napa cabbage
Takuan (yellow pickled daikon), sliced
Purple Japanese eggplant, chopped
Assorted salt-pickled vegetables

For the rolled Napa cabbage, sprinkle one teaspoon of the salt in the bottom of a glass bowl and add the cabbage, red pepper, and remaining salt. Cover with a plate, place a weight such as a light brick or a piece of wood on the plate and set aside in a cool place for 48 hours. Rinse the cabbage and red pepper, place in a medium bowl, and sprinkle with soy sauce. Roll each leaf into a cylinder and reserve with the red pepper rings.

For the cooking liquid, in a medium saucepan, add the soy sauce, sugar, mirin, and dashi and bring to a boil. Remove from the heat and set aside.

To serve, arrange some of the meat, a mushroom, some tofu, and spinach in a mollusk shell, and add some of the cooking liquid. Prepare a burner at the table and cover with sea salt. Place the shell on the sea salt and cook the ingredients at the table to desired doneness. Garnish the sukiyaki with lemon zest and serve with plain white rice, Napa cabbage and pickled vegetables.

Sirloin with Sauce Bordelaise

(Serves 2)

For the sirloin:

2 10-ounce sirloin strip steaks
Salt and freshly ground black pepper to taste
1 tablespoons unsalted butter

For the sauce:

1 tablespoon unsalted butter
1 small shallot, peeled and minced
2 cups red Bordeaux wine
2 sprigs thyme, stemmed and chopped
2 cups demi-glace
8 ounces fresh beef marrow, sliced into ¾-inch pieces
Salt and pepper to taste

For the garnish

Sautéed vegetables
Minced parsley

For the sirloin, season the steaks with salt and pepper and set aside. In a large sauté pan, heat the butter over high heat, add the steaks, and sauté for five minutes on each side. Remove from the pan and keep warm.

For the sauce, in a medium saucepan, heat the butter, add the shallots, and sauté until lightly caramelized. Incorporate the wine and thyme and bring to a boil. Reduce the heat and simmer until the liquid is reduced by two-thirds. Add the demi-glace, bring to a simmer, and reduce by half. Add the marrow, reduce the heat to low, and poach for ten minutes. Remove form the heat, season, and keep warm.

To serve, place steak on plate, and arrange the marrow on top. Pour some of the sauce over the plate and garnish with vegetables and minced parsley.

Roast Tenderloin of Beef
Venison Style

(Serves 4)

For the tenderloin:
2 cups red wine
1 tablespoon cracked black peppercorns
4 juniper berries
1 stalk celery, thinly sliced
1 medium onion, peeled and sliced
4 shallots, minced
2 carrots, peeled and thinly sliced
12 ounces beef tenderloin, trimmed and tied
Salt and pepper to taste
2 tablespoons olive oil
3 cups demi-glace
½ cup red currant jelly
2 tablespoons unsalted butter, softened
Salt and pepper to taste

For the garnish:
Sautéed chanterelles
Whole glazed chestnuts
Wild rice
Blueberry tartelettes
Vegetable pasta tossed in butter

For the tenderloin, in a medium bowl, combine the red wine, peppercorns, juniper berries, and vegetables and set aside for 30 minutes. Strain and separately reserve the vegetables and the liquid. Preheat the oven to 425 degrees. Season the tenderloin, set in a roasting pan and place in the oven to roast for ten minutes. Reduce the heat to 350 degrees and continue to roast to desired doneness. Remove from the oven and set aside to rest for ten minutes before carving. In a large sauce pan, heat the olive oil, add the reserved vegetables, and sauté until softened. Add the reserved marinade and bring to a boil. Reduce the heat and simmer until the liquid is reduced by two-thirds. Add the demi-glace, bring to a simmer, and reduce by half. Strain in to a small saucepan and incorporate the jelly and butter. Season and keep warm.

To serve, slice the roast into ½-inch pieces and place three slices in the center of a plate. Pour some of the sauce around the tenderloin and garnish with chanterelles, chestnuts, wild rice, a blueberry tartelette, and pasta.

Tournedo of Beef
with Roquefort

(Makes 4 servings)

For the sauce:
2 cups brown stock
1 tablespoon green peppercorns

For the tournedos:
4 8-ounce beef tournedos
4 ounces Roquefort cheese
4 slices blanched lean bacon
2 tablespoons olive oil
Salt and pepper to taste

For the garnish:
Julienned and fried parsnips
4 small tomatoes, broiled
Radish sprouts

For the sauce, in a medium saucepan, add the stock and peppercorns, and bring to a boil. Reduce the heat and simmer until the liquid is reduced to three-fourths cup. Remove from the heat and keep warm.

For the beef, make a horizontal incision in each tournedo, no bigger than 1-inch, and fill with some of the Roquefort. Wrap a piece of bacon around each piece and secure with a toothpick. Brush with oil, season, and set aside. Either grill or pan sauté to desired doneness, and set aside.

To serve, spoon some of the sauce on a plate and place a tournedo on top of the sauce. Garnish the plate with fried parsnips, tomato, and sprouts.

Fillet of Beef with Country Ham and Oyster Sauce

(Serves 4)

For the sauce:

7 tablespoons unsalted butter

2 garlic cloves, peeled and chopped

½ small shallot, peeled and minced

2 sprigs parsley, stemmed and minced

2 ounces country ham, finely diced

2 oysters, shucked with their liquor reserved

¼ cup dry white wine

1 quart heavy cream

1 teaspoon tomato paste

½ teaspoon curry powder

Salt and pepper to taste

4 slices country ham, finely julienned

For the dish:

4 8-ounce filet mignon medallions

Salt and pepper to taste

16 oysters, shucked and shells reserved

3 slices bacon

Blanched and julienned leek

Sautéed vegetables

For the garnish:

Minced chives

For the sauce, in a medium sauté pan, heat one tablespoon of the butter, add the garlic, shallots, parsley, and ham and sauté for two minutes. Add the oysters with their liquor and the wine, and simmer two minutes. Add the cream, tomato paste, and curry, and bring to a boil. Reduce the heat and simmer until the liquid is reduced by half. Whisk in the remaining butter, season, and strain into a small saucepan. Add the ham and keep warm.

For the dish, season the filet mignon with salt and pepper. Shuck the oysters, reserving four of the shells, and reserve the liquor for another use. In a small sauté pan, add the bacon and fry until half cooked, remove from the pan and slice transversely into four equal pieces. Wrap 12 of the oysters with bacon, securing with toothpicks and set aside.

To assemble the dish, either sauté or broil the filet mignon to desired doneness and keep warm. Preheat the broiler and arrange the bacon-wrapped oysters on a parchment-lined sheet pan. Place in the oven and bake, turning once, until the bacon is crisp. Poach the remaining four oysters in the sauce, simmering for one minute, or until the edges of the oyster curl. Remove from the heat and set aside.

To serve, place an oyster shell on each plate, fill with of a bed of julienned leek, and arrange three bacon-wrapped oysters on top. Place a filet medallion on the plate and top with a poached oyster and some sauce. Spoon some additional sauce on the bacon-wrapped oysters and sprinkle with minced chives. Serve with sautéed vegetables.

Grilled Sirloin Steak

(Serves 4)

For the Mansion on Turtle Creek Pepper Mixture:

1 cup ground black pepper

⅓ cup ground white pepper

1½ tablespoons ground cayenne pepper

For the black bean sauce:

2 tablespoons corn oil

1 medium onion, peeled and diced

½ green bell pepper, stemmed, seeded, and diced

½ poblano chili pepper, stemmed, seeded, and diced

1 dried ancho chili pepper, stemmed, seeded, soaked in hot water for
   20 minutes, drained, and diced

1 serrano chili, stemmed, seeded, and chopped

1 small jalapeño chili pepper, stemmed, seeded, and chopped

1 tablespoon ground chili powder

2 teaspoons ground cumin

2 teaspoons ground coriander

1 teaspoon paprika

1 clove garlic, peeled and minced

4 sprigs cilantro, stemmed with leaves and stems reserved

For the steaks:

4 8-ounce sirloin steaks

3 tablespoons peanut oil

Salt to taste

1 cup red wine

2 tomatoes, cored and diced

1 cup chicken stock

1½ cups brown veal demi-glace

Reserved meat trimmings

Salt to taste

1 small sweet potato, peeled and diced

1 medium red bell pepper, stemmed, seeded, membranes removed,
   and diced

1 medium yellow bell pepper, stemmed, seeded, membranes removed,
   and diced

1 medium green bell pepper, stemmed, seeded, membranes removed,
   and diced

1 cup cooked black beans, well drained

recipe continued on next page

Grilled Sirloin Steak

continued from previous page

For the garnish:
*Red bell pepper ketchup
Sage leaves

For the Mansion pepper mixture, in a medium bowl, combine all of the ingredients and mix thoroughly. Reserve some of the mixture for the steaks and place the remaining pepper mixture in an air tight jar and seal tightly.

For the steaks, trim the meat of any fat and silver skin, reserving the trimmings for the sauce. Brush the steaks with the peanut oil, season, and set aside.

For the chili sauce, in large sauté pan over medium high heat, heat one tablespoon of the corn oil, add the onion, bell and chili peppers, and sauté until softened. Incorporate the chili powder, cumin, coriander, paprika, garlic, and cilantro stems, and continue to sauté for two minutes. Add the wine and bring to a boil. Reduce the heat and simmer until the mixture is almost dry, stirring frequently to prevent burning. Add tomatoes, chicken stock, demi-glace, meat trimmings, and bring to a boil. Reduce the heat and simmer for

45 minutes, or until the sauce is reduce by one-third. Remove from the heat, strain, and keep warm. In a medium sauté pan, heat the remaining oil, add the potato, and sauté for three minutes, or until softened. Add the peppers and beans and sauté for two minutes. Incorporate the cilantro leaves and add the mixture to the sauce. Remove from the heat, season, and keep warm.

For the steaks, prepare a hot grill. Level the coals or wood and lightly brush the grates with oil. Grill steaks to desired doneness, remove from the grill, and keep warm.

To serve, spoon some of the bean sauce on a plate and place a steak in the center of the plate. Spoon some of the ketchup on either side of the plate and garnish with sage leaves.

To make the red bell pepper ketchup, take equal parts of red bell peppers and tomatoes and add one quarter of this amount in smoked red peppers. Add onions, garlic, serrano chili and cilantro to season the mixture. Sweeten with white Port. Add some chicken stock and some tomato stock and cook down. Let cool and purée.

Medallions of Beef with Ancho Chili Sauce

(Serves 4)

For the ancho chili sauce:
1 tablespoon peanut oil
1 yellow onion, medium-diced
2 shallots, chopped
2 cloves garlic, chopped
1 jalapeño chili pepper, stemmed, seeded, and chopped
4 dried ancho chilies, stemmed and seeded, soaked in hot water for 30 minutes, and drained
3 sprigs fresh cilantro
1 cup chicken stock
1 medium tomato, chopped
½ cup brown veal demi-glace
½ cup heavy cream
½ tablespoon honey
Salt to taste
Juice of a ½ lime

For the jícama-black bean relish:
1 tablespoon peanut oil
1 jícama, peeled and diced
1 red bell pepper, stemmed, seeded and diced
½ cup cooked black beans
Salt to taste

For the beef:
8 3-ounce beef tenderloin filets, trimmed of fat and any silver skin
Salt to taste
Mansion on Turtle Creek Pepper Mixture
3 tablespoons peanut oil

For the garnish:
¼ cup fresh cilantro leaves, washed and dried
Crispy fried onion rings

For the chili sauce, in a large sauté pan over medium high heat, heat the oil, add the onion, and sauté for two minutes. Add the shallots, garlic, and jalapeño, and sauté for two more minutes. Incorporate the ancho chilies, cilantro, chicken stock, and tomato, and bring to a boil. Reduce the heat and simmer for 12 minutes. Add demi-glace, increase heat slightly, and cook for an additional ten minutes or until liquid is reduced by half. Add the cream and heat just to boiling. Pour the mixture into the bowl of a food processor fitted with the metal blade attachment and purée until smooth. Return to the sauté pan, add honey to taste, and season with salt and lime juice. Keep warm.

For the jícama-black bean relish, in medium sauté pan over medium-high heat, heat the oil, add the jícama, pepper, and black beans, and sauté for two minutes or until just heated through. Remove from the heat, season, and keep warm.

For the beef, season the filets with salt and the pepper mixture. In a large sauté pan over medium high heat, heat the oil, add half of the filets, and sear for three minutes on each side. Remove from the pan and keep warm. Repeat the procedure with the remaining filets, and set aside, keeping warm.

To serve, spoon some of the ancho chili sauce on a plate and arrange two filets on top of the sauce. Sprinkle the jícama-black bean relish beside the filets and garnish the plate with cilantro sprigs and onion rings.

Bocaleoni

(Serves 6)

For the filling:
½ pound green asparagus, peeled, cooked, and finely chopped
⅜ pound smoked mozzarella, diced
1 pound ricotta cheese
4 ounces grated Parmesan cheese
2 eggs
1 small sprig sage, stemmed and chopped

For the egg pasta:
1½ cups durum flour
½ cup semolina flour
½ teaspoon salt
3 eggs

For the spinach pasta:
1¾ cups durum flour
½ cup semolina flour
¾ cup fresh spinach purée (about 1 pound raw spinach)
½ teaspoon salt
1 egg

For the beet pasta:
1¾ cups durum flour
½ cup semolina flour
¾ cup fresh beet purée
½ teaspoon salt
1 egg

For the sauce:
6 tablespoons unsalted butter
30 fresh sage leaves
6 ounces pancetta, diced

For the garnish:
Green and white asparagus spears

For the filling, in a medium bowl, combine all of the ingredients and set aside.

For each of the pastas, combine the flours on a board and mix with the salt. Break the eggs into the center and incorporate the flours using a fork. For the spinach and beet, add the purées to the eggs. Knead well, and allow the dough to rest for 30 minutes. Roll through a pasta machine, ending with a thin setting, and cut into thin strips. On a work surface, spread alternating strips of the multi-colored sheets, pressing them lightly together. Carefully roll this through the pasta machine to adhere the layers. Place one tablespoon of the filling about 3 inches apart on a dough sheet. Place another sheet on top, and cut each with a round ravioli cutter, pressing to insure that the edges are sealed.

For the sauce, in a medium sauté pan, add the butter and cook until light brown. Add the sage leaves and pancetta, and sauté until crisp. Remove from the heat and set aside.

To serve, poach the bocaleoni in salted boiling water for 30 seconds, and drain. Arrange three on a plate, and spoon some of the sauce over them. Garnish the plate with green and white asparagus.

Macaroni with Caviar and Onions

(Serves 4)

For the pasta:
5 ounces fresh spinach pasta, rolled into thin sheets
5 ounces fresh tomato pasta, rolled into thin sheets
5 ounces egg pasta, rolled into thin sheets

For the sauce:
¾ cup heavy cream
Salt and pepper to taste
1 small onion, peeled and minced
3 tablespoons Beluga caviar
1 bunch chives, sliced

For the pasta, on a lightly floured work surface, slice the dough into 1½-inch squares and wrap each square around a thin stick approximately the diameter of a pencil. Use a pasta comb to create ridges in the dough, remove from the stick, and set aside.

For the sauce, in a small saucepan over medium heat, add the cream and bring to a boil. Reduce the heat and simmer until the cream is slightly thickened. Remove from the heat, season, and set aside, keeping warm.

To finish the pasta, in a large pot of boiling salted water, add the pasta and cook to desired doneness. Remove from the heat, drain, and toss with the cream and onions.

To serve, mound some of the pasta onto a plate, spoon some of the caviar in the center, and sprinkle with chives.

Farfalle with Mozzarella and Pepper Vodka

(Serves 1)

For the pasta:

¼ cup heavy cream
8 slices zucchini, cut ⅛ -inch thick
1 cup cooked farfalle pasta
1 tablespoon pepper vodka
Salt to taste

Wild asparagus spears
1 Roma tomato, peeled, seeded, diced, and seasoned with salt and pepper
4 ½-inch cubes buffalo mozzarella
4 basil leaves
1 tablespoon shredded Gruyère

For the pasta, in a medium sauté pan over medium low heat, add the cream, zucchini, pasta, vodka, and salt, and bring to a very slow simmer. Arrange the asparagus, tomato, mozzarella, and basil and on the pasta and sprinkle with the Gruyère. When the mozzarella begins to melt, remove from the heat, and slide the pasta onto a plate.

"Alpler" Macaroni

(Serves 4)

For the dish:

2 tablespoons butter
1 10-ounce potato, peeled and diced
4 ounces ham, julienned
1 cup heavy cream
8 ounces cooked macaroni or penne
½ cup diced Emmenthaler cheese
¼ cup diced Gruyère
1 tablespoon grated Sapsago cheese
Salt and pepper to taste

For the garnish:

Fried shallots
Grated Sapsago cheese

In a large sauté pan over medium high heat, heat the butter, add the potato, and sauté until golden brown. Incorporate the ham and cream and bring to a boil. Add the pasta and continue to simmer until the cream thickens. Remove from heat, incorporate the cheeses, and season, keeping warm.

To serve, spoon some of the macaroni on a plate and sprinkle with shallots and cheese.

Angel Hair Pasta with Chanterelles

(Serves 6)

For the dish:

⅜ cup olive oil
½ small shallot, peeled and finely chopped
1 clove garlic, peeled and finely chopped
1½ pounds fresh chanterelle mushrooms, cleaned and sliced
¼ cup white wine
1 cup chicken stock
¼ cup cognac
¼ cup dry Marsala wine
2 tomatoes, peeled, seeded and finely chopped
3 tablespoons chopped fresh herbs (basil, rosemary, oregano, thyme and sage)
Salt and pepper to taste
1 recipe Egg Pasta, cut with the angel hair dye of a pasta machine

For the garnish:

Minced parsley
Chervil sprigs.

For the dish, in a large sauté pan, heat the oil, add the shallots, garlic and mushrooms, and sauté until softened. Add the wine and stock and bring to a boil. Reduce the heat and simmer for ten minutes. Add the cognac and Marsala and remove from heat. Incorporate the tomato and herbs, season, and keep warm.

To serve, cook the pasta in a large saucepan of boiling salted water for 30 seconds. Drain and toss with the sauce. Mound some of the pasta in a shallow bowl, sprinkle with parsley, and garnish with a sprig of chervil.

Risotto with Saffron and Gold Leaf

(Serves 4)

For the risotto:
2 tablespoons butter
½ small onion, peeled and diced
1 cup arborio rice
⅓ cup white wine
4 cups veal stock
Large pinch saffron threads
1 tablespoon butter
1 tablespoon grated Parmesan cheese

For the garnish:
4 sheets 24 carat gold leaf

For the risotto, in a medium sauce pan over medium-high heat, add onions and sauté until softened and translucent. Incorporate the rice and continue to sauté for three minutes, stirring constantly until the grains are well combined and evenly coated with the oil. Add the wine and simmer, stirring occasionally, until the liquid has been absorbed. Add half of the stock and again, simmer while stirring occasionally, until the liquid has been absorbed. Add the remaining stock and saffron and continue to cook until all of the liquid has been absorbed, the mixture is creamy, and the rice is still slightly firm in texture. Remove from the heat, incorporate the butter and cheese, and set aside, keeping warm.

To serve, spoon some of the risotto onto a plate and place a sheet of gold leaf on top.

Mushroom Wontons

(Serves 4)

For the dish:
1 pound fresh mushrooms, or a combination of wild and button
  mushrooms, cleaned
2 tablespoons almond oil
½ cup thinly sliced shallots
2 cloves garlic, peeled and minced
2 jalapeño chili peppers, stemmed, seeded, and minced
½ cup chopped fresh herbs
6 ounces fresh tofu, diced
32-40 3-inch round wonton wrappers
2 cups chicken stock
¼ pound snow peas, stemmed
¼ pound thin asparagus, cleaned
1 red bell pepper, stemmed, seeded, and sliced

For the wontons, reserve six ounces of the best caps, thinly slice the large ones and leave the small ones whole. Finely chop the remaining mushrooms and set aside. In a large sauté pan, heat the oil add the shallots, garlic and jalapeño pepper and sauté until golden. Add the herbs, chopped mushrooms, and tofu and sauté over high heat until the mushrooms are tender and all the liquid has evaporated. Remove from the heat, season, and set aside to cool.

To assemble the wontons, place a wrapper on a flat work surface and place a few teaspoons of the mixture in the center of each wonton skin. Lightly brush the edges with water, fold the wrapper in half to form a crescent, and crimp the edges to seal. Repeat the procedure with the remaining wrappers and filling and set aside on a parchment-lined sheet pan. In a large sauté pan, add the chicken stock and bring to just below a simmer. Add the wontons and poach for five minutes. Remove from the poaching liquid with a slotted spoon, and keep warm. Bring the chicken stock to a boil, reduce the heat and simmer until the liquid is reduced to three-fourths cup. Add the reserved mushroom caps, snow peas, asparagus and red pepper and simmer for two minutes. Add the wontons and remove from the heat.

To serve, spoon six of the wontons on a plate and arrange some of the vegetables around the plate.

Plain Brioche

(Makes 1 8-inch round brioche)

For the brioche:

⅓ ounce fresh yeast or 1 package active dry yeast

2 tablespoons warm water (110 degrees F.)

2¼ cups flour (½ cake flour, ½ bread flour)

½ teaspoon salt

2 tablespoons granulated sugar

3 to 4 medium eggs

6¼ ounces unsalted butter, softened

Flour for kneading

1 egg yolk blended with 1 teaspoon water for egg wash

For the brioche, in the bowl of an electric mixer fitted with the dough hook attachment, add the yeast and water and mix to dissolve. Add the flour, salt, and sugar and mix to combine. Incorporate the eggs and butter and knead on medium speed for six to eight minutes, or until the dough begins to pull away from the sides of the bowl. Remove from the mixer, cover with a clean and dampened kitchen towel, and set aside in the refrigerator for two to three hours. Remove from the bowl, place on a lightly floured work surface, knead for one minute, and reserve. To make brioche à tête, preheat the oven to 400 degrees and grease an 8-inch fluted brioche mold. Pinch off a piece of dough the size of a large egg and set aside. Shape the remaining dough into a smooth ball and place seam-side down in the prepared pan. With a buttered thumb, press into the center of dough, making a ¾-inch indentation. Place the pinched-off portion in the indentation, cover loosely with buttered wax paper, and let rise until doubled in bulk, about one and a half hours. Preheat oven to 400 degrees. Gently brush brioche with egg wash, place in the oven, and bake for 35 to 40 minutes. Remove from the oven, turn out onto a rack, and cool slightly, top side up.

Note: This recipe can also be made into petites brioches by placing the dough into smaller pans and dividing the dough in fourths. The procedure is the same, but the baking time is reduced. Place these balls side by side in a large loaf pan. Let rise until doubled and bake as directed above.

Fruit Brioche

(Makes 1 8-inch round brioche)

For the brioche:

⅓ ounce fresh yeast or 1 package active dry yeast

2 tablespoons warm water (110 degrees F.)

2¼ cups flour (½ cake flour, ½ bread flour)

½ teaspoon salt

2 tablespoons granulated sugar

¾ teaspoon ground cinnamon

3 medium eggs

6 ¼ ounces butter, softened

4 dried dates, pitted and chopped

4 dried figs, chopped

2 tablespoons chopped pecans

2 tablespoons pistachios, shelled and halved

Flour for kneading

1 egg yolk blended with 1 teaspoon water for egg wash

For the fruit brioche, in the bowl of an electric mixer fitted with the dough hook attachment, add the yeast and water and mix to dissolve. Add the flour, salt, sugar, and cinnamon and mix to combine. Incorporate the eggs and butter and knead on medium speed for six to eight minutes, or until the dough begins to pull away from the sides of the bowl. Fold in the fruit and nuts and remove the bowl from the mixer. Cover with a clean and dampened kitchen towel and set aside in the refrigerator for two to three hours. Remove from the bowl, place on a lightly floured work surface, knead for one minute, and reserve. To make brioche à tête, preheat the oven to 400 degrees and grease an 8-inch fluted brioche mold. Pinch off a piece of dough the size of a large egg and set aside. Shape the remaining dough into a smooth ball and place seam-side down in the prepared pan. With a buttered thumb, press into the center of dough, making a ¾-inch indentation. Place the pinched-off portion in the indentation, cover loosely with buttered wax paper, and let rise until doubled in bulk, about one and a half hours. Preheat oven to 400 degrees. Gently brush brioche with egg wash, place in the oven, and bake for 35 to 40 minutes. Remove from the oven, turn out onto a rack, and cool slightly, top side up.

Note: This recipe can also be made into petites brioches by placing the dough into smaller pans and dividing the dough in fourths. The procedure is the same, but the baking time is reduced. Place these balls side by side in a large loaf pan. Let rise until doubled and bake as directed above.

Vegetable Brioche

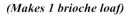

(Makes 1 brioche loaf)

For the brioche:

⅓ ounce fresh yeast or 1 package active dry yeast
2 tablespoons warm water (110 degrees F.)
2¼ cups flour (½ cake flour, ½ bread flour)
1 teaspoon salt
2 tablespoons granulated sugar
3 to 4 eggs
6¼ ounces butter, softened
1 small carrot, peeled and julienned
1 small eggplant, stemmed and julienned
1 small bunch broccoli, sliced into florets
Flour for kneading

For the brioche, in the bowl of an electric mixer fitted with the dough hook attachment, add the yeast and water and mix to dissolve. Add the flour, salt, and sugar, and mix to combine. Incorporate the eggs and butter and knead on medium speed until the dough comes together into a ball and begins to pull away from the sides of the bowl. Add the carrots, zucchini, and eggplant, knead until incorporated, and remove from the mixer. Line a #10 can or mold with parchment paper. With the can on its side, stand the broccoli florets in a row down the middle of the can. Carefully place the dough in the can, place upright on a parchment-lined sheet pan, and set aside in a warm place to rise for one hour. Preheat the oven to 400 degrees, cover the can with another sheet pan, and bake for 30 to 40 minutes. Remove from the oven, cool slightly, and remove from the can. Slice transversely through the broccoli florets into ½-inch thick rounds and serve warm.

Big Apple Dessert

200

(Serves 10)

For the apple mixture:
6 to 7 Granny Smith apples
Juice of ½ lemon
4 tablespoons butter
1½ tablespoons Calvados
2 cups apple cider reduced to ⅓ cup
1 tablespoon apple purée

For the apple bavarian:
1 tablespoon unflavored gelatin
1 cup milk
4 egg yolks
1 teaspoon sugar
2 egg whites
1 tablespoon sugar
1 cup heavy cream
1 tablespoon sugar

For the cherry sauce:
12 ounces kiln-dried cherries
½ bottle Beaujolais
1 cup sugar
2 cups water
3 tablespoons arrowroot

For the garnish:
Cookies baked into shape of heart or apple
Marzipan leaves and stems
Whipped cream
Cream puff ornaments

For the apple mixture, peel and core apples. Scoop out 30 parisiennes. Coat with lemon juice and sauté in a little of the butter until brown. Set aside. Cut rest of apple into ½-inch pieces and sauté in remaining butter until browned. Deglaze with Calvados. Blend with reduced cider and apple purée. Mince apple mixture and refrigerate.

For the bavarians, soften gelatin in a third of the milk. Set aside. Heat remaining milk. Combine egg yolks and one teaspoon sugar and stir this mixture into hot milk. Cook until slightly thickened. Do not boil. Add softened gelatin and cool mixture. Whip egg whites with one tablespoon sugar. Whip heavy cream with one tablespoon sugar. Fold whipped egg whites into cooled egg yolk mixture and fold in the whipped cream. Add cooled, chopped apples and blend without overmixing. Pipe into individual molds and refrigerate.

For cherry sauce, combine cherries, Beaujolais, sugar and water. Bring to a boil and stir until thickened. Refrigerate for two days. Drain, bring juice to a boil and thicken with arrowroot.

To serve, place apple bavarian on cookie base, surround with cherry sauce and decorate with sautéed apple parisiennes, whipped cream, cream puff ornament and marzipan stems and leaves.

Cheese Strudel with Sauce Anglaise

202

(Serves 15)

For the sauce anglaise:
2 cups milk
1 vanilla bean, split and seeds scraped and reserved or ½ teaspoon
  vanilla extract
4 egg yolks
⅔ cup granulated sugar

For the strudel:
1 pound farmers' cheese or any soft unaged cheese
1 pound cream cheese
6 ounces butter, softened
½ cup crème fraîche
12 egg yolks, lightly beaten
9 ounces granulated sugar
Zest of 1 lemon
Salt to taste
10 egg whites
10 ounces melted butter
4 ounces white bread crumbs, toasted
5 ounces raisins
1 recipe strudel dough, (recipe on page 322)
Confectioners' sugar for dusting

recipe continued on next page

Cheese Strudel with

Sauce Anglaise
continued from previous page

For the garnish:
Melted chocolate
Sliced strawberries

For the sauce anglaise, in a medium saucepan, bring the milk, vanilla bean, and seeds to a boil. In a medium bowl, whisk together the egg yolks and sugar. Remove the milk from the heat and temper the egg yolk mixture, adding one-fourth of the boiled milk while whisking constantly. Pour the tempered egg yolks back into the milk and stir over medium heat with a wooden spoon. When the mixture thickens enough to coat the back of the spoon, remove from the heat, pour through a fine strainer, and cool in an ice bath.

For the strudel, in the bowl of an electric mixer fitted with the paddle attachment, add the farmers' cheese, cream cheese, butter, and crème fraîche, and beat on high power until smooth. Incorporate the beaten egg yolks, half of the sugar, the zest and salt, and mix until smooth. In another bowl of an electric mixer fitted with the whip attachment, add the whites and remaining sugar, and beat until stiff peaks form. Fold into cheese mixture and set aside. To assemble the strudel, preheat the oven to 325 degrees. On a flat work surface lined with a tablecloth, pull the dough to desired thinness, and brush with melted butter. Sprinkle the dough with bread crumbs and raisins, cover with batter, and using the tablecloth, roll starting at the short end into a cylinder approximately 3-inches in diameter. Place on a parchment-lined sheet pan, brush with butter, and place in the oven for 30 minutes, or until golden brown and crisp. Remove from the oven and set aside to cool slightly.

To serve, dust the strudel with confectioner's sugar and slice into 3-inch pieces. Spoon a pool of sauce on a plate and drizzle decoratively with melted chocolate. Place a piece of strudel beside the sauce and arrange a few strawberries around the plate.

Grape Strudel with Riesling Sauce

(Serves 15)

For the sauce:
1 cup Riesling
1 cinnamon stick
Juice of ½ lemon
1 whole clove
4 egg yolks
1 teaspoon cornstarch
2 egg whites
4 ounces granulated sugar

For the filling:
6 ounces butter, softened
8 ounces granulated sugar
7 egg yolks
16 ounces almond flour
Juice of 2 lemons
2 tablespoons cherry brandy
8 egg whites

For the strudel:
10 ounces melted butter
4 pounds white grapes, seeded and sliced
1 recipe strudel dough, (recipe on page 322)

For the garnish:
Confectioners' sugar for dusting
Raisins
Sliced green grapes
Black grapes
Mint sprigs

For the sauce, in a medium saucepan, add the wine, cinnamon, lemon juice and clove and bring to a boil. Remove from heat and set aside for ten minutes. In a small bowl, add the yolks and cornstarch, and mix with a wooden spoon until well combined and smooth. Remove the cinnamon and clove from the reserved wine mixture and incorporate the yolks. Place the pan over low heat and cook, stirring constantly, until the mixture coats the back of the spoon. Remove from the heat and set aside. In the bowl of an electric mixer fitted with the whip attachment, add the whites and sugar and whip until stiff peaks form. Fold into the wine mixture and reserve.

For the filling, in the bowl of an electric mixer fitted with the paddle attachment, add the butter and half of the sugar and beat until light and creamy. Gradually add the egg yolks, one at a time, scraping the bowl after each addition. Incorporate the flour, lemon juice, and brandy, mix until well combined, and set aside. In the bowl of an electric mixer fitted with the whip attachment, add the whites and whip until frothy. Gradually add the remaining sugar and continue to whip until stiff peaks form. Fold the whites into the yolk mixture and reserve.

To prepare the strudel, preheat the oven to 350 degrees. On a flat work surface lined with a tablecloth, pull the strudel dough to desired thinness and brush with butter. Spread the filling over two-thirds of the dough, sprinkle with grapes, and roll into a cylinder, approximately 3-inches in diameter. Place on a parchment-lined sheet pan, brush with butter, set in the oven to bake for 30 minutes, or until golden brown and crisp. Remove from the oven and set aside to cool slightly.

To serve, dust the strudel with confectioners' sugar and slice into 3-inch pieces. Place a piece of strudel on a plate and spoon some of the sauce beside it. Sprinkle some raisins on the sauce and garnish the plate with grapes and a sprig of mint.

Apple Strudel

(Serves 15)

For the strudel:

1 recipe strudel dough, (recipe on page 322)
10 ounces butter, melted
8 ounces white bread crumbs, toasted
6 pounds tart, baking apples, peeled, cored and cut into
 ⅛-inch thick slices
10 ounces granulated sugar
1 ounce ground cinnamon
3 ounces chopped walnuts
6 ounces raisins

For the garnish:

Confectioners' sugar for dusting
Sliced apples

For the strudel, preheat the oven to 350 degrees. Pull the dough to desired thinness, brush with melted butter, and sprinkle with bread crumbs. Arrange a layer of apple slices on the dough and sprinkle sugar, cinnamon, walnuts, and raisins. Using a tablecloth, roll the strudel into a cylinder 3-inches in diameter, and transfer to a parchment-lined sheet pan. Brush with melted butter and place in the oven to bake for 30 minutes or until golden brown. Remove from the oven and set aside to cool.

To serve, dust the strudel with confectioners' sugar and slice into 3-inch pieces. Place a piece of strudel on a plate and arrange some of the apple slices beside it.

Chocolate Strudel
with Eggnog

(Serves 15)

For the strudel:

6 egg yolks
7 ounces granulated sugar
3 ounces butter, softened
6 egg whites
12 ounces bittersweet chocolate, finely grated
7 ounces almond flour
6 ounces raisins
1 recipe strudel dough, (recipe on page 322)
8 ounces melted butter

For eggnog sauce:

1½ cups heavy cream, whipped until semi-stiff
1 cup eggnog

For the dish:

Confectioners' sugar for dusting
Melted chocolate
Sliced dates
Mint sprigs

For the strudel, in the bowl of an electric mixer fitted with the whip attachment, add the egg yolks, half of the sugar, and the butter, and whip on high power until frothy. In another bowl of an electric mixer fitted with a whip attachment, add the whites and remaining sugar, and whip until stiff peaks are formed. Fold the whites into the yolk mixture, incorporate the chocolate, almond flour, and raisins, and set aside. To assemble the strudel, preheat the oven to 275 degrees. On a flat work surface, pull the strudel dough to desired thinness, and brush with melted butter. Spread the chocolate mixture on the dough and using a tablecloth, roll into a cylinder 3-inches in diameter. Place on a parchment-lined sheet pan, brush with butter, and place in the oven for 30 minutes or until golden brown and crisp. Remove form the oven and set aside to cool slightly.

For the eggnog sauce, in a large bowl, add the whipped cream, fold in the eggnog, and set aside.

To serve, dust the strudel with confectioners' sugar and slice into 3-inch pieces. Spoon a pool of the sauce on a plate and drizzle decoratively with melted chocolate. Place a piece of strudel beside the sauce and garnish the plate with dates and a sprig of mint.

Apple Cranberry Cobbler

204

(Serves 8)

For the cobbler:
3 tablespoons butter
8 ounces fresh or frozen cranberries
⅓ cup applesauce
1⅓ cups brown sugar
1½ teaspoons cinnamon
⅓ cup golden raisins
⅓ cup walnuts, chopped
7 apples, peeled and sliced

For cobbler topping:
½ cup all-purpose flour
½ cup brown sugar
4 tablespoons butter, at room temperature
1 teaspoon cinnamon

For the garnish:
Vanilla ice cream

For the cobbler, melt butter in a 4-quart saucepan and stir in cranberry sauce, applesauce and brown sugar. Mix over low heat until combined. Mix in cinnamon, raisins and walnuts. Add sliced apples and cook over medium heat for 15 to 20 minutes or until apples begin to soften but still hold their shape. Place apple filling in eight individual baking dishes or one 2-quart baking dish. Preheat oven to 375 degrees.

For cobbler topping, in a mixer, combine all the ingredients until combined. Do not over mix. Sprinkle topping over apple mixture so that it is well covered. Place in oven and cook 30 to 40 minutes or until apples are tender. If top of cobbler begins to darken before cobbler is finished, cover with a piece of aluminum foil. Serve warm with vanilla ice cream.

Salzburger Soufflé

205

(Serves 2)

For the Soufflé:
10 egg whites
6 ounces confectioners' sugar
4 egg yolks,
1½ ounces all-purpose flour
2 ounces heavy cream
1 ounce melted butter
Confectioners' sugar

For the garnish:
Mint sprigs
Raspberries
Granulated sugar

For soufflé, preheat the oven to 400 degrees. In the bowl of an electric mixer fitted with the whip attachment, add the yolks and whip until thickened and lemon colored. Add the flour and mix to combine. In another bowl of an electric mixer, add the whites and sugar and whip until stiff peaks form. Fold into the yolk mixture and set aside. In a small saucepan over medium low heat, add the cream and butter and cook until heated through. Pour into a shallow baking dish and cover with the egg mixture. Place in the oven and bake for ten minutes or until golden brown. Remove from the oven and set aside.

To serve, dust the soufflé with confectioners' sugar and garnish with a mint sprig. Sprinkle the raspberries with sugar and serve with the soufflé.

Basic Strudel Dough

(Makes 16 portions)

For the dough:
11 ounces flour
1 egg yolk
1 tablespoon vegetable oil
⅓ ounce salt
½ cup water
Vegetable oil to brush the dough

For the dough place flour, egg yolk, oil, salt and water in a mixing bowl equipped with a dough hook. Mix well until dough is completely smooth and

free of any lumps. Remove from the bowl and form the dough into a ball, place on a floured surface and brush generously with the oil. Let rest for 30 minutes.

Place a linen cloth over a 4 x 2 foot table and dust the surface with flour. Place the dough in the center of the cloth, dust with flour, and with a rolling pin, gently roll the dough until it measures about 3 x 1 foot. Now begin pulling the dough with the back of your hands until it is paper thin.

Fill strudel dough with desired filling, cut of any excess dough and with the help of the cloth, roll up the strudel. Place on a baking sheet and brush with melted butter. Baking time will vary depending on the type of filling.

Prune and Apricot Fritters with Red Wine Sauce

(Serves 1)

For the batter:
1 cup white wine
3 egg yolks
7 ounces flour
1 tablespoon vegetable oil
Salt to taste
3 egg whites
1½ ounces sugar
4 cups vegetable oil for frying

For the prune filling:
3 prunes
3 whole almonds
¼ cup prune brandy

For the apricot filling:
1 fresh apricot, peeled
½ teaspoon almond paste
1 tablespoon flour

For the red wine sauce:
1 cup red wine
1½ ounces sugar
Pinch ground cinnamon
Juice of a half lemon
⅓ ounce cornstarch
1 ounce slivered almonds

For the vanilla cream:
½ cup sauce anglaise
½ cup heavy cream, whipped to soft peaks

For the garnish:
Whipped cream
Chocolate shavings
Vanilla bean
Mint sprigs

For the batter, in a large bowl, add the wine, yolks, flour, oil and salt, and whisk until well combined and smooth. Cover with plastic wrap and set aside for 30 minutes.

For prune filling, carefully pit the prunes without slicing all the way through, insert the almonds in place of the pits, and place in a small bowl. Cover the prunes with brandy and set aside to marinate for two hours.

For apricot filling, make a small incision in the apricot to remove the pit. Fill the opening with almond paste, roll in flour, and set aside.

For the red wine sauce, in a medium saucepan over high heat, add three-fourths of the wine, the sugar, cinnamon, and lemon juice, and bring to a boil. In a small bowl, combine the remaining wine and cornstarch, and while whisking constantly, incorporate with the boiling wine mixture. Return to a boil, reduce the heat, and simmer for five minutes. Remove form the heat and strain into a medium bowl. Add the almonds, place a piece of plastic wrap on the surface to prevent a skin from forming, and set aside to cool.

For the vanilla cream, in a large bowl, add the sauce anglaise, fold in the whipped cream, and set aside.

To finish the batter, in the bowl of an electric mixer fitted with the whip attachment, add the whites and sugar, and whip to stiff peaks. Gently fold into the reserved wine batter and set aside.

To finish the fritters, in a large saucepan, heat the oil to 325 degrees. Dip the prunes and apricots in the batter, place in the oil, and fry until golden brown and crisp. Remove with a slotted spoon, and set aside to drain on paper towels, keeping warm.

To serve, ladle some of the red wine sauce on a plate and spoon some of the whipped cream beside it. Roll the prune fritters in chocolate shavings and arrange on top of the red wine sauce. Slice the apricot fritter open and set on top of the whipped cream. Halve the vanilla bean, arrange on top of the fritters and garnish the plate with mint sprigs.

Berries in Puff Pastry

(Serves 4)

For the pastry:
8 ounces puff pastry

For the berries:
2 cups sparkling wine
½ cup confectioners' sugar
2 cups wild strawberries, stemmed
2 cups raspberries
2 cups strawberries, stemmed
Juice of ½ lemon

For the dish:
½ cup whipped cream
Powdered sugar

For the garnish:
Halved strawberries with stems

recipe continued on next page

continued from previous page

For the pastry, preheat oven to 350 degrees. On a lightly floured surface, roll the pastry to 1/8-inch thickness, and using a sharp knife, cut into four 2x3-inch rectangles. Arrange on a parchment-lined sheet pan and set aside in the refrigerator to chill for one hour. Place in the oven and bake for 18-20 minutes, or until golden brown and crisp. Remove from the oven and set aside to cool.

For the berries, in a medium saucepan, add the wine and sugar and bring to a boil. Remove from the heat, add the berries and lemon juice and set aside to cool.

To serve, halve one of the pastry rectangles transversely. Place the bottom half on a plate and spoon some of the berry mixture and whipped cream on top of the pastry. Dust the top one-half of the rectangle with confectioners' sugar, place over the berry mixture, and garnish the plate with strawberry halves.

Savarin with Grand Marnier

206

(Serves 8)

For the savarin:
2½ cups all-purpose flour, sifted
1 teaspoon dry yeast
4 eggs
5 ounces unsalted butter
½ tablespoon salt
1¼ tablespoons granulated sugar
4 cups water
1 cup Grand Marnier
1½ cups granulated sugar
½ cup apricot glaze or apricot jelly thinned with water

For the orange sauce:
½ cup water
¾ cup granulated sugar
8 oranges, peeled, white membrane removed, sectioned, and seeded

For the garnish:
Whipped cream
Candied orange zest
Mint sprigs
Orange sections
Raspberries

For the savarin, lightly butter eight small savarin molds and set aside on a parchment-lined sheet pan. In a small bowl, combine the yeast and water and set aside for five minutes or until the mixture is foamy. In the bowl of an electric mixer fitted with the whip attachment, combine the flour, yeast mixture, and eggs, and mix until the dough comes together to form a ball. Switch to the dough hook attachment and continue to knead for five minutes, or until the dough is smooth and elastic. Remove the bowl from the mixer, arrange a layer of butter on top of the dough, and cover in plastic wrap. Set the bowl aside in a warm place for two hours or until the dough doubles in bulk. Preheat the oven to 325 degrees. Return the bowl to the mixer fitted with the hook attachment and incorporate the butter, salt, and sugar, mixing until well combined and smooth. Remove the dough from the bowl, divide into eight pieces, and place each piece into one of the prepared molds. Set aside in a warm place to rise for one hour. Place the savarins in the oven and bake for 12 to 15 minutes or until golden brown. Remove from the oven, unmold, and set aside to cool. In a medium saucepan over medium-high heat, combine the water, sugar, and Grand Marnier and bring to a boil. Reduce the heat and simmer for ten minutes. Remove from the heat and set aside. Arrange the savarins on a metal cake rack and generously brush with the syrup. Brush the savarins with apricot glaze and set aside.

For the orange sauce, in a small saucepan over medium heat, combine the sugar and water and bring to a boil. Reduce the heat and simmer for five minutes, incorporate the orange sections, and continue to simmer over low heat for ten minutes. Place in the bowl of a food processor fitted with the metal blade attachment and purée until smooth. Strain and set aside.

To serve, spoon some of the orange sauce onto a plate and place a savarin in the center. Spoon some whipped cream on top of the savarin, sprinkle with orange zest, and garnish with a sprig of mint. Arrange orange sections and zest around the plate and garnish with raspberries.

Ginger Custard with Warm Berries

(Serves 12)

For the custard:
1 quart half and half or light cream
1 cup sugar
4 eggs
5 egg yolks
2 tablespoons grated fresh ginger
3 tablespoons Grand Marnier or Cointreau

For the berries:
1 bunch seedless grapes
1 pint strawberries
½ pint raspberries
1 orange
2 lemons
½ cup sugar
Extra berries for garnish

Preheat oven to 350 degrees. In a saucepan, warm the cream with the sugar. While the mixture is heating, beat the eggs and egg yolks with the ginger in a large bowl. Add the warm cream to the eggs, whisking well, and then add the Grand Marnier. Strain through a fine sieve.

Pour into 12 well-buttered ramekins and place in a large baking pan. Pour water half way up the sides of the ramekins, cover the ban and bake until the custard is set, about 30 minutes.

For the sauce, remove the zest from the orange and lemon, and juice all citrus. Combine with grapes and berries in a saucepan and bring to a boil over medium heat. Simmer for five minutes, stirring constantly, and then pass through a food mill or purée in a food processor fitted with a steel blade.

To serve, invert custards onto serving plates and garnish with whole berries. Spoon sauce around sides.

Chocolate Tart

(Serves 6)

For the tarts:
7 egg yolks
½ cup sugar
9 ounces bittersweet chocolate, melted
6 ounces unsalted butter, melted
7 egg whites
1 pint fresh raspberries

For the garnish:
Crème anglaise
Confectioners' sugar
Vanilla ice cream
Cocoa powder

For the garnish:
Mint leaves

For the tart, preheat oven to 350 degrees, lightly butter and flour six 4-inch stainless steel ring molds, and reserve on a parchment-lined sheet pan. In the bowl of an electric mixer fitted with the whip attachment, add the egg yolks and half of the sugar, and whip until thickened, lemon colored, and the mixture forms a ribbon when the whip is lifted. Incorporate the chocolate and butter and set aside. In the bowl of an electric mixer fitted with the whip attachment, add the egg whites and whip on medium speed until light and frothy. Increase the speed to high and slowly add the remaining sugar, whipping until the meringue is light and glossy. Gently fold the meringue into the chocolate mixture, fill the reserved molds three-fourth full, and place in the oven. Bake for 15 minutes, remove from the oven, and set aside to cool for five minutes. In the bowl of a food processor fitted with the metal blade attachment, add the raspberries, and purée until smooth. Strain into a small bowl and set aside. Top each tart with a tablespoon of the purée, fill the remainder of the molds with the rest of the batter, and return to the oven to bake for ten minutes. Remove from the oven and set aside.

To serve, spoon some of the crème anglaise on a plate. Unmold one of the tarts and dust with confectioners' sugar. Place a tart in the center of the plate, spoon a quenelle of ice cream rolled in cocoa beside it, and garnish the plate with mint leaves.

Poached Pear
in Phyllo

(Serves 10)

For the pears:
1¾ cups granulated sugar
6 cups water
1 bottle dry white wine
Juice of 4 lemons
1 teaspoon saffron threads
10 brown-skinned Bartlett pears

For the baskets:
10 sheets phyllo dough
4 ounces melted butter

For the nut mixture:
3 cups heavy cream
1 cup honey
1 tablespoon ground cinnamon
1 cup walnuts, toasted and chopped
1 cup hazelnuts, toasted and chopped
1 cup pecans, toasted and chopped
½ cup blanched almonds, chopped
½ cup shelled pistachios, toasted and chopped

For the sauce:
½ cup black currant purée
¼ cup orange juice
¼ cup sugar
Zest of 1 orange

For the garnish:
Julienned candied orange peel
Julienned candied lemon peel
Mint sprigs
Confectioners' sugar

For the pears, in a large saucepan, add the sugar, water, wine, and lemon juice and bring to a boil. Place one-fourth cup of the poaching liquid in a small bowl, add the saffron threads, and set aside to steep for five minutes. Return to the saucepan and bring to just below a simmer. Peel the pears, starting 1-inch from the top and keeping the stem intact and core using a melon baller. Place immediately in the saucepan and poach over medium heat for 15 minutes. Remove from the heat and set aside to cool in the syrup.

For the baskets, preheat the oven to 350 degrees. Cut each piece of phyllo into fourths and brush with butter. Press the four pieces into a 5-inch tart mold and decoratively fold the edges. Repeat the procedure with the remaining phyllo and place the molds on a parchment-lined sheet pan. Set in the oven and bake for ten minutes or until golden brown. Remove from the oven and set aside.

For the nuts, in a small saucepan, add the cream and bring to a boil. Remove from the heat, add the honey and cinnamon, and whisk until cool. Stir in the nuts and set aside.

For the sauce, combine all of the ingredients and bring to a boil. Reduce the heat and simmer for two minutes. Strain and chill in an ice bath.

To serve, place two tablespoons of the sauce on a plate and set a phyllo basket beside it. Place a pear in the basket and spoon two tablespoons of the nut mixture around the pear. Garnish the plate with the candied peel and a mint sprig and dust with confectioners' sugar.

Orange Scented
Raspberry Gratin

(Serves 6)

For the pastry cream:
1¼ tablespoon gelatin
½ cup orange juice
¾ cup heavy cream
9 egg yolks
⅓ cup flour
5 tablespoons honey

For the meringue:
9 egg whites
½ cup granulated sugar
½ cup plus 3 tablespoons honey

For the dish:
10 ounces fresh raspberries
Confectioners' sugar
Orange flavored crème anglaise

For the garnish:
Raspberries

recipe continued on next page

Orange Scented
Raspberry Gratin
continued from previous page

For the pastry cream, in a small bowl, sprinkle the gelatin over one-fourth cup of cold water, and set aside to soften for 15 minutes. In a small saucepan, add the orange juice and cream, and bring to a boil. Bring a large saucepan filled with 2-inches of water to a simmer. In a large bowl, whisk together the egg yolks, flour, and honey, and place over the pan, making sure the bottom of the bowl does not come in contact with the water. Gradually add the hot cream mixture to the eggs and cook over the pan of simmering water, stirring constantly, until smooth and thickened. Incorporate the gelatin, remove from the heat, and cool in an ice bath.

For the meringue, in the bowl of an electric mixer fitted with the whip attachment, add the whites, and whip to soft peaks. In a small saucepan, add the sugar and water, and bring to a boil. Reduce the heat and simmer until thickened. Remove from the heat and while whipping constantly, gradually add to the whites, beating until stiff and glossy. Incorporate the honey and remove from the mixer. Fold the meringue into the cooled pastry cream and set aside.

To assemble the gratin, preheat a broiler, and place six 4-inch in diameter stainless steel ring molds on a parchment-lined sheet pan. Fill the molds with the pastry cream mixture leaving a ½-inch from the top of the mold and arrange a layer of raspberries on top. Cover with more of the pastry cream mixture and set aside in the refrigerator to chill for one hour. Remove from the refrigerator, dust with confectioners' sugar, and place under the broiler to brown slightly. Remove from the broiler and set aside.

To serve, spoon some of the orange crème anglaise on a plate. Unmold a gratin, place in the center of the plate, and garnish with raspberries.

Timbale of Chocolate with Berries and Mint Cream

210

(Serves 8)

For the timbales:
Butter
Flour for dusting
3 ounces bittersweet chocolate, chopped
3 ounces semi-sweet chocolate, chopped
⅔ cup plus 2 tablespoons confectioners' sugar
4 ounces unsalted butter, softened
4 egg yolks, room temperature
¼ cup raspberry preserves
2 tablespoons framboise, or other berry liqueur
4 egg whites, room temperature
⅔ cup all-purpose flour, sifted

For the berry mixture:
½ cup ripe strawberries
½ cup ripe raspberries
½ cup ripe blackberries
¼ cup raspberry purée
1 tablespoon framboise, or other berry liqueur
3 tablespoons granulated sugar

For mint cream:
2 cups heavy cream
½ cup granulated sugar
1 vanilla bean, split (or 1 teaspoon vanilla)
4 egg yolks
2 cups fresh mint leaves
¼ cup simple syrup (equal parts of sugar and water heated to dissolve the sugar)
1 tablespoon crème de menthe

For the garnish:
White chocolate shavings
Whipped cream
Mint sprigs
Cocoa powder

For the timbales, preheat oven to 325 degrees. Butter eight timbale molds, line the bottom of the molds with parchment paper, and dust the sides with flour. In a medium bowl, add the chocolates and set aside. Bring a medium saucepan filled with 2-inches of water to a boil. Reduce the heat to a simmer and place the bowl of chocolate over the water making sure the bottom of the bowl does not touch the water. Melt the chocolate, remove from the heat, and whisk until cooled. In the bowl of an electric mixer fitted with the paddle attachment, add two-thirds cup of the sugar and the butter and beat until light and creamy. Add the egg yolks, one at a time, scraping down the sides of the bowl with a spatula, and mixing well between each addition. Incorporate the preserves, framboise, and reserved melted chocolate, remove from the mixer, and set aside. In the bowl of an electric mixer fitted with the whip attachment, add the egg whites and the remaining two tablespoons of sugar and whip until stiff peaks form. Sift the flour over the chocolate mixture, fold to incorporate, and then fold in the whites. Fill the molds three-fourths full and place the timbales in a baking pan. Fill the pan with enough water to reach half way up the sides of the molds, place in the oven, and bake for 40 to 45 minutes in the center of the oven. Remove the molds from the pan and cool on a wire rack.

For the berry mixture, in a medium bowl, combine all of the ingredients and set aside for one hour.

recipe continued on next page

327

For the mint cream, in a small saucepan, add the cream, half of the sugar, and the vanilla bean, and bring to a boil. Remove from the heat and set aside. In the bowl of an electric mixer fitted with the whip attachment, add the egg yolks and remaining sugar, and whip until thickened and lemon colored. Slowly pour the reserved cream into the egg yolks, whisking constantly, and then return the sauce to the pan. Cook over low heat, stirring constantly, until the mixture is thick enough to coat the back of a spoon. Do not allow the sauce to boil or the egg yolks will curdle. Remove from the heat and set aside. In the bowl of a food processor fitted with a metal blade attachment, add the mint and simple sugar and purée until smooth. Add to the sauce, incorporate the crème de menthe, and cool in an ice bath.

To serve, unmold the timbales in the center of a plate. Spoon some of the mint cream and berries around the plate, garnish with white chocolate shavings, whipped cream, and mint sprigs, and dust with cocoa powder.

Apricot Ravioli with Peach Sauce

(Serves 6)

For the ravioli dough:

4 ounces dried apricots, softened in hot water and squeezed
1 cup bread flour
1 small egg
2 tablespoons granulated sugar
Flour for kneading

For the ravioli filling:

1½ teaspoon butter
6 fresh apricots, peeled and finely diced
¼ cup granulated sugar
¼ teaspoon vanilla

For the ravioli assembly:

Flour for rolling
1 egg, lightly beaten
3 cups simple syrup

For the sauce:

3 fresh peaches, peeled and diced
½-inch piece ginger, peeled and minced
2 tablespoon granulated sugar

For the garnish:

Raspberry coulis
Fresh apricot slices
Fresh blackberries
Mint sprigs

For the ravioli dough, in the bowl of the food processor fitted with a metal blade attachment, add the apricots and purée until smooth. Add the flour, egg and sugar, and process until the dough comes together to form a ball, adding additional flour if necessary. Transfer the dough to a lightly floured work surface and lightly knead for five minutes. Cover with plastic wrap and set aside for two hours.

For the ravioli filling, in a small saucepan, heat the butter, add the apricots, sugar, and vanilla, and sauté over medium until softened. Remove from the heat and set aside.

To assemble the ravioli, divide the dough in half and roll each piece into thin sheets using a pasta machine. Lay one sheet on a flat work surface and spoon approximately one tablespoon mounds of the filling about 2-inches apart on the sheet. Brush the second sheet with beaten egg, lay over the first sheet, and press the edges to seal. Cut out the ravioli with a cookie cutter, place on a well-floured sheet pan, and set aside for at least half hour.

For the peach sauce, in a small saucepan, add the peaches, ginger, and sugar and bring to a simmer. Reduce the heat and continue to cook until the fruit is soft. Transfer to the bowl of a food processor fitted with the metal blade attachment and purée until smooth. Strain into a small bowl and set aside.

To serve, in a medium saucepan, add the simple syrup and bring to a boil. Reduce the heat to a simmer, add the ravioli, and poach for one to two minutes. Remove with a slotted spoon and keep warm.

To serve, spoon some of the raspberry coulis in the bottom of a wide soup bowl. Alternate slices of apricot and ravioli and place beside the sauce. Place four pools of the peach sauce on the plate and set a fresh blackberry in each pool. Fan slices of fresh apricot, place on the coulis, and brush with some of the simple syrup. Garnish the plate with more blackberries and a mint sprig.

Tiramisu

(Serves 6)

For the tiramisu:
2 tablespoons gelatin
4 egg yolks, room temperature
4 tablespoons granulated sugar
4 tablespoons mascarpone cheese
4 egg whites, room temperature
2 tablespoons rum
2 cups espresso
10 ounces lady fingers
Cocoa powder

For the sauce:
4 egg yolks
1 cup sugar
1 cup dry Marsala
½ cup heavy cream

For the garnish:
Chocolate sauce
Raspberries

For the tiramisu, in a small bowl, sprinkle the gelatin over three table-spoons of cold water and set aside for five minutes to soften. In the bowl of an electric mixer fitted with the paddle attachment, add the egg yolks and sugar and beat until thickened, lemon colored, and double in volume. Add the mascarpone cheese and continue to mix for one minute. In the bowl of a food processor fitted with the metal blade attachment, add the whites and whip until stiff and glossy. Incorporate one-third of the whites into the yolk mixture, carefully fold in the remaining whites, and set aside. In a small saucepan, add the rum and reserved gelatin and simmer over medium heat until the gelatin granules dissolve. Remove from the heat, incorporate the espresso, and reserve. Dip the cookies into the espresso mixture and press in a single layer in the bottom of an 8-inch springform pan. Fill with half of the mascarpone mixture and repeat with another layer of cookies dipped in espresso. Repeat the procedure with the remaining mascarpone and cook-ies, ending with a layer of cookies. Cover with plastic wrap, and set aside in the refrigerator until set. Remove from the refrigerator, unmold, and slice into 2-inch squares. Sprinkle with cocoa and reserve.

For the sauce, bring a medium saucepan filled with 2-inches of water to a boil. In a medium bowl, add the egg yolks, sugar, and Marsala, and whisk to combine. Place the bowl over the pan of water and whip until frothy. Remove from heat and chill in an ice bath. Whip the cream until stiff peaks are formed and fold into the chilled sauce.

To serve, place a pool of sauce on a plate and drizzle the chocolate sauce decoratively around the plate. Set a piece of the tiramisu in the center of the plate and garnish with raspberries.

Rock of Hazelnut

(Serves 8)

For the praline:
⅓ cup granulated sugar
2 tablespoons brown sugar
⅓ cup water or sherry
½ cup hazelnuts, toasted and chopped

For the mousse:
1½ tablespoons gelatin
¼ cup cold water
2 cups milk
¼ pound reserved chopped praline
8 egg yolks
½ cup granulated sugar
2 cups heavy cream, whipped to soft peaks
3 ounces hazelnuts, toasted and chopped

For the ganache:
1 pound bittersweet chocolate, melted
2 tablespoons unsalted butter, softened
3¼ cups heavy cream

For the garnish:
Cocoa powder
Tuile butterfly

For the praline, in a large saucepan, add the sugars and sherry, and bring to a boil over low heat. Cover and cook approximately three minutes, allow-ing the steam to wash down any crystals that form on the sides of the pan. Uncover and continue to cook until the temperature of the syrup reaches 234 degrees. Remove from the heat, pour into the bowl of an electric mixer fitted with the whip attachment, and set aside to cool to 110 degrees. Whip the syrup until thickened and matte, stir in the hazelnuts, and pour onto a buttered and parchment-lined sheet pan. Set aside to cool, crack into pieces, and reserve.

For the mousse, line a medium bowl with plastic wrap, and set aside. In a small bowl, sprinkle the gelatin over the water, and set aside to soften for ten minutes. In a small saucepan, add the milk and praline, and bring to a boil. Remove from the heat and keep hot. Bring a medium saucepan filled with 2-inches of water to a simmer. In the bowl of an electric mixer fitted with the whip attachment, add the egg yolks and sugar and whip until

recipe continued on next page

Rock of Hazelnut

continued from previous page

thickened and lemon colored. Gradually add the hot milk to the yolk mixture, and place over the pan of simmering water. Cook the custard, stirring constantly, until it coats the back of a wooden spoon, incorporate the gelatin, stirring until all granules are dissolved, and chill in an ice bath. Fold in the whipped cream and nuts, place in the prepared bowl, and set aside in the freezer.

For the ganache, in the bowl of an electric mixer fitted with the paddle attachment, add the chocolate, butter, and cream, and beat until smooth. Set aside in the refrigerator, and when thick enough to handle, place in a pastry bag, and pipe into quarter-sized truffles onto a parchment-lined sheet pan.

To finish the mousse, unmold the mousse and cover with the truffles, beginning at the bottom of the mold and working up the sides in circles. Dust with cocoa, place on a plate, and garnish with a tuile butterfly.

Chocolate Symphony

(Serves 5)

For the chocolate mousse:
8 ¾ ounces bittersweet chocolate
2 ½ cups heavy cream, whipped

For the pistachio cream:
2 ¼ cups milk
2 tablespoons sugar
2 tablespoon ground pistachios
4 egg yolks, slightly beaten
½ cup sugar

For garnish:
Chocolate butterfly
Chocolate curls
Assorted confections

For the mousse, chop chocolate and place in a bowl. In a double boiler over low heat, stir constantly until all chocolate is melted. Remove from heat and stir occasionally. Just before the chocolate starts to set again, fold in the whipped cream and pour onto a parchment paper lined mold. Refrigerate for 6 hours. When ready to serve, dip the mold into hot water and turn over onto a cutting board.

For the pistachio cream, combine milk, half the sugar and pistachios and bring to a simmer. Remove from heat. In a separate bowl, whisk the egg yolks with the remaining sugar and while constantly stirring, slowly pour the hot milk into the eggs. Stir well and strain. Set aside and let cool.

For presentation, place pistachio cream in center of plate and cover with 2 slices chocolate mouse. Decorate with chocolate butterfly, chocolate curls and assorted confections.

Trio of Chocolate Mousses

(Serves 4)

For the dark chocolate mousse:

2 eggs, separated

2¹⁄₂ tablespoons sugar

1 tablespoon mocha paste*

3 ounces bittersweet chocolate, melted and cooled to room temperature

¹⁄₄ cup heavy cream, whipped to soft peaks

For the milk chocolate mousse:

2 tablespoons cold water

1 teaspoon gelatin

1 egg

1 egg yolk

4 ounces milk chocolate, melted and cooled to room temperature

2 tablespoons dark rum

³⁄₄ cup heavy cream, whipped to soft peaks

For the white chocolate mousse:

1 teaspoon gelatin

2 tablespoon cold water

1 egg

1 egg yolk

4 ounces white chocolate, melted

2 tablespoons cherry liqueur

³⁄₄ cup heavy cream, whipped to soft peaks

For the garnish:

2 cups crème anglaise

Mint sprigs

Toasted slivered almonds

Chopped pistachios

*Available in gourmet markets

For the dark chocolate mousse, in the bowl of an electric mixer fitted with the whip attachment, add the egg yolks and half tablespoon of the sugar and whip until thick and lemon colored. Incorporate the mocha paste and melted chocolate, gently fold in the whipped cream, and reserve. In the bowl of an electric mixer fitted with the whip attachment, add the egg whites and the remaining sugar, and whip to stiff peaks. Gently fold into the chocolate mixture and pour into a pan 2-inches deep. Cover with plastic wrap and set aside in the refrigerator for at least eight hours.

For the milk chocolate mousse, in a small bowl, add the water, sprinkle with the gelatin, and set aside to soften for ten minutes. Bring a small saucepan filled with 2-inches of water to a boil and place the gelatin over the pan making sure the bottom of the bowl does not come in contact with the water. Reduce the heat and melt the gelatin, stirring occasionally, until the gelatin is dissolved and no granules remain. Remove from the heat and set aside. In the bowl of an electric mixer fitted with the paddle attachment, add the eggs and whip until thick and lemon colored. Gradually add the chocolate and rum and mix to combine. Incorporate the gelatin and gently fold in the whipped cream. Pour into a pan 2-inches deep, cover with plastic wrap, and set aside in the refrigerator for at least eight hours.

For the white chocolate mousse, follow the procedure used for the milk chocolate mousse, substituting white chocolate and cherry liqueur, and set aside in the refrigerator for at least eight hours.

To serve, place a pool of crème anglaise on a chilled plate. Using a serving spoon dipped in hot water, scoop some of each of the mousses and arrange on top of the sauce. Sprinkle with toasted almonds and pistachios, and garnish the plate with a sprig of mint.

Ricotta Quenelles with Strawberry Coulis

(Serves 4)

For the quenelles:

2 ounces unsalted butter, softened to room temperature

4 eggs

2 cups ricotta cheese

¹⁄₂ cup white cornmeal

¹⁄₂ cup crème fraîche

¹⁄₄ teaspoon salt

Zest of 1 lemon

¹⁄₂ teaspoon vanilla extract

1 teaspoon salt

For the strawberry coulis:

1 quart strawberries, stemmed

¹⁄₄ cup granulated sugar

For the breadcrumb mixture:

2 ounces unsalted butter

³⁄₄ cup plain white breadcrumbs

2 tablespoons granulated sugar

For the garnish:

Lightly whipped cream

Confectioners' sugar

recipe continued on next page

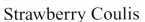

For the quenelles, in the bowl of an electric mixer fitted with the paddle attachment, add the butter and beat until smooth and creamy. Beat in the eggs, one at a time, scraping down the sides of the bowl after each addition. Incorporate the ricotta, cornmeal, crème fraîche, salt, zest, and vanilla. Remove from the mixer, cover with plastic wrap, and set aside to rest in a cool place for one hour. In a large saucepan, bring four quarts of water and one teaspoon of salt to a boil. Reduce the heat and bring the water to a low simmer. Form the quenelles with two large soup spoons, carefully set in the simmering water, and poach for ten minutes. Remove from the pan, drain on paper towels, and keep warm.

For the strawberry coulis, in the bowl of a food processor fitted with the paddle attachment, add the strawberries and sugar and purée until smooth. Strain through a sieve into a small bowl and set aside.

For the breadcrumbs, in a small sauté pan, heat the butter over medium heat, add the breadcrumbs and sauté until golden brown. Sprinkle with sugar and continue to sauté until the sugar is lightly caramelized. Remove from the heat and set aside.

To serve, spoon some of the coulis on a plate, arrange a few of the quenelles on top, and sprinkle with some of the breadcrumb mixture. Pipe a decorative pattern of whipped cream in the coulis and dust the plate with confectioners' sugar.

Apricot Ravioli
with Sabayon

215

(Serves 4)

For the ravioli:
4 ounces dried apricots
2 tablespoons apricot brandy
6 ounces fresh egg pasta dough
3 sprigs mint, stemmed and minced

For the sabayon:
2 eggs
2 egg yolks
4 tablespoons granulated sugar
¼ cup apple juice
⅛ teaspoon ground cinnamon
Juice of ½ lemon

For the garnish
Confectioners' sugar
Mint leaves

For the ravioli, in a medium saucepan, add the apricots, cover with boiling water, and set aside for one hour. Add the apricot brandy and cook over low heat for 20 minutes or until the apricots are very soft. Remove from the heat and set aside to cool in the liquid. Strain, chop finely, and set aside. Roll pasta dough through a pasta machine, until it is at its lowest setting. Arrange mint leaves on half the dough and fold the other half over the mint to enclose. Roll again through the finest setting and place on a lightly floured work surface. Cut into leaf shapes with a cookie cutter, place on a parchment-lined sheet pan, and set aside. Place one teaspoon of the apricot filling in the center of half of the leaves and lightly brush the edges with water. Cover the filling with the remaining leaves and press the edges to seal. Cover the ravioli with a towel and set aside for two hours. Bring a large saucepan of water to a boil, add the ravioli and cook for one minute. Remove the ravioli with a slotted spoon, drain on a paper towel, and keep warm.

For the sabayon, bring a medium saucepan filled with 2-inches of water to a simmer. In a medium bowl, whisk together all of the ingredients and place over the saucepan. Reduce the heat and cook, stirring constantly, until the sabayon is thick enough to coat the back of a spoon. Remove from the heat and set aside.

To serve, arrange three ravioli on a plate, slicing one open to reveal the filling. Spoon some of the sabayon on the plate and garnish with confectioners' sugar and a sprig of mint.

Frozen Apricot Soufflé
Le Cirque

(Serves 4)

For the soufflé:
8 apricots, peeled, pitted, and chopped
2 teaspoons butter
¼ cup apricot brandy
¼ teaspoon almond extract
6 eggs, separated
½ cup sugar
1 cup heavy cream, whipped to soft peaks

For the garnish
Cocoa powder
Mixed berry purée
Sugar fantasy

For the apricot soufflé, lightly butter and sugar four 4-ounce ramekins. Make a parchment paper collar for the extending 2-inches above the rim of the ramekin and secure with string. Place on a sheet pan and set aside. In a large sauté pan, heat the butter, add the apricots, and sauté until soft. Flambé with the brandy, and add the almond extract. Place in the bowl of a food processor fitted with the metal blade attachment, and purée until smooth. Strain into a medium bowl and set aside. In the bowl of an electric mixer fitted with the whip attachment, add the egg yolks and sugar and whip until thickened and lemon colored. Remove from the mixer and set aside. In a medium saucepan, bring two inches of water to a boil and set the yolk mixture over the saucepan. Reduce the heat and continue to whisk until the mixture forms a custard thick enough to coat the back of a spoon. Do not allow it to come to a boil or the egg yolks will curdle. Remove from the heat and set aside to cool. In the bowl of an electric mixer fitted with the whip attachment, add the whites and whip until frothy. Add the remaining one-fourth cup sugar and beat to soft peaks. Remove from the mixer and set aside. Combine the apricot purée and the custard, and gently fold in the whipped cream and egg whites. Pour the mixture into the prepared ramekins and place in the freezer for at least eight hours before serving. Remove form the freezer and allow to sit for 15 minutes to soften slightly before serving.

To serve, place a soufflé on a plate, sprinkle lightly with cocoa powder, and serve with purée on the side.

Bartlett Pear
Granité

(Serves 4)

For the pear:
2 cups Paul Thomas Bartlett pear wine or other dry pear wine
2 tablespoons water
2 tablespoons granulated sugar

For the garnish:
4 grape leaves
Julienned red and green Bartlett pear
Julienned plum
4 grape vine tendrils

For the granité, in a small saucepan, add the water and sugar and bring to a boil, stirring until sugar dissolves. Incorporate the wine and pour into 12 by 18-inch shallow pan. Place in the freezer for two hours, stirring frequently to break up any ice crystals that form.

To serve, remove the granité from the freezer. Place a grape leaf in a chilled champagne glass and fill with some of the granite. Garnish with julienned fruit and a grape tendril.

Passion Fruit Mousse with Orange Brioche

218

(Serves 4)

For the mousse:
5 ounces white chocolate
4 ounces passion fruit purée
1 tablespoon confectioners' sugar
5 yolks
8 ounces heavy cream

For the brioche:
6 ounces flour
¼ ounce yeast
¼ cup milk
2 ounces butter, softened
Zest of 1 orange
1 ounce sugar
1 egg
½ teaspoon salt
1 ounce melted butter
½ pint orange juice
4 ounces sugar

For the sauce:
6 ounces crème fraîche
1 cup plain yogurt
1 ounces confectioners' sugar
2 ounces Grand Marnier
4 ounces strawberry coulis
4 ounces heavy cream

For the garnish
Fresh strawberries, cut in half
Strawberry leaves

For the mousse, fill a medium saucepan with 2-inches of water and bring to a boil. In a medium bowl, add the chocolate and place over the pan so that the bottom of the bowl does not touch the water. Reduce the heat and cook until the chocolate has melted, stirring occasionally. Remove from the heat and incorporate the passion fruit purée, sugar and egg yolks. In the bowl of and electric mixer fitted with the whip attachment, add the cream and whip to soft peaks. Fold into the chocolate mixture and spoon into a shallow mold. Set aside in the refrigerator to chill for at least six hours.

For the brioche dough, using a standard brioche method, add the rind of the orange. Let proof twice, form into walnut-sized clumps and place them next to each other on a baking pan. Proof the brioche one more time, brush with melted butter and bake at 375 degrees until golden brown. In the meantime, reduce the orange juice and four ounces of sugar by tho-thirds and with this glaze, brush the brioche after they have finished cooling.

For the sauce, in a small bowl, whisk together all of the ingredients and set aside.

To serve, place some of the sauce on the plate, place two scoops of the mousse on top of the sauce, set three brioche around mousse. Garnish with strawberry halves and leaves.

Gratin of Cream Cheese with Mangoes

220

(Serves 3)

For the white mocha ice cream:
6 ounces heavy cream
6 ounces milk
3 ounces granulated sugar
2 ounces mocha beans
6 egg yolks

For the gratin:
10 ounces cream cheese, softened
7 ounces crème fraîche
1 ounce corn starch
Zest of 1 lemon
1 tablespoon dark rum
½ vanilla bean, split and seeds reserved
4 egg whites
6 ½ ounces confectioners' sugar
1 mango, peeled, pitted, and sliced
15 strawberries, hulled and halved

For the garnish
Melted chocolate
Confectioners' sugar
Chopped pistachio nuts for garnish

recipe continued on next page

Gratin of Cream Cheese

with Mangoes
continued from previous page

For the ice cream, in a medium saucepan, combine the cream, milk, and half of the sugar, and mocha beans, and bring to a boil. In a small bowl, whisk together the remaining sugar and egg yolks. Remove the cream from the heat and temper the egg yolks, adding half of the boiled cream while whisking constantly. Whisk the tempered egg yolks back into the cream and place over medium heat, stirring constantly with a wooden spoon. When the mixture thickens enough to coat the back of a spoon, remove from the heat, pour through a fine strainer, and cool in an ice bath. Freeze in an ice-cream machine according to the manufacturer's directions and reserve.

For the gratin, lightly butter three 8-ounce soup bowls, place on a parchment-lined sheet pan, and set aside. In a medium bowl, add the cream cheese, four ounces of the confectioners' sugar, crème fraîche, cornstarch, zest, rum, vanilla bean seeds and mix thoroughly. In the bowl of an electric mixer fitted with the whip attachment, add the egg whites and remaining sugar and whip to soft peaks. Remove from the mixer and fold into the cream cheese mixture. Pour into the prepared bowls and arrange the fruit decoratively on top. Place the sheet pan in the oven and bake until the edges of the gratins begin to brown. Remove from the oven and set aside. For the garnish, place a scoop of ice cream on the gratin, drizzle with melted chocolate, and sprinkle with pistachio nuts and confectioners' sugar.

Pear Strudel

219

(Serves 8)

For the pear filling:

2 pounds pears, peeled, cored and thinly sliced
½ cup currants
2 ounces almond flour
5 ounces cake crumbs
4 ounces sugar
3 ounces Pear William brandy

For the strudel dough:

11 ounces all-purpose flour
1 egg yolk
1 ounce vegetable oil
⅓ ounce salt
5 ounces warm water
6 ounces melted butter

For the Pear William sabayon:

4 egg yolks
1 cup dry white wine
3 ounces sugar
2 ounces Pear William brandy

For the praline ice cream:

6 ounces heavy cream
6 ounces milk
4 ounces hazelnut paste
4 ounces bitter chocolate
2 ounces amaretto
1 ounce brandy
3 ounces granulated sugar
6 egg yolks

For the garnish:

Confectioners' sugar
Strawberry leaf
Strawberry syrup
2 ounces chocolate shavings

For the ice cream, in a medium saucepan, combine the cream, milk, hazelnut paste, chocolate, liquor, and half of the sugar, and, and bring to a boil. In a small bowl, whisk together the remaining sugar and egg yolks. Remove the cream from the heat and temper the egg yolks, adding half of the boiled cream while whisking constantly. Whisk the tempered egg yolks back into the cream and place over medium heat, stirring constantly with a wooden spoon. When the mixture thickens enough to coat the back of a spoon, remove from the heat, pour through a fine strainer, and cool in an ice bath. Freeze in an ice-cream machine according to the manufacturer's directions and reserve.

For the pear filling, in a large bowl, add the pears, currants, almond flour, almonds, cake crumbs, sugar and Pear William brandy and set aside for one hour.

For the strudel, in the bowl of an electric mixer fitted with the paddle attachment, combine all of the ingredients and mix thoroughly. Replace the paddle with the dough hook attachment and continue to knead until the dough is smooth and elastic. Remove from the bowl and place on a floured and tablecloth-lined flat work surface. Coat the dough with a thin layer of vegetable oil and allow to rest for 30 minutes. Preheat the oven to 375 degrees. Pull the strudel dough until it is paper thin. (You should be able to read a newspaper, if placed under the dough.) Arrange the pear filling down the center, brush with melted butter, and using the tablecloth, roll the strudel into a cylinder, approximately 2½-inches in diameter. Place the strudel on a parchment-lined sheet pan and set in the oven to bake for 25 minutes or until golden brown and crisp. Remove from the oven and keep warm.

For the sabayon, fill a medium saucepan with 2-inches of water and bring to a boil. In a medium bowl, whisk together all of the ingredients and place over the saucepan. Reduce the heat and continue to whisk the sabayon until it pulls away from the sides of the bowl. Remove from the heat and set aside.

To serve, dust the strudel with confectioners' sugar and slice on the bias into 2-inch thick pieces. Arrange two pieces on a plate and set a scoop of ice cream beside them. Spoon some of the sabayon on the plate and drizzle with some strawberry syrup. Garnish with chocolate shavings and a strawberry sprig.

Chocolate-Walnut Tea Cake

(Makes one 9 inch by 5 inch loaf)

For the cake:
1 cup bread flour
¾ cup cake flour
¾ teaspoon baking powder
½ teaspoon salt
6 ounces butter
⅞ cup granulated sugar
3 eggs
½ cup milk
1 tablespoon orange flower water
6 ounces chopped walnuts
6 ounces bittersweet chocolate, chopped

For the glaze:
½ cup sifted confectioners' sugar
2 tablespoons strong tea
1 teaspoon orange flower water

For the cake, preheat the oven to 325 degrees and lightly butter and flour a 9x5-inch loaf pan. In a large bowl, sift together the flours, baking powder, and salt, and set aside. In the bowl of an electric mixer fitted with the paddle attachment, add the butter and sugar and beat until light and creamy. Gradually add the eggs, scraping down the sides of the bowl after each addition, and mix until well blended. Alternate adding the reserved dry ingredients and the milk, beginning and ending with the dry ingredients, incorporate the orange flour water, nuts, and chocolate, and mix thoroughly. Remove from the mixer, pour into the prepared pan, and place in the oven. Bake the cake for one hour and 15 minutes, and remove from the oven. Cool for five minutes, carefully remove from the pan, and continue to cool on a wire cake rack.

For the glaze, in the bowl of an electric mixer fitted with the whip attachment, add all of the ingredients and mix until smooth. Remove from the mixer and brush over the cake.

Fog City Brownie with Chocolate Sauce

(Serves 8)

For the brownies:
1 cup butter, room temperature
5 ounces bittersweet chocolate
½ cup butter, chopped
1½ cups sugar
1 teaspoon vanilla
½ teaspoon salt
1 cup all-purpose flour
3 eggs
1 cup chopped, toasted walnuts or pecans

For the chocolate sauce:
1 cup butter
¼ cup brandy
2 tablespoons triple sec
¾ cup corn syrup
Pinch of salt
1 pound bittersweet chocolate
¾ cup heavy cream

For the garnish:
Vanilla ice cream
Fresh strawberries, sliced in half
Confectioners' sugar

For the brownies, preheat oven to 375 degrees. Melt half of the butter with the chocolate. Let cool slightly. Meanwhile, mix the remaining butter with sugar, vanilla and salt until just mixed. Pour in melted chocolate and butter mixture and mix on low speed very quickly. Add flour on low speed until just mixed. Add eggs one at a time on slightly higher speed. Add nuts and mix 30 seconds. Pour batter into two greased and floured half sheet pans and bake for 30 minutes, rotating pans halfway through cooking time. Remove from oven and let cool.

For the sauce, combine butter, brandy, triple sec, corn syrup, salt and chocolate in a bain marie over hot water until melted. Don't stir. When melted, stir in heavy cream.

To serve, cut brownies into large squares and place on serving plates. Surround with chocolate sauce. Top with a scoop of ice cream and position halves of strawberries around brownie. Drizzle ice cream with a little more sauce and dust confectioners' sugar on top.

Lemon-Poppyseed Pound Cake

220

(Makes one 9x 4-inch loaf)

For the cake:
8 ounces butter
2 cups granulated sugar
6 eggs, room temperature
2 cups cake flour, sifted
2½ tablespoons lemon juice
Zest of 1 lemon
½ cup poppy seeds

For the cake, place a shallow pan of water in the lower rack of the oven, and preheat the oven to 350 degrees. Lightly butter and flour a 9x4-inch loaf pan and set aside. In the bowl of an electric mixer fitted with the paddle attachment, add the butter and sugar and beat until light and creamy. Gradually add the eggs, one at a time, scraping down the sides of the bowl after each addition. Add the flour and mix on medium speed for one minute. Incorporate the lemon juice, zest, and poppy seeds, and mix until well combined. Pour the batter into the prepared pan, place in the oven, and bake for 30 minutes. Remove the pan of water from the oven and continue to bake the cake for an additional 30 minutes. Remove from the oven and set aside to cool for 10 minutes. Remove form the pan and cool completely on a wire cake rack.

Chocolate Bag with White Chocolate Mousse

221

(Serves 6)

For the sacks:
2½ pounds imported bittersweet chocolate, chopped
6 waxed paper lined bags (the kind coffee beans come in)

For the white chocolate mousse:
4 cups heavy cream
1 pound imported white chocolate
½ cup egg whites (4 large eggs)
1 cup granulated sugar
2 cups water

For the raspberry coulis:
4 cups raspberries (fresh or frozen unsweetened)
⅔ cup sugar syrup
2 tablespoons lemon juice (1 lemon)

For the crème anglaise:
¾ cup granulated sugar
6 egg yolks
2½ cups boiling milk
1 vanilla bean, split and scraped

For the garnish:
2 baskets fresh raspberries
6 sprigs fresh mint

For the sacks, melt chocolate in bowl over hot, but not boiling water. Prepare bags. Measure four inches up from the bottom and mark bags. Cut off top at this line with pinking shears to give a finished look to bag. Open bag and tape down all edges with masking tape. This is to prevent chocolate from seeping into cracks of bags, making them difficult to remove from chocolate when complete. Working slowly, covering only one side at a time, brush melted chocolate onto inside of bags. Refrigerate after brushing each side and turn bag as you go along to prevent running. There should be three complete coats of chocolate applied to each bag. Chill until ready to serve. Carefully peel bag away from chocolate being sure to work quickly to prevent melting.

For the mousse, whip cream until thick and keep cool in refrigerator. Melt chocolate in bowl over warm water. Be careful, white chocolate burns very easily, creating lumps. Let cool slightly. Place egg whites in bowl of electric mixer with whip attachment. Meanwhile, in heavy saucepan, cook sugar in water to the hard ball stage - 248 degrees F on a candy thermometer. Slowly add sugar syrup to egg whites while mixer is on high. Continue mixing until meringue has cooled down. Quickly fold meringue into cooled chocolate. Then fold whipped cream into meringue chocolate mixture. Refrigerate until needed.

For the coulis, purée all ingredients in a blender or food processor until smooth. Strain through a fine-mesh strainer to remove seeds. If too thick, thin with more lemon juice or sugar syrup.

For the crème anglaise, gradually beat the sugar into the egg yolks and continue beating two to three minutes until the mixture is pale yellow and forms the ribbon. While continuing to beat the egg yolk mixture, gradually pour in the boiling milk in a thin stream so that the yolks are slowly warmed. Pour the mixture back into the saucepan and set over moderate heat, stirring slowly and reaching all over the bottom and sides of the pan, with a wooden spatula until the sauce thickens just enough to coat the spoon with a light, creamy layer. Do not let the custard come anywhere near the simmer. Maximum temperature is 165 degrees on a candy thermometer. Then beat the sauce on the heat for a minute or two to cool it. Strain through a fine sieve. Cool. Makes three cups.

To serve, cover plates with raspberry coulis, using a two to three ounce ladle. Using squirt bottle, place drops of crème anglaise in circle around edge of raspberry sauce. Using toothpick or skewer, swirl through dots to create design. Using piping bag fitted with large star tip, fill chocolate sacks with white chocolate mousse. Place sacks in center of plate. Garnish with fresh raspberries and a sprig of mint, if desired.

Index

"Your life and career are two different things,

but real success-not necessarily happiness-comes

from fusing the two."

-Jeremiah Tower, *Becoming a Chef*